OUT OF THE ROUGH

OUT OF THE ROUGH

Ted Rhodes and His Fight against Golf's Color Barrier

BY DAN TAYLOR

BLOOMSBURY ACADEMIC
NEW YORK • LONDON • OXFORD • NEW DELHI • SYDNEY

BLOOMSBURY ACADEMIC

Bloomsbury Publishing Inc, 1359 Broadway, New York, NY 10018, USA
Bloomsbury Publishing Plc, 50 Bedford Square, London, WC1B 3DP, UK
Bloomsbury Publishing Ireland, 29 Earlsfort Terrace, Dublin 2, D02 AY28, Ireland

BLOOMSBURY, BLOOMSBURY ACADEMIC and the Diana logo are
trademarks of Bloomsbury Publishing Plc

First published in the United States of America 2026

Copyright © Dan Taylor, 2026
Cover images: © United States Golf Association

All rights reserved. No part of this publication may be: i) reproduced or transmitted in any form, electronic or mechanical, including photocopying, recording or by means of any information storage or retrieval system without prior permission in writing from the publishers; or ii) used or reproduced in any way for the training, development or operation of artificial intelligence (AI) technologies, including generative AI technologies. The rights holders expressly reserve this publication from the text and data mining exception as per Article 4(3) of the Digital Single Market Directive (EU) 2019/790.

Bloomsbury Publishing Inc does not have any control over, or responsibility for, any third-party websites referred to or in this book. All internet addresses given in this book were correct at the time of going to press. The author and publisher regret any inconvenience caused if addresses have changed or sites have ceased to exist, but can accept no responsibility for any such changes.

Library of Congress Cataloging-in-Publication Data Available

ISBN: HB: 979-8-88180-042-0
ePDF: 979-8-88185-780-6
eBook: 979-8-88180-043-7

Typeset by Deanta Global Publishing Services, Chennai, India
Printed and bound in the United States of America

For product safety related questions contact productsafety@bloomsbury.com.

To find out more about our authors and books visit www.bloomsbury.com and sign up for our newsletters.

Thank you, Keith.

AUTHOR'S NOTE

The words "Negro" and "colored person" are used only in direct quotes or titles and for historical purposes.

CONTENTS

Acknowledgments x

Introduction 1

1 Rags 7
2 The Champ's Inner Circle 21
3 A New Star 39
4 Please Go Away 55
5 A Worthy Pioneer 65
6 Critical Eyes 75
7 Swinging at a Star 85
8 The Bomber's Battle 95
9 He's Too Good 109
10 Get That Champagne Ready 121
11 The Money Dries Up 133
12 Breaking the Barrier 143
13 Fighting for His Life 153
14 Mentor to the Next Wave 163
15 So Long, Old Pro 173

Epilogue 179
Notes 184
Bibliography 198
About the Author 219
Index 220

ACKNOWLEDGMENTS

So many offered so much with such great enthusiasm. For that I am grateful. Thank you to Jim Ayers, Barb and Tom Balcom, Chuck Bandelian, Winslow and Pattie Chase, Bruce Cramer, Artie Harris, Rod Kraft, Gary Mintz, Ron Munvez, Renee Powell, Charles Sifford, Jr., Bruce Slutsky, and Irina Ventresca. My thanks to Terri Garst of the Los Angeles Public Library, Kathleen Feduccia, Laura Scott, and Eva Wurst of the Nashville Public Library, John Calhoun with the Billy Rose Theatre section of the New York Public Library, Elayne Bascotti, Jose Lopez, Victoria Nenno, Julia Pine, and Stacy Shiff with the United States Golf Association, and Erin Barnhart with the Carnegie Museum of Art. The time afforded, effort made, suggestions offered, and direction extended were tremendously helpful. Very special thanks to Deborah Rhodes for the wonderful stories, continued motivation, and most of all your trust. To my wife Eve, my deepest gratitude for your unwavering support, attention to detail, and succinct suggestions. I aced the hole of life the day I met you.

Introduction
I Won't Forget

Tiger Woods sat in a chair never before occupied by a person of his ethnicity. He had been whisked to Butler Cabin, a quaint, colonial-style structure on the grounds of Augusta National Golf Club moments after signing his scorecard in the presence of a playing partner and the event's official scorer to codify a historic 1997 victory at The Masters.

Woods' triumph came from a rare and scintillating exhibition of golf, one that stoked flames of frenzy among not just the most ardent fans of the game but those at the far opposite end of the spectrum, who would only label their interest in golf casual or passing at best. Amid the picturesque azaleas and sixty-one dogwoods that lined the historic Georgia course, Woods produced 270, the lowest seventy-two-hole score in the event's sixty-three-year history—18 under par. He won the tournament by a record twelve strokes. And nobody had ever before conquered this daunting challenge at such a young age, twenty-one years, three months, and fourteen days. So great was the fervor over Woods' accomplishment that *Variety* reported forty-three million viewers watched the CBS telecast of the final round, a 53 percent increase over the year before.

For all the fervency that rippled about the country, Woods' victory at The Masters held far greater significance to a generation of African Americans. The son of an African American father and a Thai mother had triumphed in an event and on a golf course that steadfastly denied a person of color the right to hit a golf ball in competition during the first forty years of its existence. Woods' win also came in a state that, until April 1949, would not allow Black and White athletes to compete against one another on the same playing field, a solidity fractured when Branch Rickey defied the Ku Klux Klan and sent Jackie Robinson and Roy Campanella to play in an exhibition game for the Brooklyn Dodgers against the minor-league Atlanta Crackers. Augusta National and The Masters were so synonymous with bigotry that for decades few questioned whether the course and event co-founder, Clifford Roberts, did or did not once say, "As long as I'm alive all the golfers will be White, and the caddies will be Black."[1]

As Woods sat in front of the fireplace within Butler Cabin, he was flanked by Nick Faldo, the 1996 champion who readied to present the winner's green jacket. About the room, cables, cameras, monitors, and other broadcast equipment littered a structure that for fifty-one weeks of the year offered accommodations to visiting Augusta National members. Once April and The Masters annually arrived, Butler Cabin became a television studio. A few seconds before 8:00 p.m. on Sunday, April 13, 1997, the flick of a stage manager's right hand, index finger extended, illumination of a red light, and images on nearby monitors signaled to all in the room they were live on CBS.

Following opening remarks by CBS sportscaster Jim Nantz, Joe Ford, vice-chairman of Augusta National Golf Club, offered congratulations to Woods, who broke into a broad smile. A recitation of the golfer's momentous tournament achievements then led Nantz into his interview of the new champion. Ultimately, the topic delved into the matter of race.

> "Also, you're the first African American to ever win The Masters, a Grand Slam event, the first Asian American. What does all of this mean to you?"
>
> "It means a lot. I was the first, but I wasn't the pioneer. Charley Sifford, Lee Elder, Teddy Rhodes, those guys were the ones who paved the way. I thank them. If it wasn't for them, I may not have had the chance to ever play golf."[2]

Within the golfing community the names Elder and Sifford were well known. Those familiar with their career history understood why Woods might acknowledge them on such a historic occasion. Elder, in 1975, became the first Black golfer to play in The Masters. Sifford, eighteen years before, was heralded the first Black golfer to win a Professional Golfers' Association (PGA)-sanctioned tournament when he won the Long Beach Open. But most among the millions who watched the CBS interview with Woods had never heard of Ted Rhodes, an ignorance that rankled Elder and Sifford. "You never heard of Ted Rhodes!" Elder once snapped at a sportswriter. "How long you been covering golf?"[3]

Part of the reverence was personal. Elder and Sifford were professional golfers because of Ted Rhodes. They were inspired and mentored by Rhodes, who showered both men with his generosity. Elder lived with the Rhodes family for three years, during which time he caddied for, received hours and hours of instruction from, and all the while developed his game under Rhodes' guidance. Sifford grew so close to Rhodes his sons knew the man as "Uncle Teddy." But much more swelled the regard held by the two men into reverence—notably the golfing awe that came whenever Ted Rhodes swung a club. With uncanny accuracy from what 1968 Masters champion Bob Goalby called "a classic golf swing," Rhodes reaped tournament title trophies at an unheard-of rate.[4] Over a five-year span he won a staggering 79 percent of the tournaments he entered, an achievement unmatched by the men held up over time as the greatest to ever play the game: Ben Hogan, Bobby Jones, Jack Nicklaus, Arnold Palmer, Gene Sarazen, Sam Snead, and Tiger Woods.

Why Rhodes' name isn't routinely mentioned in the same breath with the game's all-time greats has much to do with the when and where of his career. Jim Crow laws and a "Caucasian-only" clause in the PGA's membership policy relegated Rhodes to the all-Black United Golfers Association (UGA) circuit for the peak years of his professional career. He, like other golfers of his race, was made to scrape, claw, and fight to make a living. With winnings on the UGA circuit being a fraction of those on the PGA tour, gambling and instructing helped to pay the bills.

Once the PGA was finally forced to open its doors to Black golfers, Rhodes was in his forties. His best golf was behind him. Had he been able to play his entire career in the PGA, Charley Sifford suggested, "you would have seen an Arnold Palmer in technicolor 20 years ahead of time. Nobody could play as consistently as Teddy."[56] Legendary *New York Daily News* sports columnist Dick Young wrote, "Ted Rhodes might have been the greatest golfer who ever lived if he had been born 30 years later."[7]

As with those who followed Jackie Robinson into baseball, the path to professional success for Tiger Woods and other Black golfers was paved with perseverance, sacrifice, and fortitude. The early Black PGA golfer endured acrimony, hostility, dehumanizing enmity, and amoral indignities. Black golfers, said James Black, a onetime professional, "didn't have the freedom to play without having their lives threatened. They had to change in the car, couldn't use the facilities in the clubhouse, and couldn't play the course until the day of the tournament."[8]

Unlike the case of Robinson, Black professional golfers had no teammates from which to draw support. They were alone, playing in a field of more than one hundred, some of whom teemed with contempt and boiled with disdain at their involvement in their game. As difficult as the trait was to exercise, restraint was paramount. Deference, while normally a weakness, became a tool to diffuse volatility.

In 1948 Rhodes became the first African American golfer to play in the modern era of the US Open. That same year he was part of a lawsuit that unsuccessfully sought to force the PGA to remove the Caucasian-only clause from its membership policy. In 1952 at the Phoenix Open, Rhodes became the first Black golfer to turn in a scorecard, make the cut, and play all four rounds in a PGA tournament. The following year he was the first to play on the PGA tour. Commercially, Black golfers had no endorsement opportunities, that is, until 1954, when a club manufacturer took a chance and struck a deal with Rhodes.

In the press conference that followed his Masters victory, Tiger Woods continued to extend gratitude to Rhodes, Sifford, and Elder. "Coming up 18, I said a little prayer of thanks to those guys. Those guys are the ones who did it. They came down and inspired me," he said.[9] Nike and other sponsors raced to capitalize on their client's momentous victory. In the July 1997 issue of *Ebony* magazine, Nike took out a two-page advertisement to celebrate Woods. A picture of Ted Rhodes appeared in the ad. Corresponding copy attributed to Woods read, "Thank you, Mr. Rhodes," and "You the man, Mr. Rhodes."[10] The ad culminated with the tag line—"I won't forget."[11]

1

Rags

Clamor echoed about the walls of Union Station. Uniformed soldiers spilled from coaches. Porters and conductors hastily moved into position to off-load luggage. The military men, with merriment in mind, scanned the platform for directions to the Soldiers and Sailors Lounge. Women who fanned themselves and men whose khakis were tinged with sweat stains gave evidence to the sweltering 92-degree August day. Misery was exacerbated by a stifling level of humidity.

The influx of uniformed men came from an organized campaign to bring soldiers by the hundreds to Nashville. A number of local organizations as well as the city itself invested thousands of dollars on advertising and hospitality programs in the hope soldiers from nearby Camp Forrest in Tullahoma would spend their three-day leave—and most importantly, their money—in the burgeoning city. The local YWCA held dances. Churches offered lunches. Recreation, which covered everything from swimming to attending movies and minor-league baseball games, was promoted. It all became far more successful than expected, particularly when family members and friends of soldiers—some from as far away as Chicago—flocked to the city to spend time with their sons and loved ones. From mid-April through summer in 1941, more than twenty-five thousand responded to the campaign. At times so many arrived that hotels could not handle their numbers. The city was forced to scramble and set up tents and cots in a public park to provide accommodations.

As soldiers meandered about the platform, a flow of people surged in the opposite direction. It brought together a mass of those soon to embark with the just-disembarked in one chaotic scene. Among those in the wave of the departing was a man toting luggage some may have considered peculiar, at least for a Black man in 1941 Nashville—golf clubs.

Only days earlier, while at the North Nashville nightclub where he held a second job, Ted Rhodes picked up a newspaper. Leaping from a page was news that Joe Louis, the renowned heavyweight boxing champion, was to stage a tournament for Black golfers in his hometown of Detroit. Almost without hesitation Rhodes told his boss he would have to find someone else to serve as his emcee for the next two weeks. The next morning the boss at his day job received a similar message. It was a spontaneity driven by conviction, the product of an almost inconceivable marriage in the American Deep South between golf, the game of Whites with money, and a Black youth on an impoverished trail who held an unquenchable zeal for the sport.

As the 27-year-old Rhodes prepared to board the Dixie Limited for Chicago, it had been almost two decades since an improbable intersection made him smitten by the game of golf. An uncle was responsible. Rhodes' youthful pursuit was an exhibition of resourcefulness and wit. He lacked the strength to swing a regulation golf club and the money to buy one, so he turned to creative measures to satiate his budding obsession. With deft hands the youth reshaped wire coat hangers. Once straightened and with one end bent, the modified hanger became his club. But his ingenuity did not stop there. Wielding a pocketknife, the youth whittled cork bottle caps into the shape of golf balls. Then there was the matter of where young Ted Rhodes could practice the game. Golf in 1920s Tennessee was for the folks in Franklin, Germantown, or the Belle Meade area of town. The White folks. Particularly those with money. It was not a game for those who resided in the 9th Ward, Edgehill, a section of Nashville originally settled by former slaves. Then there was instruction. Golf lessons and green fees required money, a commodity in short supply to folks in Edgehill. Even if they had money, there was Jim Crow to contend with.

Jim Crow did not refer to a man, per se, but rather an insidious prejudice that infested the Deep South of America. The name was actually an onerous euphemism born of a skit, "Jump Jim Crow," performed by a popular comedian in the 1830s that mocked a Black man. The popularity of the comedian led to his character's name becoming synonymous with denigration and ostracism.

Following the abolition of slavery in 1865, the seventeen southern states in which it was practiced adopted a series of laws that rendered Blacks second-class citizens. Their intent was to prohibit the co-mixing of Blacks and Whites in public facilities. Proponents touted the laws as "separate but equal." What they did, however, was make it legal to give Blacks inferior products and service and to limit opportunities. Their edicts, called Jim Crow laws, were affirmed by the United States Supreme Court in an 1896 case, *Plessey v. Ferguson*. The case upheld a Louisiana law that confined Blacks to designated railcars, separate from Whites. Writing for the majority, Justice Henry Brown stated, "If the civil and political rights of both races be equal, one can not be inferior to the other civilly or politically."[1]

Twenty Jim Crow laws were enacted in the state of Tennessee. The first called for Blacks and Whites to be educated in separate schools. In the following years more such laws were introduced. Blacks and Whites were made to use separate public restrooms and drinking fountains, separate mental health hospitals, different railcars on trains, and separate seating areas on city trolleys and buses. Blacks were barred from city parks, swimming pools, and tennis courts. Private business owners, too, were made to keep the races separate. While the Knickerbocker Cinema boasted of being the "Cool and Healthful" place to take in a movie, and the Loews attempted to lure moviegoers by calling itself the "cool Loews," those summertime comforts were actually only available to White patrons. Blacks were restricted to films that played at the Black-owned Bijou.

Jim Crow involved more than laws alone. It was a general malignancy, a pietism that infested thinking, perverted behavior, and distorted judgment. While Pastor Richard Nowen would espouse 1 John 4:7, "Beloved, let us love one another," from his Sunday pulpit, that love did not extend to Nashville's African American population, which was barred from his First Baptist Church on Broad Street.[2] The editorial page of the local newspaper, the *Nashville Tennessean*, regularly urged youth to exhibit greater discipline, excoriated the actions of Adolf Hitler in Germany, and urged Christians to remain strong in their faith. Yet between these admonishments the newspaper regularly exhibited hypocrisy in the form of *Sunflower Street*, a degrading cartoon that painted Blacks as ignorant and mocked their diction. This was the world Ted Rhodes was born into.

On a day when light rain bathed the city of Nashville and temperatures barely crept above freezing, November 9, 1913, Frank and Della Rhodes celebrated the birth of a son who would be their only child. They christened the boy Theodore Nathaniel. The family home at 1602 Patterson was little more than a shack, small, and comprised just three rooms—a bedroom, living room, and kitchen. Behind the dwelling, an outbuilding stood in lieu of a bathroom. The home was crowded. Its occupants included a fourth, Mary, who was Della's daughter from a previous relationship and eleven years older than her new baby stepbrother. Money was scarce, so much so that the family could not afford a telephone. To reach them, one had to phone a neighbor and ask that a message be relayed.

Life for the Rhodes family was hardscrabble. Frank Rhodes was part of a large Black workforce at Federal Chemical Company's fertilizer plant, where he performed exhausting physical labor in a grimy, noxious environment amid animal manure and volatile chemicals for low pay. Opportunities for betterment were limited by an inability to read or write. While the plant did offer schooling for its employees, Frank Rhodes chose to spend his spare time on other pursuits, one of which was the activities at Stringer Lodge Number

6, where he was part of the Knights of Pythias, a Black fraternal organization created not long after the abolition of slavery.

The meager wages Frank Rhodes brought home made it imperative Della Rhodes juggle the demands of raising a family with full-time employment. Each day she traveled to North Nashville and the four-story Weyman-Bruton Tobacco warehouse. There, she toiled in the operations stemming room as part of a team of women who plucked stems from tobacco leaves. Della Rhodes carried a degree of weariness home at the end of a shift. But rather than being from the sort of physical exertion that exhausted her husband, Della Rhodes' fatigue was a product of tedium.

Hours spent at work and away from her child failed to diminish the guidance and direction Della Rhodes imparted to her son. She was a strong woman. With each passing year friends saw in her son the product of her teaching. They also recognized traits from her own character. Ted Rhodes was easygoing. He exhibited an abundance of patience, a tendency to let bygones be bygones, yet teemed with a steely determination to achieve.

Once in school Ted Rhodes' interactions with others his age led to participation in sports. The youth enjoyed baseball. Though slight of build, he roughhoused on the schoolyard and played football. But by the age of eight, Rhodes' interest began to narrow its focus toward one sport in particular—golf. But for Blacks in the South, golf came with restrictions. They were barred from playing on any of Nashville's public golf courses. Neither were they welcomed as members at the area's private country clubs, Belle Meade and Richland. So, young Rhodes improvised. With the creativity exhibited to bridge the expense chasm and concoct his own golf club, Rhodes overcame a second obstacle. He forged his own golf course. Rhodes searched for pieces of fabric and sticks, then attached them. At a schoolyard, then later at two Nashville parks that did welcome Blacks—Watkins Park in North Nashville and Frederick Douglas Park in East Nashville—Rhodes played an improvised sort of golf. He drove his sticks into the ground at selected spots and went about swinging his coat-hanger club to whack the cork bottle-cap ball. "There were no holes," explained a friend, who added that the youths could "only practice for distance and hitting the ball at designated targets."[3]

For Rhodes, the frivolity of youth came to a disquieting end on a brisk March morning in 1929, when the tremor of death shook the family household. A debilitating gastrointestinal ailment plagued Frank Rhodes for several weeks. As the problem worsened, the family patriarch became unable to work, then was incapacitated and ultimately confined to bed. At 10:11 a.m. on Sunday, March 17, with his family at his bedside, Frank Rhodes passed away. Two days later, after the funeral for his father at Olivet Baptist Church, Ted Rhodes found himself thrust from adolescence to adulthood.

Grief that enveloped the family was compounded by crisis. Loss wasn't simply that of the family patriarch but also an income. Though only twelve and having completed just the sixth grade, Ted Rhodes was faced with little choice. He had to go to work. Rhodes dropped out of school. Over the previous three years, an uncle had, on occasion, helped him earn money from work as a caddy, carrying clubs for the golfers who played at Belle Meade Country Club. Ted Rhodes went to the man in the hope of working full time.

John Lee Bates was caddy master at Belle Meade Country Club. The man, known around the club as "Pap," had overseen Belle Meade's caddies dating back to 1917. He agreed to add his nephew to the exclusive club's cadre. The daily 6-mile trolley journey from his home to Belle Meade took Rhodes into an entirely different universe. While Edgehill was awash in hardship, Belle Meade Country Club sat among a bastion of Nashville-area wealth. Situated southwest of downtown, the club stood on what had once been the grounds of a 2,500-acre plantation that was home to some of the finest racehorses in America. The plantation's centerpiece was a two-story Greek Revival mansion that was built using 136 slaves. After the death of the plantation's owner, William Hicks Jackson, who had been a brigadier general in the Confederate

Army during the Civil War, the plantation was sold to pay off debts. Nine years later, in 1915, Belle Meade Country Club opened its doors.

Belle Meade was a place of opulence. The club took pride in its refined, dignified culture. It was a place of white dinner jackets, tuxedos, and gowns, of afternoon tea, ladies' day on Tuesdays, and dinner dances on Saturday nights. Belle Meade was where young women dreamt of holding their wedding receptions, where visiting dignitaries were entertained, and where people yearned to be when the clock struck midnight on New Year's Eve. Golf was important to Belle Meade. When the club was made host of the State Golf Championship in 1920, then the Southern Amateur Championship a year later, it brought validation and a reputation as one of the finest facilities for golf in the South.

Belle Meade did not accept Black members, nor could Blacks play golf, enter the pro shop, or even dine at the club as guests. They could, however, work as caddies, janitors, dishwashers, and busboys. Strict rules applied. There were boundaries and limitations, areas where they were not permitted to go, and behavior that had to be followed. For Rhodes, the formal education he forsook paled when compared to the golf training he embraced. Pap Bates assigned a senior caddy to initiate the teen. Rhodes quickly learned being a caddy involved much more than toting a 10-pound bag with fourteen clubs. He was schooled in the elementary aspects of the role, the proper stance, when and how to hold the flagstick, the importance of following the flight of the ball, and being able to quickly identify where it landed. There was proper etiquette to adhere to.

1. Don't speak unless spoken to.

2. Never cast a shadow on your golfer's lay.

3. Clean the club after a shot.

4. Never lag behind. Walk slightly ahead of or alongside your golfer.

5. Do nothing that would distract your golfer.

Far more important, though, were the lessons necessary to forge a new caddy into one whom members would seek out and tip well as opposed to a laggard whom Pap Bates would have to dismiss. "Every bag lugger is a coach, must know every shot, and must know capabilities of the man for whom he's working," explained veteran caddy Jimmy McMurry. "A golfer should trust the caddy's judgement over his own."[4] A good caddy's knowledge was akin to a PhD in physics, a master's degree in human behavior, and a doctorate in agronomy and meteorology. It was imperative he know every aspect of Belle Meade's eighteen holes from yardage to daily pin placements, landscape, angles, traps and roughs, wind tendencies, and what impact weather could have. Vital, too, was an understanding of equipment. A successful caddy never waited for a golfer to request their club. It was important to know the best club for the shot at hand. That meant understanding the type of shot every club was designed for. Along with club selection, the caddy had to size up the skills of the golfer and take into consideration the strengths and weaknesses of their game when selecting the proper club. Golf balls weren't exempt from schooling either. Every manufacturer had unique characteristics that produced differing tendencies. The schooling was daunting, if not overwhelming, and made so because every bit of know-how could only come from on-the-job observation and experience rather than from a lecture or textbook.

Additional challenges often came from the golfers whom a caddy served. Bad shots could evoke fury. In a part of the country that considered Blacks inferior, a hook, slice, or missed putt could mean a serenade of profanity that might continue for several holes, if not the entirety of a round. It was no secret some golfers were made so angry by a perceived mistake they'd lose self-control and physically punch or even beat their caddy. In Texas, a golfer became so upset at losing a bet he shot his caddy. In Memphis, two golfers became enraged to such a degree they doused their caddy with gasoline and lit him on fire.

The job came with natural hazards as well. Reaching to pull a flagstick from a hole only to find a 2-foot green snake curled up inside was the least dangerous. Each year in Nashville and around Tennessee, caddies were struck by lightning and killed. A Belle Meade caddy was struck on the head by an errant shot, rendered unconscious, and later died from the blow. The golfer could not understand why the caddy failed to respond when he cried "fore!" It was later that he learned the teen was deaf.

For those caddies able to absorb the knowledge, put up with the abuse, and consistently practice the craft at a high standard, there was good money to be made. An eighteen-hole round in 1929 could net a caddy at least one dollar, even more if the golfer was a generous tipper. There were senior caddies, ones popular for their skill and consistency who, with 153 golfing days a year for Belle Meade's five hundred members, had the potential to take home decent pay.

Overseeing a staff of several dozen caddies was laborious at best. For Pap Bates, days at Belle Meade Country Club began long before sunup and extended far beyond the bag room. A plethora of set-up tasks could equate to a full day's work even before the first member showed up. A slender man of average height, often clad in a flat cap, Bates was a patient man with an ability to size up the strengths and weaknesses of the young men who worked for him. It didn't take long for Bates to notice that one of his caddies in particular "was different. That's for sure."[5] In Rhodes he saw a teen with a voracious zeal for golfing knowledge. Bates noticed how Rhodes watched the golfers as he caddied, building awareness by soaking up the selections and strategies employed by the men. It impressed Bates to see Rhodes eschew the games of marbles some caddies played during downtime and, instead, use his spare time to size up the golfing skills, the mental acuity, and the self-control or lack thereof exhibited by the club's member golfers.

In time Rhodes was bringing home seventy-five cents a day. He was known around the course by a new nickname. While evidence of acceptance from the older Belle Meade caddies, it was not a nickname Rhodes particularly liked. It came from the threadbare clothing he wore and his raggamuffin appearance. The older youths called him "Rags."

After watching his newest caddy for several weeks, Pap Bates initiated what for him was an uncommon step. He took Ted Rhodes under his wing. Bates became a mentor and golf tutor to the young caddy. The man was considered the best Black golfer in Nashville. Early in the morning and sometimes late in the afternoon when no one was playing, Bates would go out on the course and work on his game. In time he invited Rhodes to join him. Bates was selective on which holes to play, careful not to be seen lest they upset White members. Beneath the oak trees Bates and Rhodes discussed club selection. As they walked Belle Meade's Bermuda fairways, questions and answers flew back and forth. Rhodes learned how to navigate the rough, hit out of bunkers, and read the bent grass greens. When the pros came to Belle Meade for the Southeastern Professional Golfer's Championship, Rhodes was an ardent observer. Similarly, when the Whitefoord Cole Trophy was contested or the city championship came to the course, he focused intently. Rhodes knew that the better the caddy, the better the golfer you got to caddy for. That meant the more money the caddy could make.

At the end of a shift, Bates would slip Rhodes an old worn club that had been discarded by a member along with some scuffed golf balls. The teen would then beat a path to Watkins Park, Douglas Park, or, if time allowed, Sunset Park to practice. Located 20 miles from Nashville, Sunset Park was an oasis for the area's African American population. Carved out of 11 acres near the community of Nolensville by a successful shoemaker and his wife, Sunset Park featured the only baseball diamonds in the region available to Blacks. Picnic tables, barbeque pits, and open space drew people by horse-drawn cart and special buses, especially on weekends. It was here that Rhodes spent hours whacking balls and honing his skills.

Keen to find a more convenient place where he could improve his game, Rhodes identified an open space a mile away from his home where he could set up his own course. At Washington Junior High School, he crafted a four-hole layout on which he could master his iron skills and become adept with the one-through-four woods. But for all his ever-improving skills, Ted Rhodes was a golfer on the outside looking in. Barred from tournaments by the color of his skin, Rhodes could only read or hear tales about area tournaments. If he was angered by the exploits of other caddies, such as nineteen-year-old John Ed Reed or the redheaded, freckle-faced, fifteen-year-old phenom Herschel Spears, who excelled in area junior events and the city amateur championship, nobody ever knew. Rhodes was never one to complain.

The spoils of Rhodes' golfing growth came instead through his work as a caddy. Practical know-how improved his ability to counsel Belle Meade members. Demand for Rhodes grew, not only from members of the country club but also some of the area's best golfers. Mac Brothers, a Nashville grocery executive, regarded by *Nashville Tennessean* columnist Will Grimsley as "the town's finest shot maker," insisted Rhodes be his caddy for the city championship.[6] When US Open qualifying came to Belle Meade in 1936, the Arkansas sensation "Dutch" Harrison, with Rhodes on his bag, shot the second-lowest score among all qualifiers in the nation. Even Herschel Spears sought Rhodes when trying to qualify for the National Public Links championship. "That guy can show me plenty about this game," he said.[7]

By the time Rhodes reached the age of twenty-one, financial pressures tugged at him. The Great Depression was wreaking havoc on American households. Nearly one-fourth of all able-bodied men of working age struggled to find a job. Wages for those who had jobs fell by an average of more than 42 percent. In an effort to create jobs, President Franklin D. Roosevelt created the Civilian Conservation Corps. The program was designed to employ 250,000 unmarried men between the ages of eighteen and twenty-five. Ted Rhodes signed up.

Men were assigned to camps, initially in Virginia, then as the program grew, Alabama, Illinois, Michigan, North Carolina, and Pennsylvania. Camps were segregated. The work was backbreaking. Projects spanned the gamut from building bridges and airfields to planting trees and stocking lakes and streams with fish. Each participant served a six-month term. They worked forty-hour weeks and were paid thirty dollars a month, twenty-five of which was automatically sent home for family members.

Once Rhodes' stint in the Conservation Corps concluded, he returned to Nashville and Belle Meade Country Club. Opportunities in golf remained constrained by the citadel that was Jim Crow. Through much of his twenties, Rhodes remained content to earn his living as a caddy. Demand took him to a second Nashville-area country club: Richland.

During the summer of 1941 the 26th Tennessee State Amateur Championship came to Belle Meade. With it came tales of near-mythical proportions about a new golf phenomenon in the western part of the state. Cary Middlecoff had been filling his trophy case for four years, since he turned sixteen. He was the son of a Memphis dentist who gifted clubs to his son for his seventh birthday. Middlecoff attended an all-White private high school and honed his skills at Chickasaw, the country club where his parents were members. At the age of seventeen the teen won the Memphis high school title, then beat all comers to take the city golf championship. Upon graduation from high school, Middlecoff enrolled at the University of Mississippi, where in 1938 he became the school's first all-American in the sport of golf. In July of 1940 Middlecoff, then nineteen and married, entered the Tennessee state championship with few expectations. As he concluded the front nine holes on the final day of match play, his wife strode onto the course, wrapped her arms around her husband's neck, and gave him a kiss. The golfer reacted sheepishly at first, then inspired, proceeded to win six of the next seven holes from his opponent and take the title.

Drawn perhaps by tales of the long-driving Memphian, large throngs of fans turned out for the Belle Meade event. Middlecoff's drives and precise putting took him to the final of the match play tournament against Nashville favorite, Mac Brothers. Middlecoff did not use a caddy. Brothers had drawn Dan

Robertson from the Belle Meade caddy clutch when the tournament began, and as he continued to win, stuck with Robertson for luck. Along with Pap Bates, Rhodes joined the crowd, estimated to be two thousand, the largest ever to witness the final day of the state championship. They watched as Middlecoff finished the morning round 2-up. Then, on the thirty-second hole, in driving rain, Middlecoff unleashed a second shot that wound up inches from the hole. When he tapped in an eagle putt, Brothers conceded to give the Memphian his second consecutive state title trophy.

In the wake of Middlecoff's triumph, sportswriters were effusive in their praise. "The finest amateur in Tennessee, one of the outstanding players of the past decade," opined Bob Rule in the *Nashville Banner*.[8] Will Grimsley, writing in the *Tennessean*, proclaimed Middlecoff "one of the greatest champions in Tennessee golf history."[9] Pap Bates bristled at the acclaim. The Belle Meade caddy master was insistent he knew a player who was better. Ted Rhodes, Bates told a reporter, "hits 'em as long as Middlecoff off the tee and he is death with the irons." And if the two were to play head-to-head, "I'd bet a week's salary on 'Rags,'" Bates said.[10]

It was two weeks later when Rhodes informed Bates he wanted time off. He had learned of an all-Black tournament in Detroit and wanted to enter. Eager to help, the caddy master approached his boss, Belle Meade's long-time pro, George Livingstone. A tall, slender native of Scotland, Livingstone's heavy accent could release an uproarious sense of humor or offend with razor-sharp curtness. The man was more than just the club pro. He designed Belle Meade's course when he arrived in Nashville in 1915. Bates explained to Livingstone Rhodes' opportunity and that he didn't own any golf clubs. Bates asked for permission to let the caddy pick through a barrel full of clubs Belle Meade members had discarded, a total he estimated was close to three hundred. Peering through round, wire-rimmed glasses, Livingstone replied, "You let him pick any he wants and if he doesn't find what he needs, tell me and I'll give him a set myself."[11]

Toting his bag of five used clubs into Union Station, Rhodes was awash in conflicting emotions. His eagerness was tempered by a tinge of apprehension. Never before had he traveled by train, let alone out of state. Tales abounded in the Black community of appalling conditions in the railcars set aside for African American riders. Insolent conductors were known to spit chewing tobacco juice on seats in the so-called Negro Cars. Some lines allowed White farmers to store their livestock alongside Black passengers rather than place them in the luggage car. It drove some Black passengers to wear coveralls to protect their clothes. Dining cars were off-limits to Black passengers, so many carried a shoebox filled with food and, in some cases, brought a small table to eat from. There were even extreme cases where riders brought with them a small gas stove on which to cook.

As Rhodes boarded the train, ambition and anticipation were silent cargo that accompanied his golf clubs and a suitcase. Over the next day and a half, he would cover 760 miles over the American Midwest, a journey of more than just traversed geography. Leaving Nashville meant escape from the specter of Jim Crow. Arrival in Detroit would represent an embodiment of liberation. As Rhodes gazed out the window of his railcar, he pondered. Never in his two decades of golfing zeal had he been able to play in a tournament. The dream of doing so was coming into focus.

Soon the shrill sound of a loud whistle and hissing of released steam filled the air all about Union Station. Cars hitched together jerked to the initial movement of the locomotive. The squeal of wheels on steel rails and the clatter of churning pistons accompanied the Dixie Limited from beneath the roof of Union Station and out into a town painted bright colors by a setting sun. The board inside Union Station listed the departing train's final destination as Chicago. For Ted Rhodes, his destination was a new way of life.

2

The Champ's Inner Circle

By the summer of 1945, there were few stars more popular or well celebrated in American sports than Joe Louis. It was a mantle assumed by the boxer from Babe Ruth in the summer of 1935 upon the home run slugger's retirement from baseball. It came at a time when Louis was in the final stages of a mercurial rise from obscurity to the heavyweight championship. Over a span of eleven months, Louis had gone from knocking an unknown opponent, Jack Kraken, out of the ring in his professional debut before 1,133 spectators in Bacon's Arena in Chicago to pummeling the former heavyweight champion of the world, Primo Carnera.

The Carnera fight brought a raucous crowd of fifty-seven thousand to New York's Yankee Stadium, more than fifteen thousand of whom were Blacks. Following the bout, twenty-five thousand fans celebrated noisily with cowbells, whistles, and dishpans outside the Savoy Club on Seventh Avenue in Harlem. Cars that drove past the revelers carried license plates from Illinois, Tennessee, Georgia, Maryland, Washington, DC, and even provinces in Canada, a reflection of the breadth of the boxer's popularity. The fight held major significance. It was noted by Wilfrid Smith of the *Chicago Tribune* as the "first major contest between Black and White."[1] William G. Ness, writing in the *Pittsburgh Courier*, viewed Louis's victory on a higher realm. "We know that Joe is an answer to our prayers . . . the prayers of a race of people who are struggling to break through a dense cloud of prejudice and studied misunderstanding."[2]

Three months later the popularity of Joe Louis swelled to even greater heights. An eye-popping turnout of more than ninety-one thousand filled Yankee Stadium to see Louis knock out Max Baer in the fourth round of their bout. The crowd on that night was dotted with movie stars who traveled from Hollywood, mayors who came from big cities, and even governors of several eastern states. They were joined by the wealthy and titans of industry from all across the country. Each victory saw Louis become more than just America's biggest sports star. To Black Americans he was a beacon of hope. Dean Hancock, writing in the *Birmingham Weekly*, called Louis a "supreme interracial influence on our country."[3] As each win saw the boxer's popularity grow among mainstream America, so too did the dream that his most impactful knockout would be one over Jim Crow.

Yet as he rose in the heavyweight ranks during the 1930s, many saw Louis as antithetical to the personality traits many Americans expected in a popular Black sports hero—"a great capacity for gaiety, that he is emotionally high strung, and a natural showman," in the words of syndicated columnist Heywood Broun.[4] That was not Joe Louis. He was a man the popular sportswriter Grantland Rice described as "quiet, almost shy, on the retiring side."[5] It was a cultivated image.

Born Joe Louis Barrow, the grandson of slaves in rural Alabama, he told people his father died when he was an infant. In truth, Munroe Barrow, who picked cotton for a living, was committed to a mental institution before his son's second birthday. A speech impediment kept the youth mostly silent for the first six years of his life. When Joe was seven Lillie Barrow gathered her seven children and moved the family to Detroit. The city was a bastion of manufacturing, and during his teenage years Joe became immersed in it. He worked on the assembly line at Briggs manufacturing and later at the Ford Motor Company's Rouge plant. His mother prodded him to take violin lessons, but after dropping into Brewster's Gym behind Stroh's Brewery in downtown Detroit, Louis was exposed to the pugilistic arts, and a passion for boxing was unleashed. He secretly used the money his mother gave him for violin lessons to box. Impressed by what he witnessed, a trainer in the gym, Duke Ellis, took the teenager under his wing. Other fighters marveled at the teen's natural punching power. "If he hit you, you were down," stated Stanley Evans, a fellow fighter.[6] Ellis developed Louis's left hook into a feared weapon. Louis took the punch a step farther. He added a right cross to create a combination known around Brewster's Gym as the DOA punch. "If you couldn't get out of the way of both of them at the same time, you'd be dead on your ass . . . that's what it really stood for," grinned Walter Smith, another Brewster Gym boxer.[7] Finally, in 1932 Ellis decided Louis was ready to enter an amateur tournament. The teen fretted. He had kept the boxing dalliance from his mother and feared the consequences should she find out. To ensure his secret the teenager dropped his last name when he registered and fought as Joe Louis.

As Louis drew ever so close to a heavyweight title fight, and each win made more money jingle in his pocket, he developed a fervor for an entirely different sport. From an innocent introduction to the game of golf came an interest that grew to near obsession. In time, the boxer would seek a golf mentor. It was a role that would land in the lap of Ted Rhodes.

Joe Louis's initiation to golf came in June of 1936. While he was training for his fight with Max Schmeling, newspaper columnist Ed Sullivan suggested he take up the sport. He gave Louis a golf instruction book along with a promise. If, after reading it, he wanted to take up the game, Sullivan would buy him a set of clubs. It didn't take long before the boxer was infatuated. After his loss to Schmeling in what was considered an enormous upset, more than a few sportswriters suggested Louis's training suffered because of the time he spent on the golf course.

By Louis's third year as heavyweight champion, quality opponents were becoming scarce. Known universally by the nickname "The Brown Bomber," Louis won three consecutive fights by first-round knockout. While the quick knockouts and relative ease by which he won built a sterling reputation and an impressive record, the numbers at the box office dwindled. When, in March 1940, he knocked out Johnny Paycheck forty-four seconds into the second round, Grantland Rice called the bout the "worst heavyweight championship fight in the history of all time."[8] Worse still, only 11,620 paid to see the fight. Louis's promoter, Mike Jacobs, pondered ways to stimulate ticket sales. He finally came up with a plan to take the champ's fights out of New York and to cities around the country. Jacobs hoped a rare opportunity to see Louis fight in person might overshadow the dullness of an obvious mismatch. Louis fought in Los Angeles, Miami, Chicago, and Detroit. But traveling to new locations had little effect at the box office. Braven Dyer put it aptly in the *Los Angeles Times*: "Louis outclasses the field so completely that all of his fights are apt to be tabbed as mismatches for a long time to come."[9]

It was during this time of waning challenges in the boxing ring that Louis's enthusiasm for golf grew. Obsessed with improving his game, Louis hired his very own teaching professional. In the summer of 1940, Clyde Martin left his position as head pro at the all-Black Langston Golf Course in Washington, DC to take on the role. He found his pupil to be stiff, using a stance akin to delivering a boxing punch and with an overly long swing. Martin went to work to shorten the boxer's swing and loosen his arms. By the following spring Louis's average score dropped from 125 to 81. "You've got to play golf every day," Louis said, "and then there is a question whether you can get anywhere, especially in my case."[10]

Playing led to further investment. In the early days of 1941, at the suggestion of a golfing friend, Louis announced plans to stage a tournament, The Joe Louis Open. His event would be a seventy-two-hole tournament over three days in August at Rackham Golf Course, a public course adjacent to the city's zoo in the Huntington Park section of Detroit. Louis wanted the event to be special, akin to the Negro National Open, the national championship for Black golfers. "This event will prove to the Whites that we have our [Walter] Hagens and [Gene] Sarazens too," he said.[11] The tournament would have both amateur and professional sections. Louis put up $1,000 for prize money, $500 of which would go to the winner.

Golfers arrived from as far west as San Francisco and Seattle to New York City and Massachusetts in the east. A large contingent traveled from below the Mason-Dixon Line. One in particular who stepped from the Chicago Mercury when it arrived at Michigan Central Depot was a relative golfing novice, Ted Rhodes. Newspaper headlines bore evidence of the challenge that faced him. "Biggest golf tourney opens here," screamed the *Detroit Tribune*, which called Louis's tournament "the greatest link event sponsored by colored for colored golfers."[12] Once he arrived at Rackham Golf Course, Rhodes found himself among more than two hundred golfers—and not just any golfers. This was a gathering of America's best Black golfers—Pat Ball, the former national champion, Edison Marshall, a three-time winner of the Midwestern Open, as well as Howard Wheeler and John Dedy, former Negro National Open winners. For a newcomer to make his tournament debut against such a field was daunting at the very least.

When play teed off, betting was rampant. Wagers were placed, both among the spectators in the gallery and the golfers themselves. Louis put quite a bit of money on Dedy. But the betting favorite was Howard Wheeler. An Atlantan by birth who now lived in Southern California, where he worked as a chauffeur to a motion picture executive, Wheeler utilized a peculiar cross-handed swing. Rather than tees, he hit his drives off of a matchbox, one into which a small hole was cut to balance the ball. Wheeler, who had once caddied for the legendary Bobby Jones, was a golfer with an impressive résumé: winner of the Negro National Open in 1933 and again in 1938. On the first day of the tournament, the men played thirty-six holes. Windy conditions caused many of the scores to balloon. Rhodes, who did not own a pair of golf shoes and played with just five used clubs, nine fewer than a full set, tallied 155, which put him nine strokes behind the leader. The next day, however, he shot 74 to leap past much of the field and into title contention.

Drama was in abundance throughout the final eighteen holes of the tournament. It enveloped the two men who contested the lead—Clyde Martin and Calvin Searles. Martin began the round with a one-shot lead. A double bogey on the sixth hole dropped him into second, two strokes behind Searles. Martin regained the lead when Searles double bogeyed the seventh hole. A crowd estimated at more than one thousand followed the pair. The men were tied when they reached the green on the eighteenth hole. Loud groans wafted when Searles missed his putt for a birdie. When Martin sank his to ensure victory, Louis moved to shake his hand, only to be pushed aside by an onrushing crowd. The fans lifted Martin onto their shoulders and carried him away to the clubhouse.

While the large gallery left Rackham having seen a climactic spectacle, many missed out on the most astonishing performance of the day. With long drives and accurate iron play, Ted Rhodes burst from obscurity. Devoid of fanfare he shot an even par 72. His was the second-lowest score of the day. It was an extraordinary performance that catapulted Rhodes to a third-place finish, nine strokes behind the winnér.

Frivolity reverberated throughout the post-tournament awards event. Louis, the host, was the center of attention, doling out trophies and prize money. A photographer's flashbulb lit up the room just when Louis hoisted the 2-foot-tall winner's trophy and presented it to Martin while the tournament champ flashed his booty, five one-hundred-dollar bills. As Rhodes pocketed his third-place prize money, he had no idea an even bigger reward loomed on the horizon. Privately, Joe Louis faced a dilemma. His schedule for the coming days was filled with a string of commitments. He had business in Chicago and New York City, after which he was to begin training for his next fight. Louis wanted to golf whenever possible. But Martin, his instructor and golfing partner, also had commitments, one of which was to play in the biggest Black golf event of the season, the Negro National Open.

Ted Rhodes may have arrived in Detroit an unknown, but he did not finish the Joe Louis Open in anonymity. He was recognized by the host himself.

On the second day of the tournament, Louis suffered a finger injury and was forced to withdraw. Relegated to the role of spectator, he circulated the course and watched the competition. One golfer in particular caught his attention. Now, as he pondered a temporary replacement for Martin, Louis thought of that golfer whose play and demeanor had impressed him. That was how Ted Rhodes found himself on an airplane days later traveling to New York City.

For someone who had been, only two weeks earlier, a nondescript caddy in Nashville, Tennessee, the beckoning into the inner circle of the greatest sports star in America was overwhelming. On arriving in New York, Rhodes found a place like nothing he had ever seen before. His awe at the city's skyscrapers and gawking at the hustle and bustle of Forty-Second Street and Fifth Avenue readily identified Rhodes as an out-of-towner to locals. But the sights and sounds represented revelation far more than spatial difference. Traveling in such company brought introductions and brushes with celebrity. It meant entrée; the previously inaccessible became available. Being with Joe Louis meant only the finest.

Though north of the Mason-Dixon Line, New York City still held limitations for African Americans in 1941. Many hotels and more than a few restaurants were not welcoming. Louis and Rhodes stayed in Harlem. Home base was the Hotel Theresa, an all-Black hotel known as the Waldorf of Harlem. Stepping from the hotel's front door was to enter a neighborhood far different than Edgehill back home. Frank's Famous Oyster and Chop House was a stone's throw away. Farther up 125th Street the Apollo Theatre was reopening, with The Ink Spots billed as its headliner. Over on Lenox, the Savoy was the place to go if you liked to dance, which Rhodes did and did very well. It was altogether wondrous if not extraordinary.

A day after arriving, Louis had an appointment at the Boxing Commission headquarters in the State Building. Contracts were signed for his fight with Lou Nova. He spent a day at Speedway Gardens to take in the Harlem Blue Ribbon Horse Show and watch his own entry, "Flash," compete. But regardless of the major commitment of the day, Louis always made time for golf. He bought Rhodes a brand-new pair of golf shoes and a new set of clubs. The men played frequently. When the two weeks ended, and it came time for Louis to begin serious training for the Nova fight, he invited Rhodes to stay on and join him at his training camp in picturesque Greenwood Lake on the New York–New Jersey border.

It was during the training camp that Louis received notification that would bring an end to the halcyon-like late summer days of 1941. His military draft status had been reclassified. It was now 1-A, the draft board's highest level. It was very likely Joe Louis would soon be inducted into the United States Army.

The night of September 29 brought Rhodes' trip to its apex. Stepping into the Polo Grounds, home to New York's baseball Giants, was to be bathed in wonderment. The boxing ring was erected in what for the Giants was centerfield. Chairs, thousands of them, covered every single blade of grass. A crowd of 56,549, one-third the population of Rhodes' hometown, poured into the cavernous venue. Men, women, Black, White, celebrities, and Joes—everyone heavily invested, shouting, and screaming their lungs out for Louis to successfully defend his heavyweight title. The night's decisive moment came in the sixth round. It was 10:54 p.m. when the punch, a lightning strike, a quick yet vicious right hook described the next morning by Art McMahon in *The Herald News* as "probably the hardest, most savage right hand wallop delivered by man since he came down out of the trees," struck Lou Nova square on the jaw.[13] Nova's head bounced from the canvas. His legs splayed in the air. Delirium erupted. The referee raised Louis's left hand in the air to signify his victory. Almost three hours later a throng put at more than ten thousand celebrated outside the Hotel Theresa. They roared when Louis appeared. He offered humble thanks for their support, then quietly retreated inside. And just like that it was over. A fairy-tale vacation ended. Joe Louis received his orders.

Louis was directed to report to Provident Hospital in Chicago on October 14, for a pre-induction physical exam. Full induction into the army would likely come soon after. "I'm ready and anxious to go," he told friends.[14] But first, he wanted to take his wife on a vacation. Rhodes packed for home, a man infused with confidence from the experience. Naivete was erased. He was transfigured by this newfound friendship and acceptance into the inner circle of greatness. But before Ted Rhodes could take any of these new attributes into another professional golf tournament, forces far beyond his control would come into play and send his life in another direction.

On December 7, 1941, Japan attacked Pearl Harbor, the American naval base in Hawaii. Less than twenty-four hours later, the United States declared war on both Japan and Germany. Days later, Joe Louis became registrant number 374 at Fort Jay in New York, one of a group of more than four hundred men formally inducted into the army. Both his boxing career and golf tournament were put on hiatus.

Mere days after the attack on Pearl Harbor, Secretary of the Navy Frank Knox ordered the creation of a plan for the recruitment of five thousand Black men. As part of this plan, it was decided Blacks would serve only as cooks, mess attendants, and stewards out of concern that widespread integration might cause friction and impact efficiency. President Franklin D. Roosevelt agreed and gave orders to implement the plan beginning June 1, 1942. Within six months close to thirty thousand Blacks were in the navy. Among them was Ted Rhodes.

Rhodes was sent to Naval Station Great Lakes near Chicago. The installation was the largest navy base in the country and the navy's largest training station. It was a massive complex, so big it encompassed sixteen hundred acres with its buildings connected by 69 miles of roads. Construction at the base took on a frenzied pace, both to accommodate a large influx of recruits and also to create separate accommodations for those who were Black.

Hostility toward the Black recruits permeated. Many who came from integrated backgrounds saw the treatment as demeaning. Service was limited to menial roles. Theirs was called the "Steward" Branch and involved serving Whites by waiting on tables, cooking, and cleaning.

Wartime service ended for Rhodes on January 6, 1944. Over the preceding weeks reoccurring kidney stones left him racked with pain. He was unable to carry out his prescribed duties. Though fighting still raged in Europe and in Asia, Rhodes was discharged from the navy on medical grounds. He opted to remain in the Chicago area for a time. It was there he made a fortuitous introduction, one with the popular singer Billy Eckstine. Fresh from setting box office records at the Apollo Theatre in New York, Eckstine and his fifteen-piece orchestra, one that included a young trumpeter, Dizzy Gillespie, and Charlie Parker on alto sax, set out on a tour of the Midwest. After sellout dates in Cincinnati and Cleveland, Eckstine and company arrived to play the Regal Theatre in Chicago. What brought Rhodes and Eckstine together was golf. By the time the singer's tour left the Midwest, Rhodes was hired to be Eckstine's golf tutor.

In the fall of 1944, Joe Louis received a twenty-one-day furlough from the army and returned home to Detroit. His leave came after a seven-month stretch of boxing exhibitions at military bases throughout Europe. The tour put the staff sergeant on a grueling schedule, often up by 5:00 a.m. and rarely to bed before 2:00 a.m. Officers who traveled with Louis marveled at the boxing champion's stamina. Never once, they said, did he complain or refuse a visit, even when told there might not be many men on hand.

Louis's base visits were impactful if not emotion-filled. In Italy, he beamed while he watched the red-tailed P-51 Mustangs of the 15th Army Air Force—the Tuskegee Airmen—return from a mission. "These fellows sure can fly," he said to the lieutenant who was escorting him. When the boxing sensation met the pilots, Louis told the gathering, "I have visited many airfields and spoken to a lot of pilots, they all speak well of you and give you all the credit."[15] At a base hospital on the French coast, a wounded soldier pleaded with his doctor to remove bandages from his eyes so he could see Louis. Upon feeling Louis take his hand, the soldier sobbed, "This is the happiest moment of my life."[16] While visiting a base in England, a B-17 that was shot up over Germany crashed at the edge of the airstrip. Louis raced to the wreckage. He placed the head of the unconscious pilot on his knee. When the flyer came to, he looked up, then astonished by what he saw, muttered, "Well, I'll be damned—Joe Louis!"[17] An army private stationed in the Mediterranean wrote of Louis, "I daresay his trip overseas has done a world of good for our boys."[18]

While home Louis huddled with the men who helped run his inaugural golf tournament. Riding a sense of optimism that the war was nearing an end, he announced the resumption of the Joe Louis Open for the fall of 1945. Prize money would be raised from $1,000 to $1,500. The winner would receive $700 in war bonds.

On May 8, 1945, celebrations erupted to news that Germany had surrendered. The war in Europe was over. In July, while war continued to rage in the Pacific, Louis was granted a twenty-day furlough and returned home to host his second Joe Louis Open. The tournament brought a reunion for Rhodes and Louis, who had not seen each other in three years. Louis recruited Rhodes to join him in a challenge. As a prelude to the actual tournament, Louis staged a best ball match-play event. Two Black golfers would compete with two White golfers. For the White tandem, Louis recruited two of the best golfers in the state of Michigan, 1926 British Open runner-up Al Watrous and multi-time Michigan state amateur champion Chuck Koscis. Louis would be one half of the opposition. From the field of 165 entrants in his tournament, Louis chose Rhodes as his partner. Amid rampant wagering, Louis and Rhodes came up short and lost to Watrous and Koscis, 6 and 5.

Rain greeted the golfers on the first day of the full tournament. Rhodes made the best of difficult conditions to shoot 76. It put him third, four shots off the lead. On the final day Rhodes produced one of the better rounds, 75. It gave him a fourth-place finish, seven shots behind the surprise winner, a 38-year-old waiter from Minneapolis, Solomon Hughes.

Noticeably absent from the field was the defending champion, Clyde Martin. While Louis's personal instructor did attend the tournament, his health would not permit him to play. Martin spent much of the previous year bedridden in a Washington, DC hospital, seriously ill with a lung ailment. By the summer of 1945, there was still no timetable for his return to golf and thus no idea when he would be able to work again with Louis. Anxious to resume playing regularly upon his formal discharge from the army, Louis decided to hire a new golf instructor.

Three weeks after the tournament Rhodes was visiting friends in Dayton, Ohio. He learned there was to be an all-Black tournament in the city and entered. To the surprise of event organizers, Joe Louis turned up to play. In the amateur division Louis lost a sudden-death playoff for third place. In the pro division, Rhodes finished in fourth place, six shots behind the winner. After the event Louis offered Rhodes the job as his personal golf instructor.

Accepting the offer put Rhodes on Louis's payroll. It also thrust him into a distinct inner circle, one that traveled everywhere and did everything with the heavyweight champ. Freddie Guinyard, Louis's best friend from childhood, a diminutive man whom the champ liked to say was "tough and slick," served as Louis's bodyguard and handled travel arrangements.[19] Leonard Reed, a tap dancer who choreographed the acclaimed "Shim, Sham, Shimmy" routine and later emceed at the Apollo Theatre in New York, was Louis's personal secretary and coordinated all of his appearances. Irwin Rose was Louis's publicist and Marshall Miles his manager. Rhodes' job title would be personal valet. The bulk of his work, however, was to help Louis improve his golf game and play whenever and wherever the heavyweight champion desired.

Rhodes' new job began in the early days of October. Six weeks after Japan announced its surrender to bring an end to the war, Joe Louis received an honorable discharge from the army. At 4:00 p.m., on October 1, he hurriedly left Camp Shanks, New York, to return home. "I'm catching the first train to Detroit to see those Tigers," he told reporters. "Then I'm off to California for two or three months."[20] Aside from watching his favorite baseball team play in the World Series, Louis told reporters he planned to "play a lot of golf."[21]

Louis was cheered at Briggs Stadium before Game One of the World Series. Clad in civilian clothes, a gray suit and red tie, for the first time since 1942, he predicted the Tigers would defeat the Chicago Cubs in six games. It was only after Detroit achieved the feat in seven that he set out for the West Coast.

Arriving with Louis in Los Angeles, Rhodes stepped into a city flush with golfing opportunity. Los Angeles and many of the surrounding towns offered a plethora of courses, both private country clubs and municipally owned public courses. It was also an area devoid of discriminatory Jim Crow laws. The public golf courses were open to all. Only a small few of the area's country clubs—Los Angeles Country Club in Beverely Hills and Wilshire Country Club in particular—restricted play by Blacks and Jews.

Not only did the area's warm winter weather make it possible to golf year-round but it also allowed for a busy calendar of tournaments. Los Angeles, several surrounding towns, and a number of clubs staged pro-am events throughout the fall and winter months. Each offered enticing prize money. Upon their arrival in Los Angeles, Louis and Rhodes learned one of the bigger such tournaments—the Southern California Open—was just over a week away and still accepting entries. Rhodes decided to enter.

When play teed off at Fox Hills Golf Course in Culver City, 190 golfers—71 pros and 119 amateurs—made up the field. Among the bigger names were former Wimbledon tennis champion Ellsworth "Elly" Vines, who was making a switch to golf, and Bob Crosby, the bandleader and brother of singing sensation Bing. In addition to a who's who of Southern California standouts, eleven Black golfers were in the field. All were competing for $1,750 in prize earnings, a mixture of cash, war bonds, and redeemable stamps.

Rhodes was placed in a threesome with two local Black golfers, Bill Spiller and Elmer Williams. The three hit it off. Spiller found the newcomer "a friendly man, a real entertainer, and a good dresser."[22] Rhodes endured a challenging first round. He shot a 76. His score was nine strokes behind the leader. Far more concerning than the lead, though, was the cut. The fifty-four-hole format

Joe Louis steps from a train in Los Angeles. He was accompanied by Ted Rhodes. The trip would change the trajectory of Rhodes' career. Courtesy Los Angeles Herald Examiner *photo collection and the Los Angeles Public Library.*

called for the large field to be chopped to just forty golfers after two rounds. Rhodes' score put him perilously close to the cut line. The next day, the gallery and his opponents saw an entirely different Ted Rhodes. He shot 69, the lowest score of the round, to vault into fourth place, five strokes behind the leader. Any optimism that Rhodes might challenge for the $300 winner's prize was quashed twenty-four hours later. On the final day he endured his poorest round of the tournament. Rhodes shot 77, to finish in a three-way tie for ninth place. Still, his top-ten finish earned $41.66 in prize money. One of the area's Black newspapers, the *California Eagle*, introduced Rhodes to its readers with "Theodore Rhodes, Joe Louis's traveling pro, making his debut in Los Angeles Tournament play was our best performer in the Open."[23]

Rare was the morning during their Southern California stay when Louis and Rhodes weren't on one golf course or another by 9:00 a.m. They almost never made it back to the Hotel Watkins before sunset. As one sportswriter observed of Louis, "Joe plays like any other good amateur, bets wildly, frequently loses, finds consolation in the law of averages."[24] With Louis a magnet for the famous, he and Rhodes frequently golfed with celebrities—Brooklyn Dodgers manager, Leo Durocher, and his pal, the actor George Raft, one day; Bruce McCormick, the California Amateur champ and fellow amateur standout Smiley Quick on another. Adolphe Menjou, who starred along with Rita Hayworth and Fred Astaire in *You Were Never Lovelier*, invited Louis and Rhodes to play a round at his club. When Al Williams of The Four Step Brothers fame used a five-iron to card a hole in one on the 145-yard second hole at Sunset Fields, it was Rhodes, his playing partner, who signed the scorecard to make the feat official.

Louis loved to gamble. Games frequently involved high stakes. It was not uncommon for Louis to wager $2,000 with a foe on the outcome of the front nine, another $2,000 on the result of the back nine, and $2,000 for all eighteen holes. Stories of staggering losses—$6,000 to a frequent playing partner, Judson Grant, $12,000 to another—circulated local courses. Hustlers salivated. The most brazen jockeyed for a chance to play the boxing champ. Newspaper columnists subtly told of one who fleeced Louis for enough money—$22,000—to buy an apartment building and new car. Feeling particularly confident one morning, Louis bet Rhodes $20,000 that he could beat him. Rhodes gave him four strokes. Rhodes shot 67, Louis 73.

By mid-November the paths of Louis and Rhodes diverged. Louis's vacation was interrupted. His publicist arranged promotional appearances at boxing matches, football games, and sports banquets, some of which necessitated travel from Los Angeles. A promoter convinced him to front a jazz band and tour several cities in the West. While Louis followed these new pursuits, Rhodes remained behind. He took advantage of the area's busy tournament schedule to gain more competitive experience. Rhodes entered the Montebello Open but finished out of the money. Same, too, in a tournament staged by the area Produce Growers Association that offered an enticing $5,000 in prize money.

When the calendar flipped to the new year, Rhodes pursued an even bigger challenge. Prodded by Louis, who offered to back him financially, Rhodes entered the Los Angeles Open. Where the Southern California Open drew the best golfers from around the Los Angeles area, the Los Angeles Open, with the lure of a $13,333 payout in war bonds, attracted many of the best players in the country. Byron Nelson, winner of a PGA record eighteen tournaments in 1945, eleven of which came in a row; Sam Snead, who won six events that same year; and Ben Hogan, just out of the army, headlined those who arrived to play.

Being entered in the tournament was one thing, qualifying to play in the three-day, fifty-four-hole event was an entirely different matter. In all, the entry list numbered 430. It was the largest number of entries in the event's twenty-year history. All but forty-three who met criteria to receive exemptions were made to play a thirty-six-hole qualifier. Such a large field meant playing qualifying events at seven different Los Angeles-area courses.

Rhodes was assigned to play his qualifier at Sunset Fields Golf Club. It was a course he played often since arriving in the area. He shot a 144, third best among the entries and comfortably among the ninety-five who qualified to play in the main draw.

When Rhodes along with his playing partners, Bill Spiller and Roscoe Jones, arrived at Riviera Country Club's first tee, the biggest turnout of spectators in the event's history was scattered about the course. Riviera Country Club presented a stiff challenge, the likes of which Rhodes had never tackled before. He had scant experience playing a country club course. They were far more challenging than the public municipal courses, the product of greater expense and more intricate layout. Riviera was one of the toughest of all, rated the third-toughest course in the world. Rhodes' first foray was a struggle. He shot 79, which was thirteen shots behind Snead, who led. The next day, Rhodes shot 81 and failed to make the cut.

Joe Louis saw in Rhodes the potential to be better. He arranged for one of Southern California's best instructors, Ray Mangrum, to fine-tune Rhodes' game. Mangrum, the pro at Sunset Fields, was primarily known for being the brother of Lloyd Mangrum, runner-up in 1940 at The Masters. Ray Mangrum himself was one of the area's best players and had a sixth-place finish at The Masters in 1936 on his own résumé. Louis paid Mangrum to provide Rhodes with forty instruction sessions to try to better his game.

By March, a two-month vacation that was stretched to four came to its conclusion. Joe Louis had to return to work. Contracts were signed for a much-ballyhooed comeback fight. His bout with Billy Conn would be his first since the early days of the war. Predictors suggested the fight would break boxing attendance records. Larry McPhail, president of the New York Yankees, said every effort would be made to see that Yankee Stadium could accommodate one hundred thousand fans on fight night in June. First, though, was a forty-five-day training camp at West Baden Springs in rural Indiana to get in fighting shape. In negotiations to use the place, the local resort agreed that Louis could have unlimited access to their golf course. As Louis and Rhodes left Los Angeles, warm California winter sunshine had painted surrounding hills green. His time in the region illuminated a path for Ted Rhodes, one with visions of another kind of green. The groundwork was laid. Ted Rhodes was about to become a full-fledged professional golfer and go on the professional golf circuit.

3

A New Star

The still of a quiet morning was interrupted by the rumble of a car engine. Golfers on number eight and the adjoining ninth hole paused to take in the sight of a brand-new gleaming Buick Super that turned onto the palm-lined entry road. The driver's right foot pressed on the accelerator to help the eye-catching red vehicle power uphill before it finally came to a stop in a parking space. The man who exited offered almost as much dazzle as the car itself. Two-tone shoes appeared first, then pressed, pleated slacks, followed by a colorful sweater and a flat-back cap. A pair of dark glasses in a black frame shielded the man's eyes from bright California sun. Ted Rhodes had arrived at Fort Washington Country Club north of Fresno, California, a different man from the one who left California eight months before.

Rhodes' just-completed journey over 220 miles of Central California highway compared little with the remarkable distance his golf game soared during the previous summer. The Ted Rhodes of February 1947 had trophies, money—or "that bread" as he liked to call it—in the bank, and a new car gifted by Joe Louis. He carried acclaim and, most of all, confidence. It was a product of an amazing metamorphosis.

The transformation began from his sessions with Ray Mangrum. Added polish came from Chris Brinke, a PGA standout of the 1920s who approached Rhodes at a tournament with advice. "You've got a fine game son, but you'll never be a great golfer until you learn to putt," Brinke said.

"Keep that blade low and stroke the ball smoothly. You have a tendency to lift the putter on your back stroke. Stop that fault and you'll round out your game."[1]

It was in July of 1946 when Rhodes put Mangrum's and Brinke's lessons to the test. He had accompanied Joe Louis to Cleveland for a golfing vacation after the boxer's eighth-round knockout of Billy Conn. Once in the city Rhodes learned several professional tournaments would soon take place in the region. For Black golfers, opportunities to make money in golf, particularly outside of California, were limited. Events staged by the PGA—the Professional Golfers' Association of America—were off-limits to Black participants. For the Black golfer, opportunity meant the UGA.

In 1925 Robert H. Hawkins, a onetime caddy, spent $25,000 to purchase a manor and 160 acres of land in the Boston, Massachusetts, suburb of Stow. He turned his purchase into Mapledale Country Club. It was the first country club in America exclusively for African Americans. In August of 1926 a frustrated golfer from Chicago, Walter Speedy, met with Hawkins. Over the previous five years Speedy attempted to play on several Chicago-area municipal courses, only to be assaulted by angry White golfers and even arrested by police. The meeting of Speedy and Hawkins led to the formation of an all-Black version of the PGA, the UGA.

Initially, the men viewed the UGA as a way to promote the growth of Black country clubs. Tournaments were staged that matched members of one club against another. Their competitions led to the formation of golfing clubs. Mapledale in Boston, Forest City in Cleveland, Pioneer and Sunset Hills in Chicago, New Amsterdam and St. Nicholas in New York, Douglass Golf Club in Indianapolis, Lincoln Golf Club in Atlanta, and Fairview Golf Club in Philadelphia staged tournaments with their matches capped by a national championship tournament, the Negro National Open. In April 1927 the UGA grew to include several events that would award prize money, and a series for Black professional golfers was born.

Played during summer months, the UGA circuit consisted of between eight and ten tournaments. The number of events depended upon the organization's ability to secure local backers. Jim Crow laws restricted play to Northern and East Coast states where events were held on publicly owned municipal courses. Self-deprecation and derision spawned several nicknames for the series—the Chitlin' Circuit, the Neckbone Tour, and the Peanut Circuit.

In mid-July Rhodes and Louis retreated to Detroit for Louis's third annual tournament. Now firmly established, the Joe Louis Open was a crown jewel of the UGA tour. Once again, Louis increased the prize money. In all, $2,000 would be paid out, $750 of it to the winner. In addition to men's professional and amateur sections, Louis added a women's division. The largest field yet—more than three hundred—registered to play. Rhodes toured the course at a torrid clip. By completion of the final round, he had established a new record score for the tournament, 290, and earned his first professional tournament win.

From Detroit, the men hurried to Chicago, where one of the great promoters of golf in the entire country wanted badly for Louis to play in his tournament. George S. May's All-American Open at Tam O'Shanter Country Club offered the biggest payday in golf—$50,875—with the winner getting $10,500 of it. May, a business consultant by trade and owner of Tam O'Shanter, eschewed tradition. He brought new ideas to the game—grandstands near the putting greens, scoreboards so fans would know who was leading, generator-powered lights to illuminate the eighteenth green for late finishers, and red, white, and blue bunting around the course to create a festive atmosphere. May also refused to work with the PGA. He was adamant about running his tournament his way without interference. And he wanted it open to whomever he wanted. Sportswriters called May's tournament zany and a three-ring-circus, yet it annually lured the best golfers and generated the biggest crowds of any golf event in the country.

May's contrivance for 1946 sparked controversy. He wanted fans to be readily able to identify the golfers. To achieve this, players were instructed

Rhodes (right) receives the winner's trophy from Joe Louis (left) after he had captured the 1946 Joe Louis Open. It was Rhodes' first-ever tournament title and the first of many titles he would earn. Courtesy Charles "Teenie" Harris, Hines Family Fund, Carnegie Museum of Art.

to pin numbers to their backs. Ben Hogan was among many who bristled. He felt May's idea would make a mockery of the game. Faced with backlash, the promoter declared any player who did not wear a number would see a reduction from the prize money they earned. "And if I don't wear a number?" Byron Nelson asked. "About sixteen percent less," was May's answer. "That's all I want to know," Nelson said.[2] May arranged for NBC radio to broadcast the final round nationwide with Bill Stern at the microphone. Perhaps the most bizarre of his ideas was taken from a page in professional wrestling's handbook. May announced that a "tall, dark, and handsome" gentleman who is also "a whale of a golfer" would circulate the course with a police escort wearing a black hood to conceal his identity.[3] He called him the "Masked Marvel" and teased fans to try to guess who the man was.

George S. May was also a man who did not discriminate. In the five years of his tournament, he never refused entry to a Black golfer. Rhodes accompanied his boss to Chicago, took part in qualifying, and easily made it through to be one of 170 professionals in the main event. Louis, however, threw a wrench into the promoter's plans. He had a poor qualifying round and failed to make it into the main field of forty-five amateurs. Ever the quick thinker, May announced that Louis would join the main field as an exhibition entry and would be partnered with Rhodes and the Masked Marvel.

When the 1946 All-American Open began, May's disposition was as radiant as his floral print Hawaiian shirt. There wasn't an open parking space anywhere on the grounds. More than twenty-eight thousand spectators milled about the course, a large percentage of whom followed Rhodes, Louis, and May's Masked Marvel. They watched Rhodes play the first nine holes better than anyone else in the field. His 2-under-par score was two strokes better than Sam Snead and three better than Ben Hogan. But on the back nine, holes ten through eighteen, Rhodes shot 3 over par to finish the day five shots behind the leader, Herman Barren.

On the second day Rhodes shot 73 in each of the two rounds, then followed with an even par 72 on Saturday. While a 79 on the final day may have been disheartening to some and put Rhodes' score for the tournament at 297, seventeen strokes behind the winner, his place was high enough to receive prize money. It made him the first African American golfer to earn prize money in the five-year history of May's prestigious event.

Two weeks later in New Castle, Pennsylvania, Rhodes entered another UGA event, the Colored Elks Tri-State Invitational. There he earned his second professional tournament win. It took a dramatic finish to achieve it. After fifty-four holes Rhodes was tied with Zeke Hartsfield, a professional from Atlanta. The contest took five extra holes to decide a winner. Rhodes birdied one, two, and three to take a four-shot lead and send the crowd into stunned silence. It was a performance described by the *New Castle News* as "one of the finest seen in many a day at the Sylvan Heights course. He seemed to warm to his task like an orchid on the bosom of a debutante. All he needed, apparently, was a gallery."4

Rhodes rode his hot streak into the Yorkshire Golf Club in Pittsburgh and the biggest all-Black golf tournament in the country, the Negro National Open. He was installed as the tournament favorite by no less an authority than the influential *Pittsburgh Courier* newspaper. Rhodes was five shots off the lead after the first round but rallied on day two to pull into a tie for first place with the two-time winner of the event, Howard Wheeler. On the thirty-six-hole final day, Wheeler recorded two even-par rounds. Rhodes was 1 over par for his two rounds and finished in second place behind the veteran pro.

Not only was professional golf a new experience for Rhodes but so was travel. His tournament schedule took him places he had never been before. He journeyed in ways he had never gone before. Aside from a few trips by train in the company of Louis, most of Rhodes' travel was done by automobile, specifically in a new Buick that was a gift from Louis. Rhodes called the car Alexander. By the latter part of the 1940s, more Blacks were achieving middle-class status, buying cars and taking vacations. Yet America's roadways were still not altogether welcoming to them. Roadside gas stations refused Blacks the use of their restrooms. Diners, motels, motor courts, and drug stores denied service. Stories abounded of Black motorists being robbed and even assaulted by hitchhikers. In several parts of the country were the spiteful who threw rocks at passing cars driven by Blacks.

Among Black motorists was a distrust of law enforcement. Many felt traffic stops were nothing more than harassment. In Mississippi numerous complaints were lodged with the Department of Public Safety alleging brutality and intimidation of motorists by law enforcement. In Tennessee one man, after being pulled over by police, bolted from his car and ran into the woods. A forty-man posse was assembled to search for the motorist. When he was found he said he ran because he feared he would be lynched.

If necessity is indeed the mother of invention, Victor Green reinforced the 1519 musing of the famous Greek philosopher Plato with *The Negro Motorist Green Book*. First published in 1936, the work of the New Jersey postal employee became a staple of Black travelers throughout the country. Green's publication provided Black travelers a list of welcoming roadside establishments in every state in America.

With each trip Rhodes gained more insight and took more steps to protect himself. As important to Rhodes as Green's *Negro Motorist Green Book* was the gun he carried for protection when traveling. He never used the weapon, and in the entire time he had it, the pistol was only discharged once. That happened when a hotel desk clerk dropped it. On impact with the floor the gun fired. When Rhodes stayed in a hotel, he insisted upon a second-floor room. Ground floors, he learned, could be a magnet for theft. On hot summer nights it was common to sleep with a window open. This proved inviting to bandits. While the occupant was asleep, the thief would extend an arm through the open window and snatch a pair of trousers draped across a nearby chair, then make off with the money-filled wallet that had been in the back pocket.

Rhodes' first summer of professional golf concluded with the Forest City Golf Association Classic in Cleveland. He won it by five strokes. His three wins and a second-place finish in the five summer tournaments he entered led the *Pittsburgh Courier* to crown Rhodes its Black Golfer of the Year. The *Los Angeles Sentinel* put Rhodes on its honor role of outstanding athletes for 1946. "Ted Rhodes is perhaps the greatest Negro golfer in the country and rates high with the Whites," the *Sentinel* declared.[5] Of Rhodes, Russ Cowans of the *Michigan Chronicle* observed, "His ambition is to become the outstanding golfer in the country. And he'll hit that spot if he continues to improve as he has done in the past two years."[6] For Rhodes it was the culmination of a dizzying ascension previously considered unattainable in any form but a dream.

Warm weather during winter and access to courses prompted Rhodes to make Los Angeles his new home. At the courses and clubs around Southern

California, a much different Ted Rhodes appeared. Instruction, practice, and more tournament play brought polish to his game. Winning infused confidence. More importantly, Rhodes now knew how to win. Where six months earlier the unheralded Rhodes impressed by being in the upper third of a tournament field, now it was not uncommon for him to occupy the top spot on a leader board during an event. Rhodes arched eyebrows at Baldwin Hills Golf Course when he shot a 7-under-par 65 round. Playing with Louis at Hillcrest Country Club, he shot 69. When the area's schedule of winter tournaments began, Rhodes battled gusting winds and more than eighty competitors to win the Cosmopolitan Open at Western Avenue Golf Course, then finished in the money at the Montebello Open.

Fresno and the California State Open would close out the West Coast portion of Rhodes' schedule. In a field with many professionals with whom Rhodes had competed in Southern California as well as entertainers Bob Hope and Zeppo Marx, Rhodes finished in the middle of the pack, out of the money, and nineteen strokes behind the winner, two-time state champion Art Bell.

During the first week of June, Louis and his entourage of Rhodes, Leonard Reed, and Judson Grant, a 52-year-old amateur golfer from Los Angeles, traveled to the Mexican border town of Tijuana to play a round of golf. Louis moved over his ball on the sixth tee when he was interrupted by a messenger. After reading the note, he stuffed the paper in his pocket, positioned himself, then smacked his tee shot. Once he observed where his ball landed, Louis began to walk the fairway to catch up to his partners. With a deadpan look in a matter-of-fact tone, Louis told the others his wife had just given birth to a son. The men looked at one another in disbelief. Such was Louis's general reticence to talk about family that none was aware Marva Louis had been pregnant.

As Rhodes assembled plans for his golfing summer, the mayor of the city of Houston suddenly became indirectly involved. A promoter in the South Texas city sought to create a festival to commemorate Juneteenth. The man envisioned a large golf tournament as part of the city's annual celebration of the end of slavery. Don Robey, owner of one of Houston's most popular nightclubs, the Bronze Peacock, didn't want to put on just another golf tournament. He wanted to make a UGA tournament part of the festival. And Robey wanted the tournament held on the crown jewel of Houston golf courses, Memorial Park. Doing so, however, would be a problem. Memorial Park was for Whites only. Robey knew that, but he had a plan. If he could deliver Joe Louis, Robey felt confident he would secure use of Memorial Park. Robey cajoled city leaders. Houston's mayor, Oscar F. Holcombe, had fared poorly with Black voters during his re-election six months earlier. Robey's pitch resonated. "It is a great pleasure for the city to grant use of Memorial for such a gigantic event," Holcombe said. "I sure hope Joe Louis can be here."[7]

For weeks, Robey sought help to try to land Louis. He turned to Jimmie Lunsford, the orchestra leader, who promised he could secure him. Chesterfield had recently struck a deal with Louis to appear in their advertisements. The cigarette maker was the first company to use a Black athlete in a national advertising campaign. Their regional manager badly wanted Louis at the golf tournament and promised to produce him. But as the tournament drew near, neither Lunsford nor anyone with Chesterfield had come through. Now the mayor was pressing for an answer. Desperate, and with only one week before the tournament was to tee off, Robey had no alternative but to take his plea directly to Joe Louis. He caught a flight to Los Angeles.

Robey arrived in Southern California carrying a personal invitation from the mayor of Houston. He sought out Ted Rhodes, convinced the golfer could put him together with Louis and convince his friend to come to Houston. But when the men met, Rhodes burst Robey's bubble. Louis, he told the promoter, had just become a father and was on his way to Chicago to meet his son.

Much of the Thousand Dollar Open was played under ominous Houston skies. If it wasn't rain, then temperatures that approached 90 degrees and high humidity chased spectators away. For the golfers, Memorial Park was challenging, if not downright intimidating, even without weather being part of the equation. In total, the course covered 1,500 acres—an area larger than Central Park in New York City. Its layout favored long hitters, and for three days Rhodes outdrove everybody. In every round his shots off the tee consistently traveled 280 yards or more in spite of wind, rain, and stifling humidity. Fans were in awe at the sight of such a lithe 5-foot-11-inch, 155-pound competitor driving balls farther than anyone else in the field. While weather interruptions frustrated many, Rhodes took them in stride. He breezed through the three rounds and won the tournament by eleven strokes. At the awards dinner at the Bronze Peacock, Rhodes received yet another gleaming trophy and prize earnings of $500. Despite bad weather and not having Joe Louis involved, organizers were pleased and said they would happily stage the event again the following year and offer three times more in prize money.

The summer of 1947 would see Ted Rhodes burst forth into the most dominant performer in the twenty-year history of the UGA. His second event of the UGA season, the Miami View Open in Dayton, Ohio, was won in much different fashion than the first. Temperatures that topped 100 degrees left golfers drenched in sweat and struggling with fatigue. Rhodes began the final round trailing Bill Spiller by one shot. At the twelfth hole Rhodes hooked his drive into a sand trap. He found his ball in a precarious spot, inches from the lip of the trap. After surveying the possibilities, Rhodes positioned himself, ground his feet into the sand to secure his footing, then swung. Sand flew in the air. Spectators eyed the green for sight of his ball. It never appeared. Rhodes looked down to see he missed it entirely. Irritation came over him. He spit on his palms. Gathered himself. Swung. And again, missed the ball. Soft laughter and a smattering of snickers came from the gallery. One more time Rhodes swung and this time sent the ball to within inches of the hole. "That just goes to show you what will happen in this game," a chagrined Rhodes said. "If someone had told me some months ago that I would miss a ball as I did that one, I would have told them that they were crazy but now I believe anything can happen in golf."[8]

Before Bill Spiller's name could be engraved onto the title trophy, he ran into troubles of his own. A series of bogeys erased the advantage he gained from Rhodes' sand trap troubles. Then, on fifteen, Rhodes rammed in a 40-foot putt for a birdie to assume the lead. He added to his advantage over the final three holes to defeat Spiller by two strokes. The win brought Rhodes $400 in first-prize money.

A week later, Rhodes won his third successive tournament of the 1947 UGA season, the *Pittsburgh Courier*-Yorkshire Golf Club Open. It came in dominant fashion by seven strokes over second-place Howard Wheeler. Such was the gap between Rhodes and the rest of the field that much of the gallery turned its attention to the amateur competition, where Joe Louis won his first tournament title. It was a double victory for Rhodes, who received praise for his golf course tutoring of Louis.

Through much of the tournament the influential *Pittsburgh Courier* sports editor Wendell Smith followed Rhodes. In subsequent columns Smith heaped praise. "Rhodes is a stylist on the links. He hits a long ball and plays his irons like a champion. In another year he should be able to compete in the big tournaments against the best White golfers and hold his own."[9]

Smith's column was just one of many to offer laudatory words. With each tournament win, renown grew. While general-circulation newspapers around the country frequently mentioned Rhodes' successes, it was rarely done as anything more than a single sentence or short paragraph. In newspapers that served a Black readership, such as the *Courier*, *Chicago Defender*, *New York Age*, *Baltimore Afro-American*, *California Eagle*, *Detroit Tribune*, *St. Louis Star*, and *Los Angeles Sentinel*, Rhodes jockeyed with baseball stars Jackie Robinson and Satchel Paige for the large headlines. In columns and articles Rhodes' play was described using words such as "brilliant," in glowing terms like "a smooth golf artist," and with declarations like one by the *Cleveland Call and Post* that he was simply "the best colored golfer."[10]

When Ted Rhodes showed up at a golf course, he was the essence of flair. To watch his swing was to marvel. Accuracy from his iron play was uncanny. His skills spawned nicknames such as "Mr. Swing," "Sweet Swinger," and from Joe Louis, "Straight Arrow." As flashy as were Rhodes' golf swing and remarkable accuracy, his wardrobe was even flashier. Nobody, not one golfer on the PGA circuit or in the UGA, dressed in more style or pizzazz than Ted Rhodes. From knickers one day to pleated, pressed slacks the next, colorful sweaters, knit Tam O'Shanter caps, flat caps worn backwards, berets, two-tone and solid-color golf shoes in varying colors, Rhodes turned heads whenever he arrived on a golf course. Columnists regularly used space to regale their readers with details of Rhodes' attire. During an East Coast tournament, Ralph Trost of the *Brooklyn Daily Eagle* wrote that Rhodes wore "a riot of color." Trost explained, "He wore brown alligator shoes, green pants, yellow shirt, and topped things with one of those multi-colored checked hats that looks like a shrunken tam with a peak." Trost noted that Rhodes bought golf bags to match his attire. "Rhodes goes in for those flashy bags. He has green for his green pants, yellow for his yellow, red for his violent trousers and blue for his somber days."[11] Still other newspapers devoted paragraphs in their tournament coverage just to describe Rhodes' attire. "But few spectators were more colorful than player Ted Rhodes," wrote Peg Johnson in the *Minneapolis Star Tribune*. "He wore iridescent red trousers with his white shirt and shoes, and a floppy gray Tyrolean hat with a feather."[12]

When a newspaper columnist heard someone refer to Rhodes by his old Belle Meade nickname "Rags," he assumed it was a compliment and used it in print. Far from the intended pejorative of the 1930s in Nashville, the nickname stuck and became a standard adjective used whenever Rhodes was written about from that day forward.

A week after Rhodes' win in Pittsburgh, acumen and flair took a backseat to outright humiliation on the golf course. In the opening round of the Sixth City Open in Cleveland, Bill Spiller set the gallery abuzz by breaking the five-year-old

There were few men in professional golf who dressed with more flair than Ted Rhodes. During tournaments he was known to change his attire after playing the front nine and match his clothing with color-coordinated golf bags. Courtesy of the author.

record for low score at Highland Park Golf Course with a 5-under-par 67. His score might have been lower had a 10-foot putt on eighteen not caught the edge of the cup and spun out. At the end of the round, Rhodes was fourth, nine strokes behind Spiller. The wide gap sparked talk that Rhodes' win streak might end. That conversation topic as well as Spiller's course record would last less than twenty-four hours. The following afternoon Rhodes left fans astounded. He shot 66. His round not only eclipsed Spiller's course record but erased the man's lead in the tournament. By the time the tournament ended, Rhodes was the winner by a shocking margin of seven strokes.

At the Joe Louis Open, Rhodes established yet another record, shaving ten strokes off his winning score from the previous year. As in Cleveland, Rhodes had to come from far behind to win. He trailed by five strokes at the beginning of the final round. When Rhodes made the turn after completing the first nine holes, he had pulled into a tie with Spiller for the lead. Rhodes put an exclamation mark on a three-stroke margin of victory with his shot making on the final hole. First, 10 feet from the green, Rhodes used an iron to place his ball 15 feet from the hole. He then rammed home a putt to complete a 3-under-par round and win first prize.

Rhodes made Louis's event a platform to express gratitude to his benefactor. "I'd like to say that without Joe Louis I probably never would have played golf as I do today," he said. "He made it possible for me to practice, play during the winter, and summer. So if there's any credit due me, I'd like for Joe Louis to receive it. He's the guy who deserves it."[13]

By the time the season-ending Negro National Open arrived, Rhodes added to a remarkable 1947 résumé with wins at the Chicago Open and Wake Robin Golf Club Invitational in Washington, DC. It was no surprise when bookmakers tabbed Rhodes the overwhelming favorite to win the UGA's championship event. But the host course, Fairview Golf Club in Philadelphia, was now Howard Wheeler's home course. Wheeler had left Southern California to become the pro at Fairview. He knew every inch of its layout and used that knowledge to his full advantage. Jack Saunders of the *Pittsburgh Courier* described the duel. "Wheeler turned Rhodes every which way but loose, and by trying to match strokes with the elongated champion, Rhodes played way off his game."[14] Wheeler prevailed. It was his fourth Open championship. Rhodes could do no better than fourth place, eleven strokes behind.

Despite the season-ending finish, Rhodes' 1947 campaign, his second in professional golf, was nothing short of extraordinary. He won eight of the nine UGA tournaments in which he played. Throughout the 1947 season, Rhodes was the only UGA golfer under par in every event. Over a two-season span

Rhodes took away winner's trophies from eleven of the thirteen UGA events he entered.

New winter projects were on the horizon. Another boxing champion—Sugar Ray Robinson, the welterweight champ—had been bitten by the golf bug. He wanted Rhodes to be his instructor. But as Rhodes returned to Los Angeles, ominous clouds portended stormy days ahead.

4

Please Go Away

The last man to putt bent down and reached into the cup. With two fingers he pulled out his ball. A clattering sound accompanied the flagstick being shoved back into the hole. Ted Rhodes and Bill Spiller walked from the green, their practice round complete. The men had made the long drive from Los Angeles to this town on the eastern side of San Francisco Bay to learn the ins and outs of Richmond Golf Club before play would get under way later in the week for the Richmond Open.

A breeze cooled by ocean waters teased the open pores of the men on what was an unseasonably hot mid-January day. As Rhodes and Spiller chatted about their round, a man walked to intercept them. George Schneiter, chairman of the PGA tournament committee, had come to deliver a message. Brusque, with a no-nonsense demeanor, Schneiter was an accomplished golfer and businessman from Ogden, Utah, who counted among his spoils a 43,000-acre ranch in Montana. Sportswriters considered him a fair-minded man who, in the words of Harold Ratliff of the *Associated Press*, tackled golf's problems "with the idea of doing what is right and doing what will be for the good of golf."[1] Schneiter himself liked to say, "Justice must be tempered with common sense."[2]

When Schneiter stopped Rhodes and Spiller, he asked them to meet in his office. There, he delivered a message both blunt and direct. The men would have to leave. Neither Rhodes, Spiller, nor a San Francisco amateur player,

Madison Gunter, would be permitted to play in the Richmond Open. When reporters learned of the action, they pressed Schneiter. They found him evasive and vague. He said Rhodes, Spiller, and Gunter were not members of the PGA, yet he admitted there were golfers allowed into the Richmond Open who were not members either. Schneiter spoke of rules and requirements, barked that he didn't make policy, and insisted he was merely doing his job to enforce what was PGA policy. Behind the façade was the ugly truth. The only PGA policy Rhodes, Spiller, and Gunter were in violation of was not being White.

The crux of the matter involved the membership policy of the PGA. Implemented in 1934, Article III Section I of the PGA policy guide, it stated membership in the organization was open only to the following:

> Professional golfers of the Caucasian race, over the age of eighteen (18) years, residing in North or South America, and who have served at least five years in the profession (either in the employ of a golf club in the capacity as a professional or in the employ of a professional as his assistant) shall be eligible for membership.[3]

Four weeks after *The Boston Globe* declared Jackie Robinson's integration of big-league baseball the sports highlight of 1947, and three weeks after Kenny Washington, who reintegrated the National Football League, scored the final touchdown in the Los Angeles Rams 34–10 win over the New York Giants, the PGA was an organization firmly entrenched on a different path.

An impetus for the controversy in Richmond was an agreement struck between two tournaments. To create incentive for golfers to play in its 1948 tournament, the Los Angeles Open made an agreement with the Richmond Open. The top sixty finishers would receive automatic entry at Richmond. None would have to play a usual midweek qualifying round to get into the field.

For twenty years, the Los Angeles Junior Chamber of Commerce rebuffed the PGA's attempts to take over management of the Los Angeles Open. They, much like the All-American Open in Chicago, felt there was no need to pay the organization for little more than the provision of an official starter, a scorekeeper, and to stage a golf clinic using ten to fifteen of its member players as instructors. The Junior Chamber wanted the right to determine entries, pairings, and tee times and to retain the $20,000 to $30,000 it made each year in profit. The PGA rarely missed a chance to criticize the operation of the Los Angeles Open. Ironically, however, the two most highly attended and profitable professional golf tournaments in the country were the two that rejected a management contract with the organization: the Los Angeles Open and the All-American Open.

On January 2, Bill Spiller generated headlines. On the opening day of the 1948 Los Angeles Open, Spiller shot 68 to tie Ben Hogan for the first-round lead. When he teed off the next day, Spiller was, by his own admission, "shaking like a leaf."[4] Throughout the previous night he had been beseeched by phone calls and telegrams from well-wishers. Spiller became rattled by the attention. His game suffered and he faded from contention. Hogan went on to win the tournament. Spiller finished twelve strokes behind him and one behind Rhodes. But both Spiller and Rhodes finished high enough to qualify for the incentive promoted by the Los Angeles Open—automatic entry into the Richmond Open.

Driving to Richmond, Rhodes and Spiller wondered aloud if they would be permitted to play. "We were pretty sure we'd be barred," Spiller said.[5] On their arrival at Richmond Golf Course, both men paid their ten-dollar tournament entry fee and were hospitably welcomed by Dan Markovich, the club pro. Local newspaper and radio reporters interviewed the men. In subsequent articles and broadcast reports, their results in the Los Angeles Open were promoted. The next day, Rhodes and Spiller played a practice round with Smiley Quick. It was then that they were summoned by Schneiter and told they and Gunter were barred from the tournament.

Schneiter told the men they could apply for a special exemption. Rhodes and Spiller agreed, only to be told the PGA executive did not have the proper forms with him. He promised to mail a copy to their homes. When asked how long the process would take, Schneiter explained exemptions would have to be reviewed by the general assembly of the PGA. A meeting was planned at The Masters in April, but it was doubtful action would be taken before the national body met in November in Chicago.

As Rhodes and Spiller left the meeting, they were stopped by several golfers, each of whom expressed solace and dismay. The following morning, news of the expulsion hit the press, and a firestorm erupted. Bill Steel, a leading sportscaster in Los Angeles, suggested the tournament rename the winner's prize the "Hitler Trophy." Steel added, "What a proud day in sports. This is America. The land of the free."[6] *Oakland Tribune* columnist Alan Ward wrote, "The Professional Golfers Association did not cover itself in glory in refusing permission for three Negro players to play in the Richmond Open."[7]

Already angry with the PGA for its failure to deliver on a promise that Ben Hogan would play in their tournament, the management of Richmond Golf Course became incensed by the adverse publicity. Dan Markovich fought to distance the club from the banishment of the Black players. He pointed an accusatory finger in Schneiter's direction and explained that a contract with the PGA forced Richmond Golf Club to follow the organization's rules. Markovich went on to say he had been courteous to Rhodes and Spiller, that many of his friends were Black, and pointed out that Blacks had played in local tournaments at the club.

For his part, Schneiter chafed at criticism. He tried to lay blame on Rhodes and Spiller. "I heard Spiller say on the radio during the Los Angeles Open that he wasn't eligible to play in a PGA tournament. So, he obviously knew about the situation."[8] The reactions of Rhodes and Spiller reflected their personalities. "If I had my preference," Rhodes once said, "I'd take the nice way, because when you get something that way, it's a lot sweeter to have."[9] Bill Spiller, on the other hand, was a combative sort, quick to tackle a slight head-on and unafraid of a fight. A native of Oklahoma, Spiller was a standout in basketball and track and field at Booker T. Washington High School in Tulsa and at Wiley College in Texas. Golf, however, was never of interest to him. Not, at least, until he was in his late twenties and working as a baggage porter at Union Station in Los Angeles. A fellow porter suggested Spiller take up the game. Reluctant at first, Spiller developed a zeal and skill for the sport. He enjoyed so much success in amateur tournaments he gave up his job to play professionally. After being rebuffed by Schneiter, Rhodes prepared to pack his bags and drive back to Los Angeles. Spiller, on the other hand, girded for a fight.

At Richmond Golf Course, Schneiter and Markovich fretted. There were rumors of threats. Rhodes and Spiller, they were told, might show up at the first tee to try to force their way into the tournament as play was to get underway. Spiller was known to be unpredictable. What's worse, on occasion he carried a gun, something that traced back to his early years in Oklahoma when, as a nine-year-old, he was slapped by a White shopkeeper. Fears of a first-tee showdown failed to materialize, but it didn't mean the firestorm wasn't about to turn into a raging inferno.

Soon after their expulsion Rhodes and Spiller met with an area attorney. Jonathan Rowell was a partner in a Redwood City law firm with renowned consumer rights litigator Melvin Belli. While Belli focused his energies on negligence cases, Rowell built a reputation for representing the disenfranchised. The son of a newspaper publisher, Rowell was adept at generating publicity. When he declared his intent to sue the PGA on behalf of Rhodes, Spiller, and Gunter, it produced headlines in almost every newspaper in America.

Coverage of the first two days of the Richmond Open were buried beneath paragraphs about Rowell's impending lawsuit. The attorney exposed the PGA's Caucasian-only clause. He said the organization met the definition of a closed shop, one that restricted membership. This, Rowell emphasized, put the PGA in violation of the 1947 Taft-Hartley Act. He promised to file his legal action quickly so Schneiter would be served before leaving town.

As golfers completed play in the third round of the Richmond Open, the newsworthiness of their results paled in comparison to what John Rowell was doing in a nearby town. The attorney filed three separate lawsuits with the Contra Costa County Superior Court. Each suit sought $105,000 per plaintiff. The suits charged the PGA with preventing the three golfers from earning a living and being an organization in violation of federal statutes by the barring of Blacks. Rowell also sought damages from Richmond Golf Club. He named Schneiter, Markovich, five PGA administrators, and ten members of the Richmond Golf Club board of directors as defendants in the case.

For the first time, professional golf was under assault for its discriminatory practices. Rhodes, Spiller, and Gunter found themselves surrounded by supporters. Gene Sarazen, three-time PGA champion and 1935 Masters champion, said, "I do not go along with the PGA on its ban on Negro golfers."[10] Lloyd Mangrum said he would fight to make Rhodes an approved player. "This discrimination should not be practiced by the PGA."[11] One of Rhodes' biggest supporters was George S. May, head of the All-American Open. "I think the PGA was entirely wrong. You know I have always insisted that Negroes should not only be welcomed on the golf course but also should be entitled to clubhouse privileges accorded to any competitor. I believe this suit will do much to erase the 'Caucasian clause' from the bylaws," he said.[12]

Subterfuge became a weapon in the PGA arsenal. When trophies and prize money were doled out following the final round of the Richmond Open, competitors were handed blank checks. Schneiter feared Rowell might obtain a court order to seize the tournament's prize money, so golfers were promised their prize money would be distributed once everyone was outside of California at the Phoenix Open the following week.

In the days that followed the Richmond Open, ire simmered. Rhodes took his anger out on a golf course in Los Angeles. Playing with Spiller, Leonard Reed, and a visitor from Illinois, "Red" Wiley, the week after the Richmond Open, Rhodes set a course record shooting 62 at Western Avenue Golf Club.

A high level of fury permeated the boardroom at Richmond Golf Course too. It manifested in the form of acrimony toward the PGA. Finally, in May, Fran Watson, chairman of the tournament, declared there would not be another Richmond Open. Money, normally the reason for a tournament's demise, was not the prevailing factor in this case. Watson insisted every one of the four tournaments the club had staged made a significant profit. *Oakland Tribune* sportswriter Ed Schoenfeld reported the larger problem was unhappiness with the PGA. "The PGA didn't make the Richmond Golf Club look too good by ruling out two Los Angeles Negro pros, Bill Spiller and Ted Rhodes," he wrote.[13]

The topic of integration came up at a PGA meeting. "It's something we're going to have to make our minds up on someday," said one pro. "We might as well start now."[14] The president of the PGA, Bill Dudley, sought to allay growing enmity. "I'm pretty sure something can be done about this situation," he said.[15] While the matter was being mulled over, Rhodes resumed play on the UGA circuit. In July, while in Minneapolis for the Midwest Negro Elk's Open, Rhodes stayed in the home of a local golf pro. After winning the tournament, his host suggested the two of them enter an upcoming PGA event in the area, the St. Paul Open. Rhodes' host, Solomon Hughes, mailed entry fees to the tournament organizer, the St. Paul Junior Chamber of Commerce. As quickly as they were received, the entries and money were sent back.

When the decision to bar the two golfers was learned, controversy broke out. Whitney M. Young, a member of the St. Paul Urban League, was its catalyst. Young had only recently joined the St. Paul Junior Chamber of Commerce. When he was recruited to sell tickets and help promote the St. Paul Open, he made a point to ask if the tournament was truly an "open" event. It was only after he was assured it was, that he agreed. Feeling he had been lied to, Young complained to the chairman of the tournament committee. Bill McMahon initially called the omission an oversight. Almost as soon as he gave that explanation, McMahon's story hastily changed. It was the PGA who was at fault, he said. The organization did not recognize Rhodes or Hughes as eligible golfers.

Young took his concern to the publisher of the local newspaper, the *St. Paul Pioneer Press and Dispatch*. Ben Ridder declined to get involved. He said he feared the PGA would withdraw its member players, which would wreck the tournament. Young next took his concern to the mayor of St. Paul, Edward Delaney, and pointed out the tournament was to be played on a city-owned course. "It is a matter of principle," Young said. "I feel that the local Junior Chamber officials are making themselves a party to discrimination."[16] The mayor convened a three-hour meeting of the tournament committee to try to work out a solution. It was stressed that only a month earlier the United States Supreme Court issued a ruling that stated no municipality could lease a public facility to a private organization that discriminates against a segment of the tax-paying population. In a subsequent call to Crane, the mayor was told the local Jaycees could not extend an invitation to Rhodes or Hughes to play. To allow them into the St. Paul Open might jeopardize the PGA's ongoing legal case in California.

Attendance and revenues for the 1948 edition of the St. Paul Open dropped. George Schneiter was summoned to a meeting with the tournament committee, where he received a blistering rebuke. Delaney, the mayor, vowed not to sign any future agreement with the PGA that would discriminate. The PGA pondered a way to get around the mayor's declaration. Rather than agree to allow Black golfers, the tournament committee instead plotted to move the St. Paul Open from a public to a private course.

As fall approached, the case of *Rhodes, Spiller, and Gunter v. the PGA* loomed on the Contra Costa County Superior Court calendar. Finally, on September 20, Judge Hugh Donovan announced a ruling. The case, he said, was dismissed. A settlement had been reached. Dana Murdock, attorney for the PGA, declared the "PGA will not in the future refuse tourney play privileges to the plaintiffs on account of their color or otherwise discriminate against them."¹⁷ As part of the settlement Gunter, Rhodes, and Spiller dropped their pursuit of financial redress. Rowell explained his clients did not initiate legal action for money but to "break down racial barriers."¹⁸

The news drew praise, particularly in newspapers that served Black readership. The *Detroit Tribune* ran a large page-one headline which read, "BILL SPILLER, RHODES WIN PGA GOLF SUIT."¹⁹ Conklin Bray, the *Tribune*'s sports columnist, called the outcome, "Some of the most encouraging news since Jackie Robinson crashed the big leagues."²⁰ The *Pittsburgh Courier* headline read, "JIM CROW ROCKED BY 3 STUNNING BLOWS."²¹ Columnist A. S. "Doc" Young wrote in the *Cleveland Call and Post*, "It's another mark of progress, another sign that maybe, down the road a piece, a man can really believe he is an American and then prove it. It's another step, men. A lot of credit should go to Rhodes and Spiller for instituting the suit."²²

But while a social milestone was celebrated, members of the PGA hierarchy were privately pleased as well. The organization had no intention to open its ranks to people of color. They had quietly pulled one over on Rowell and his clients. A strategy based on subterfuge was launched mere hours after Rowell filed his lawsuit. It was an idea first raised by an influential PGA member, Maurie Luxford. Known throughout Southern California for his bow ties and the title of "Mr. Golf," Luxford pointed out that Bing Crosby ran his tournament as an invitational. Only those invited were permitted to play. While an "open" event meant anyone who wished to play must be given the chance to qualify, PGA leadership saw a twist of language as the solution to their legal predicament.

At its winter meeting in Dunedin, Florida, the PGA urged those staging 1949 tournaments to replace "Open" with "Invitational" in their title. George Schneiter further explained a new plan—an approved player list. Any player not on the list was not eligible to play in a PGA tournament. Schneiter called it part of a new code of ethics but when pressed for details said, "This entire structure is rather difficult to explain in writing."²³

Contrary to the announced settlement, there would be no change. Preservation rose above contrition. Gall and arrogance smothered integrity and fairness. While baseball and football were widely celebrated for integration, the PGA chose, instead, to cling to its policy of exclusion. It was several months before Rhodes, Spiller, Gunter, and other Black golfers realized what had happened. Once they did, that realization harkened the words of a fellow UGA member who said he felt what the letters PGA really stood for was "Please go away."[24]

5

A Worthy Pioneer

Los Angeles was a city abuzz, far more so than usual. Sports had elbowed Hollywood and the movie industry from its place as the usual fervor generator. The second week of June 1948 began with excitement, the kind activated almost automatically whenever the schedule brought the city's professional baseball combatants, the Los Angeles Angels and Hollywood Stars, together. By midweek, however, it was the sport of golf and its plethora of stars that pushed baseball from the larger share of newspaper headlines. Specifically, the United States Open, an event Ward Gilliland described in the *Pomona Progress Bulletin* as "the biggest thing in golf that ever happened on the Pacific coast."[1]

Thursday, June 10, brought special buses winding their way down Sunset Boulevard to deposit spectators at Riviera Country Club. Cars carrying hundreds more filled the club's adjacent polo field. The nation's leading sports broadcaster, Bill Stern, arrived by train from New York to describe the action. In the days prior, golf's stars sparked the buzz with public appearances around the Los Angeles area. Ben Hogan signed copies of his new book at Bullock's Department store. Sam Snead visited Paramount Studios, where he posed for publicity pictures with Bob Hope. Lloyd Mangrum conducted a clinic at Fox Hills Golf Course. None of the 171 golfers in the field needed any special activity to remind them of the significance of the tournament. "To win the U.S. Open is the greatest honor that can come to a golfer," said Gene Sarazen, a two-time winner of the event.[2]

Once 8:15 arrived on the morning of June 10, history was made. When play teed off, the 48th United States Open was the first ever contested on the West Coast. History of a different kind would be made three hours later. It was the tee shot struck by the second man in the twenty-eighth threesome of the day that would become a celebrated event. Ted Rhodes, wrote Herman Hill in the *Pittsburgh Courier*, was "the first person of his race ever to compete in the United States Open golf tournament."[3]

Hill's assertion provoked pride, though it was not entirely accurate. In 1896, barely two years after the formation of the United States Golf Association (USGA), the second US Open was held at Shinnecock Hills Golf Club on New York's Long Island. Two Black caddies from the club, Oscar Bunn and sixteen-year-old John Shippen, entered the event. A number of professional golfers balked. The protesters delivered a petition to USGA leaders demanding Bunn and Shippen be barred. It went ignored. Shippen, the son of a former slave, wound up in fifth place and earned ten dollars.

But the event of 1948 bore little resemblance to the early US Opens. The 1896 event was primarily an amateur tournament. Play was contested by only eighty-five entrants who came from twenty-six USGA-member clubs. They competed only in medal play. On the final day, a Saturday, a group of professionals joined to compete in a thirty-six-hole format. Such was the growth of golf's popularity that by the 1920s, thirty-six-hole, one-day qualifying tournaments were needed in seventeen US cities to pare 600 entrants to a field of 163. In 1948 those numbers had exploded. Forty-eight qualifying events were held to chop 1,418 to the 140 who would come to Riviera Country Club.

In the fifty-one years since Bunn's and Shippen's participation, not a single Black golfer had competed in the US Open. Ted Rhodes ended that five-decades-long ostracism. His inclusion in the field was not without protest. Threats to withdraw were made by a small handful of golfers. But the USGA did not subscribe to any sort of exclusionary policy. When Joe Dey, executive secretary of the USGA, stood firm, the protesters backed down. Rhodes was heartened by Dey's support, and when he overheard a caddy ask a White golfer, a southerner, what he thought of a Black golfer being in the tournament, "No one has the right to stop a man from making a living," the golfer said.[4]

Rhodes caused an even bigger stir forty-eight hours before the Open was to tee off. Golfers were given access to Riviera for a practice round. Even though it took place on a Tuesday, the event brought a large crowd of spectators. Several hundred followed a celebrity foursome comprised of the game's biggest stars: Ben Hogan, Gene Sarazen, the colorful two-time Masters winner Jimmy Demaret, and the hugely popular entertainer Bing Crosby. Chicago golf magazine mogul Herb Graffis called the following the largest he had ever seen.

When those who spent their day following the foursome opened a copy of the *Los Angeles Times* the next day, they were shocked to learn what they had missed. "SNEAD, RHODES SHOOT 67S ON RIVIERA COURSE."[5] Ted Rhodes had matched the 1947 US Open runner-up, Sam Snead, for the lowest score of the practice round, 4 under par. Yet despite Rhodes' spectacular score, nobody, not a single sportswriter or columnist with any newspaper or wire service, rated him among the favorites to win the tournament. While national columnists such as Grantland Rice and Joe Williams extolled the skills and successes of Hogan and Snead, neither they nor anyone else pointed out that there wasn't a single golfer in the sport who had achieved the degree of success Rhodes had in winning eight tournaments the previous year.

Rhodes did have supporters. Joe Louis was away training for a rematch with Jersey Joe Walcott, yet managed to make a sizeable wager on Rhodes. Even more eyebrow-raising was the offer made by Lew Clayton, manager of entertainer Jimmy Durante. Clayton promised to pay Rhodes $50,000 were he to win the US Open. Should Rhodes be among the top twenty finishers, Clayton would reward him with $1,000. To earn it would mean conquering a difficult challenge.

Unlike many of the first-time competitors, Rhodes was familiar with Riviera Country Club. He had played the course in the Los Angeles Open three times.

But the US Open presented a far greater challenge. The USGA wanted a more demanding course than what members played throughout the year. At their instruction the rough was allowed to grow. By Open week it was calf-high, even knee-high in spots. Fairways were narrowed, some by as much as 20 yards. Greens went unwatered and were faster. Tees were set back 5 feet. Hole placements were changed to heighten the putting challenge. "No rank outsider will win this tournament," predicted Gene Sarazen, who called Riviera "one of the great golf courses of the world."[6]

USGA standards or not, a country club course alone represented a challenge to Rhodes. Both the color of his skin and the amount of money in his pocket meant most of his golf was played on city-owned municipal courses. They were designed and constructed with the novice golfer in mind. Country club courses were made for a more serious golfer. They featured more bunkers, water hazards, hills, knolls, elevation changes, and trees than most municipal courses. Their fairways were often more narrow and their greens made trickier by undulation. Then there was a championship course. "A fellow must develop an entirely different game when playing on a real championship golf course," explained a fellow pro, Bob Seymour. "The fairways are like velvet. The finer courses have big, fast greens with innumerable breaks and rolls. It takes skill to 'read' those greens and get those putts down. Green reading is an art developed from constant practice and experience gained from playing on them."[7]

The authoritative yet somewhat mellow voice of Bill Stern was five minutes into the first of his three scheduled radio broadcasts from Riviera Country Club when Rhodes stepped to the first tee. A three-deep crowd of spectators stretched into a half circle behind the tee box. Stylishly clad in white knickers with argyle socks, two-tone golf shoes, blue golf shirt with a blue beret atop his head, Rhodes surveyed the terrain to the green, 513 feet away. In a valley 75 feet below was the fairway. This geographic feature made the hole appear easy and the green reachable in two shots. With a superb swing Rhodes sent a majestic tee shot soaring over the middle of the fairway. Once he had tapped in his putt for an even par 5, Rhodes turned his attention from a hole considered Riviera's easiest to one most felt was its toughest. Number two ran alongside the first hole, only in the opposite direction. It had an uphill grade with the semi-sloped green at the base of a hill. Rhodes conquered the challenge with aplomb. While many golfers were counseled to be happy to escape the par-4 hole with a bogey, Rhodes recorded a birdie.

Beneath the fairway trees, behind the tee boxes, and near the greens, large clusters of spectators amassed. Many took advantage of the topography to gain distinctive vistas from hillsides, atop knolls or plateaus. Among their numbers were movie stars, directors, and athletes. Johnny Weissmuller, the star of Tarzan films, was swarmed by young females. The green checked suit worn by Adolphe Menjou made one sportswriter crack that it must have been stitched from a blanket belonging to the racehorse Seabiscuit. Contemporaries greeted the prolific director Sidney Lanfield while Cal Eaton, the boxing promoter, seemed to be forever shaking hands with fans. Novice fans, ignorant about course etiquette, were frequently shushed, lest they break a golfer's concentration with chatter. Those more adroit cringed when a large four-engine airplane thundered overhead. Play descended to a state of catastrophe when a stray dog, a frisky German Shepherd, ran onto the course and snatched up and chewed a competitor's ball. Through it all Rhodes exhibited intense concentration. Over and over, he thrilled spectators with long and precise drives. With masterful repetition he sent balls slicing through the air and over the middle of Riviera's fairways. A bogey on the final hole put his tally at 1 over par through the front nine. That's when he went on a tear.

Rhodes began the back nine with a birdie on the tenth hole, then followed it with a birdie on eleven to lower his score to 2 under par. When Rhodes sank a putt for birdie on thirteen, his third birdie in four holes, it caused excitement to spread through Riviera Country Club. Ben Hogan had just finished his round. On Hogan's scorecard was the lowest score of the day, 4 under par. Ted Rhodes was 2 under par and five holes remained.

Large crowds enjoy the 1948 United States Open. It was the first US Open contested on the West Coast. Courtesy Los Angeles Herald Examiner *photo collection and the Los Angeles Public Library.*

By the time Rhodes reached the fifteenth hole, the gallery was filled with a mixture of curiosity and enthusiasm. Little did the golfer know, though, that this particular hole, a 440-yard par 4, had bedeviled golfers all day long. Hogan himself sent a drive into the rough and wound up with a bogey 5. Sam Snead overshot the green with his second shot. The hole in the shape of a dogleg angled to the right. It featured a deep bunker at the bend, a tricky green made up of two sloped sections, and as if that were not challenge enough, wind blew from the Pacific Ocean and into the golfer's face. In all, seventy-seven golfers would run into trouble and bogey the fifteenth hole. Ted Rhodes wound up being one of them.

Rhodes was quick to brush aside his frustration and took advantage of Riviera's shortest and straightest hole, the 145-yard sixteenth. Ignoring the menacing bunkers that bordered the front of the green, Rhodes placed his tee shot 10 feet to the left of the hole. After consultation with his caddy, Russ Mains, Rhodes calmly sank his putt for birdie to return his score to 2 under par.

From the shortest hole on the course, attention turned to Riviera's longest, all 585 yards of the seventeenth. Rhodes bogeyed the par-5 hole to fall back to 1 under par. He missed a chance for birdie on eighteen. As Rhodes exited the course to turn in his scorecard, he was serenaded with loud applause from hundreds of fans perched on the hillside behind the green. His 1-under-par score was among the best recorded thus far. It would be several hours before the entire field finished. Once the last player left the course, shortly before nightfall, the final tabulations produced surprising results:

1. Ben Hogan −4
   Lew Worsham −4
2. Sam Snead −2
3. Ted Rhodes −1

The first-round lead was shared by the pre-tournament favorite, Ben Hogan, and the defending US Open champion, Lew Worsham. The 1947 runner-up, Sam Snead, was second. But it was news of who was in third place that astounded. An outlier, an upstart, the man nobody gave a chance, Ted Rhodes trailed Sam Snead by one shot. The *Chicago Tribune* praised Rhodes' round as "one of the major surprises of the day."[8] In her golf column in the *Sacramento Bee*, Beth Hightower put in print, "There were those who wondered how the PGA would feel if a non-Caucasian took USGA's blue ribbon event."[9]

Early the next morning Riviera's head pro, greenskeeper, and hole cutter accompanied men from the USGA on a survey of the course. The USGA viewed golf as a game of skill, precision, and technique. It was their goal to make the open course provide a "championship test without being tricky."[10] As the men walked the course, they reviewed how those in the field attacked the greens during first-round play. At 6:00 a.m., two and a half hours before the second round was to tee off, Richard Tufts, the USGA man in charge of hole placement, gave instructions to the Riviera Country Club crew. Hole locations on every green were to be changed. New holes were dug. Holes used the previous day were replaced. The USGA was tightening the screws.

Hole placements and greens made faster by another day without water played a part in the rise of both frustration and scores during the second round of play. When he missed his third putt on the thirteenth green, Johnny Dawson turned to his playing partner, Jimmy Demaret, and muttered, "What do I have to do to get it in?"[11] After his first round 67, Ben Hogan shot 72, a score buoyed by missed short putts on seven and eighteen and a three-putt on eight. Observers were convinced Sam Snead was overcautious on the green much of the day. Yet, despite missing several short putts, particularly makeable ones on four and fifteen, he took over the tournament lead and in doing so, set a tournament scoring record, 138, through thirty-six holes. Like both Hogan and Snead, Rhodes' score rose too. And, like Hogan and Snead, putting was Rhodes' Achilles' heel. He endured a day with putts that shot across the green and past the hole, others that stopped frustratingly short of the hole, and even a few that lipped out of the hole.

For all of Rhodes' second-round struggles, there were moments of distinction, shots that could only be executed by a player whose skills were unquestionably among the best in the game. The greatest of those, maybe the most memorable of the entire tournament, was produced by Rhodes on the ninth hole. While a seemingly simple, straight, 422-yard-long, par-4 hole, the challenge came in the form of bunkers in the middle of the fairway that required careful consideration of tactics. Rhodes' tee shot sailed some 220 yards but carried slightly to the right. It traveled just enough offline that when it bounced on the edge of the fairway, it caromed into the tall, thick rough. Pondering a plan, Rhodes took a two-iron from his caddy. Simply trying for a better lay was not on his mind. Rhodes was going for broke. He unleashed a mighty swing. His ball exploded from the tall grass, strands of which flew into the air. Rhodes' ball shot on a line directly toward the green. Its line and arc wrought awe. Then, with startling astonishment, the hush of suspense was punctured by the sound of a hard-hit golf ball smacking the flagstick. Amazement erupted into thunderous applause as Rhodes' ball caromed, dropped to the green and stopped a mere inch from the hole. When Rhodes tapped in his putt for birdie, applause rained from the gallery. His shot would be lauded in newspaper stories the next day as the greatest shot of the tournament.

Soaring second-round scores made thoughts of contention give way to concern about making the cut. Prize money was at stake. At the end of the second round, only the top fifty golfers would make the cut to advance and play the final thirty-six holes and compete for prize money. The rest, 121 in all, would go home. Once a large volume of scorecards was turned in, chatter grew that a score of 148 would be the likely cut line. Those with scores higher than that figure would be eliminated. When Rhodes walked from the eighteenth green, he tabulated his totals, then scrawled a 76 onto his scorecard. The 5-over-par score put him in a group of eight who shared twenty-seventh. He was eight shots behind the leader, Sam Snead. Rhodes could exhale. He made the cut and would play on Saturday to compete for prize money.

Bright sunshine, an 80-degree forecast, and the promise of a duel for the title between Sam Snead and Ben Hogan brought the largest crowd yet, fifteen thousand, to Riviera Country Club for Saturday's final day of the US Open. Adding to the challenge of the event, the USGA made the day the final day of the tournament with two eighteen-hole rounds. When pairings for the day were revealed, Rhodes was placed in a threesome that included his former tutor, Ray Mangrum. Tee times sandwiched the group between the two featured threesomes, one with Sam Snead and the other, a group with Ben Hogan.

From almost the very first hole, Rhodes was serenaded by the sounds of groans and cheers. They came from the groups ahead and behind and filled the air for many of the six hours he spent on the course. While playing the second hole, loud groans rose from the hole ahead when Sam Snead missed a 7-foot putt. On the very next hole it happened again, when Snead three-putted the fourth hole, costing him the tournament lead.

While Rhodes played the seventh hole, he heard loud groans from the gallery behind. Ben Hogan had struck a drive that landed in a bunker on number six. A few minutes later a loud roar went up after Hogan sent his shot out of the bunker onto the green. The alternating sounds accompanied Rhodes throughout the final day. As he finished up on the eleventh hole, he heard cheers from the hole behind. Hogan had knocked in a 15-foot putt and was now leading the tournament. As Hogan and Snead dueled for the lead, Rhodes struggled. He followed his second-round 76 with a score of 77 in the third round. As Rhodes turned in his final scorecard with a 79 final-round score, a loud roar could be heard from the eighteenth hole as celebration broke out for Ben Hogan, who had won the 1948 US Open.

Rhodes may have left Riviera Country Club disappointed with his final placement but was shrouded in praise. Herman Hill, the West Coast correspondent for the *Pittsburgh Courier*, wrote that Rhodes "acquitted himself well, demonstrated flashes of sheer brilliance, and gave definite promise of future championship caliber."[12] Even more important than Rhodes' play, Hill declared, was that he was responsible for "the crumbling of one of the few remaining citadels of race bias in the world of professional sports."[13] The *Tampa Bay Times* put Rhodes' achievement on par with the Cleveland Indians signing Satchel Paige, Harrison Dillard's victory in the Olympics, and Joe Louis's knockout win over Jersey Joe Walcott as one of the outstanding sports achievements by a Black athlete in 1948. The *Pittsburgh Courier* offered a salute to Rhodes with a succinct headline: "Golfer Ted Rhodes, a worthy pioneer."[14]

6

Critical Eyes

Chatter among those in the gallery stopped as Ted Rhodes stood over his ball on the green. His glance flicked back and forth between the ball and the hole just a few feet away. Rhodes positioned his feet, then bent his knees slightly. He leaned forward until his head was over the ball. As he drew his putter back, the area around him became flush with utter silence, so much so that the tap from the metal head of Rhodes' putter striking the ball could be heard from several feet away. Eyes, hundreds of them, were transfixed on the small white ball as it rolled quickly across the poa annua grass, a surface cut to barely one-eighth of an inch in height. Anticipation grew as Rhodes' ball rolled toward the hole. But as it neared its intended target, the path suddenly changed, altered ever so slightly by an infinitesimal bump. When the ball rolled past the hole, Rhodes snapped. With a sweep of his left arm, Rhodes flung his putter through the air. Profanity spewed from his lips. Shocked looks filled the faces of spectators. Two women recoiled in horror at the outburst. Many were made wide-eyed and open-mouthed by the piercing of the man's self-control. Caddies shot glances. They had seen Rhodes snap a club in two during a fit of anger earlier in the round.

The outburst seemed out of character for a golfer who was popular with fans and whom sportswriters described as likeable, honest, unassuming, and in the words of the *California Eagle*, "a true gentleman golfer."[1] Fellow golfers found Rhodes fun to be around. In social games of golf, he was quick with a quip. Rhodes could leave his friends flabbergasted at his ability to crack a joke, then, while the men were laughing, turn and whack a tee shot straight down the fairway without taking time to set up.

It was hardly uncommon for a golfer to lose their composure, throw or snap a club, and utter or even shout profanity in the privacy of a country club or a public course. But what might have been commonplace throughout America was not entirely acceptable when done before hundreds of spectators during an event with the profile of the 1949 Los Angeles Open. In the case of Ted Rhodes, his outburst involved more than a violation of golf etiquette. It had to do with the portrayal of an entire race, and in the case of Rhodes and the 1949 Los Angeles Open, it was an eruption that triggered strong reaction from those who felt it their duty to act as arbiters of such behavior.

In the days that followed, sportswriters and columnists with newspapers that served a Black readership were angered by Rhodes' actions. In their eyes, Rhodes was much more than just a successful golfer. *New Journal and Guide* columnist Cal Jacox said Rhodes "had awakened an interest among colored players," adding that participation in golf by Blacks was "growing by leaps and bounds."[2] Rhodes, they insisted, was an example to others, a role model. Because of that the press let him have it. None was more harsh than the *Los Angeles Sentinel*. In an editorial the paper stated:

> Rhodes is no ordinary golfer when he steps out on the links. He is, plainly, a Negro golfer. And he is on trial. Golfers and fans are looking at him with critical eyes. And, his actions will determine to a large extent the progress we make in our fight for democracy in the PGA and other golfing and sports set-ups. Therefore, we must condemn the actions of Rhodes in the recently-conducted LA Open. Ted, you can't do it! Button your lip and down your indignation.[3]

The following night, *Sentinel* sportswriter A. S. "Doc" Young was at home. Music played while he read the newspaper. The telephone rang. "This is Ted

Rhodes," stated a stern voice clearly tinged with anger. "Why did you people do such a write up?"[4] Thus began a terse back and forth between writer and golfer. Young explained that the writeup was not personal. He reminded Rhodes his paper had complimented his play in the tournament. "Fact is people called to protest. You're a pioneer, like Jackie Robinson. Every little bit of action must be watched."[5] Neither Young's explanation nor admonition was salve to Rhodes' wound. "Look," he snapped. "I was a caddy in the south for fifteen years—did it to earn my living at seventy-five cents a day. I have been golfing for years. I know how to act. I'm no fool. I wouldn't do anything to hurt our cause."[6] The brusque back and forth continued. Rhodes pointed out that many golfers, pros and amateurs alike, throw their clubs. He even rattled off names of some of the top players in the PGA and said he personally witnessed them curse and throw a club every now and then. That's when Young invoked the plight of Jackie Robinson and his work to develop self-restraint. "If you know Jackie Robinson, then you know that he was naturally quick-tempered and aggressive."[7]

Ted Rhodes needed no lecture about Jackie Robinson. A voracious reader, Rhodes digested the myriad press accounts of Robinson's ascension to major-league baseball. He was well aware that Branch Rickey, president of the Brooklyn Dodgers, strongly stressed the importance of demeanor and conduct, saying, "We can only win if we can convince the world that I'm doing this because you are a great ballplayer and a fine gentleman. But, let me tell you it's going to take an awful lot of courage."[8] What Rhodes also knew about Robinson was the advice he received and the blueprint he followed came from the same man who steered him: Joe Louis.

The heavyweight boxing champ and the future baseball pioneer met in the winter of 1942. Both were stationed at Fort Riley, Kansas. Robinson had applied for Officers' Candidate School. He felt a decision, not just about him but several other Black applicants, was taking far too much time. He sought out Louis and appealed for help. Though only a private, Louis was able to bring the matter to the attention of the right people. By the end of the year, Robinson was commissioned a second lieutenant.

Their paths would not cross again. Louis and Rhodes arrived in Los Angeles just days after Robinson became the subject of major news throughout America. He was signed by the Brooklyn Dodgers for their farm team in Montreal. Robinson would be the first Black player in minor-league baseball. By all accounts, there seemed little doubt about Robinson's ability to make the grade. The big questions involved attitudes. How would Robinson be accepted by White players, particularly those who hailed from the South? "If Robinson's presence leads to racial strife on the ball field," wrote Tommy Holmes in the *Brooklyn Daily Eagle*, "the experiment will fail."[9] Then there was the importance of Robinson's attitude and demeanor. An editorial in the *Alabama Tribune* reminded, "If a negro turns out to be a bad actor; jostles a White passenger in his haste to secure a seat, or if he commits some outrageous crime, almost always American prejudice charges it up to Race."[10]

Robinson fully understood that he was about to undertake a challenge far greater than simply succeeding as a ballplayer. Not only could his play open the door of opportunity to more Black ballplayers, his actions and comportment both on the field and away from it could change widely held misconceptions and false perceptions about a race. "There are no less than 14 million Negroes involved in this thing," he said. "I am their representative, and I can't afford to let them down."[11]

William Tucker, a columnist with the *United Press* news syndication service, offered Robinson a guide in print. He suggested Robinson would succeed, "if he just models his deportment after Joe Louis."[12] Throughout his ten-year professional boxing career, Louis was considered by the press to be a model of exemplary conduct. Columnists extolled him as humble. He was never mentioned in context to any sort of trouble. His was an image carefully crafted by his manager, John Roxborough. When, in 1934, a twenty-year-old Louis agreed to let Roxborough manage his career, he was presented with a list of seven commandments for personal and professional conduct:

1. There will be no soft fights.
2. He must live and fight clean.
3. There will be no fixed fights.
4. He must never gloat over a fallen opponent.
5. He must keep a "dead pan" demeanor in front of the camera.
6. He must never go into a nightclub alone.
7. He must never be photographed with a White woman.[13]

Roxborough's list was prompted by the public's reaction to the first Black heavyweight champion, Jack Johnson, twenty years earlier. A loud and gregarious Texan, Johnson shocked and angered the public with his boastfulness. He was frequently ticketed for speeding, served jail time for consorting with prostitutes, and was married three times, each time to a White woman. When Johnson lost to Jess Willard in 1915 and relinquished the heavyweight title, promoters became reluctant to give title shots to Black fighters. It was a trend Roxborough wanted to change with Louis.

Louis's trainer, Jack Blackburn, reinforced Roxborough's message with his own. "You're colored, Joe, and the colored fighters got to be lots better than the other man—if he's gonna go places. You gotta do the right thing and never leave yourself open so people can talk about you."[14] It was a message Louis often shared to Rhodes and other Black athletes.

Weeks after Louis and Rhodes arrived in Los Angeles, the *Pittsburgh Courier* held a sports award banquet in the city. Before a large crowd at the local Elks Club, Robinson's recent signing with Montreal was celebrated. Louis was the banquet's headliner. The event gave him the chance to speak with Robinson. Robinson was no stranger to abuse, both in the area of his upbringing, Pasadena, California, and when he played football at UCLA, particularly in games against opponents from the South: SMU, Texas A&M, and TCU. But being the first of his race to enter minor-league baseball would offer a far greater challenge. Louis had been down that road and offered advice from experience.

It was a year before Louis and Robinson met again. By then, Robinson had won a batting title and led Montreal to the International League pennant. The *Kansas City Star* was among many to predict bigger things for his future. "It's almost a foregone conclusion that Jackie Robinson will be in a Dodger uniform next season, the first of his race to play in the major leagues. His able play and quiet manner win esteem."[15] In March 1947 Joe Louis was on a multi-country tour staging boxing exhibitions in Central, South American, and Caribbean countries. His trip brought him to Cuba, where Branch Rickey arranged for the Brooklyn Dodgers to conduct spring training so Robinson would not be subjected to Jim Crow laws in Florida, where the ballclub usually trained.

Louis surprised Robinson and his teammates when he turned up at Havana Military Academy, where the Dodgers and their farm team, the Montreal Royals, were training. Players broke from drills and sprinted to greet the boxing champ. "How's your golf?" Louis asked Robinson.[16] Their conversation alternated between humorous and serious. When it came time to leave, Louis explained that he was expected at a ceremony to receive the key to the city from the mayor of Havana. "Why if he gives you the keys to the city, every ice box in the city of Havana is liable to be raided," Robinson grinned. Louis peered over his sunglasses and said, "He knows who to give the keys to and who not to give them to." When Robinson replied "What makes you say that?," Louis broke into a sheepish grin and said, "He hasn't given 'em to you, has he?"[17] As he left, Louis invited Robinson to continue their visit at his hotel the following night and promised he would be in the stands when Robinson broke into the major leagues.

It was on Tuesday, April 15, 1947, when another wall of division crumbled. Jackie Robinson debuted for the Brooklyn Dodgers. "The great day has arrived," declared Rube Samuelson in Robinson's hometown newspaper, the *Pasadena Star-News*.[18] That he scored the winning run in the Brooklyn Dodgers' 5–3 triumph over the Boston Braves was cheered by 26,623 fans in Ebbets Field. That he played in the game was a source of pride among millions more. "This was a historic occasion. For the first time ever, an acknowledged Negro played in a major league championship game," Tommy Holmes explained in the *Brooklyn Daily Eagle*.[19] The most popular sport in America was integrated.

Two weeks later, during a game between the Dodgers and New York Giants, applause broke out during the bottom of the fourth inning when the heavyweight champion walked through the stands. As Louis took his seat in a box next to the Dodgers' dugout, he waved to Jackie Robinson. Following the inning Robinson ran from his position to shake Louis's hand. Later, with the press, Robinson was effusive in his gratitude to Louis. "Joe Louis gave me the benefit of his long experience and showed me how to avoid the troubles that anybody under pressure can get in to. If it hadn't been for Joe I'd probably have aged ten years."[20]

By the beginning of 1949, Jackie Robinson was established as a full-fledged star. He helped the Dodgers reach the World Series, received votes for Most Valuable Player, and opened the door with his play and comportment for six other Black ballplayers to receive the chance to play in the major leagues. A poll conducted by the Mutual Radio Network rated Robinson the sixth most popular person in America behind singers Bing Crosby and Frank Sinatra, General Dwight D. Eisenhower, Father Flanagan of Boy's Town in Nebraska, and Mrs. Eleanor Roosevelt, wife of the late president.

Ted Rhodes was well versed in the Robinson story. He knew Robinson. The ballplayer was an avid golfer. On a good day he could score in the high 70s. He sought instruction from Rhodes. The need for a highly visible Black athlete to be beyond reproach in his conduct had been drilled into Rhodes since he began working with Joe Louis. In the three years since, his play and conduct had been laudable, even praised by Wendell Smith in the *Pittsburgh Courier*, all of which made him fume at the editorial decision of the *Los Angeles Sentinel* to illuminate a singular outburst.

Rhodes' fury toward the *Sentinel* may have reduced from a boil, but it was still on simmer when he ran into Doc Young two months later. The men met quite by accident at the Watkins Hotel, where Rhodes resided in Los Angeles. Young tried to mend fences with questions about Rhodes' play in recent tournaments. The men spoke for almost fifty minutes, during which the topic of Rhodes' behavior on the golf course was never broached.

Rhodes' anger toward the press seemed to cool until comments in a national magazine erupted what had been a small spat into a full-fledged industry-wide fury. *SPORT* magazine, one of the more widely read sports publications in the country, ran a story in its July 1949 edition that featured Rhodes and the plight of Black professional golfers. When the article's writer, Hannibal Coons, a prolific author, writer, and Hollywood screenwriter, asked Rhodes about coverage of his success by Black newspapers, he replied, "Naw, they don't care about golf. All they're interested in is who's dancing at the Savoy or who sat where in the streetcar."[21]

Almost immediately, columnists with papers around the country reacted with ire. Russ Cowans of the *Michigan Chronicle* shot back, "He should pull his head out of the fog and come down to earth. He's still a little colored boy from Nashville."[22] Leon Snead of the *Baltimore Afro-American* said Rhodes "apparently pays more attention to his putts than his tongue."[23] Knowing Rhodes was entered in an upcoming tournament in Chicago, Sam Lacy, the *Afro-American*'s sports editor, traveled there to prod Rhodes about his comments. He confronted Rhodes at the Pershing Hotel and found a man who firmly stood his ground. "The colored papers don't bother to cover the golf tournaments we play in," Rhodes said. "They get what little they do write about us by calling me in the middle of the night."[24] In his column Lacy criticized

Rhodes. He called the golfer lucky, that his success was down to "a stroke of luck," a chance meeting with Joe Louis.[25] Lacy went on to claim Louis never would have uttered such criticism of the press.

Amid the venom and controversy, a different kind of publicity swirled about Ted Rhodes. His name began to appear not on the sports pages but in gossip columns, linked to a popular dancer. It was Joe Louis's doing. He was secretly seeing a shake dancer in a Detroit nightclub show who performed under the name of "Chee Chee." Louis invited Rhodes to the show. But when the women came onstage, Rhodes' eyes became riveted to a dancer in the chorus line. He asked Louis who she was. Claudia Oliver was the reply. After the show Louis introduced the two. It was not long before a full-fledged romance blossomed.

Claudia Oliver was acclaimed "the fastest feet in show business."[26] Critics hailed her as one of the best Black female dancers, if not the best, in the country. She filled the role of the flirtatious chorus line soubrette in shows produced by popular empresario Joe "Ziggy" Johnson. Born in the tiny western Mississippi town of Scott, Oliver was of mixed race, the product of a tryst between a Black woman and White man of Irish and German ancestry. In Mississippi at the time of Oliver's birth, miscegenation, the marriage of a Black person to a White, was not just against the law. It was a felony punishable by life in prison. Oliver's birth was never recorded. Three months after the girl was born, her mother inexplicably wandered off during a snowstorm. She was later found dead, the victim of hypothermia. When the infant's father appeared at the family home, the girl's grieving grandfather brandished a shotgun and threatened the man if he ever came around again. John and Elsie Oliver then took their granddaughter to their hometown of St. Louis, where they raised her as their own.

At the age of sixteen, Claudia Oliver dropped out of school to become a dancer. She performed at a local St. Louis club, the Golden Lilly. Soon after, glowing reviews appeared in the *St. Louis Argus*, "She has personality and lively dancing feet."[27] Two years later, in April 1938, Ziggy Johnson brought his popular review to the Plantation Club in St. Louis. When he saw Oliver perform, he added her to the chorus line in his show. Johnson's show toured the Midwest and East. Oliver was featured at the Apollo Theatre in New York, the Three Sixes in Detroit, the Crystal Caverns in Washington, DC, and the Flame Show Bar in Chicago. She traveled to Los Angeles, where she performed in a show produced by Bill "Bojangles" Robinson which enjoyed lengthy runs at the Biltmore and Mayan theatres. Columnists and reviewers described her performances with words like "dynamic," "captivating," and "sizzling." The *Chicago Defender* called Oliver one of the best chorus-line dancers in the country. "Claudia kicks out and then how. Rounds and rounds of applause greet her every appearance."[28]

In 1941 Oliver left Johnson's show to become chorus director for a nightclub in Chicago. It was reported the parting was dotted with acrimony. On the anticipated opening night of her new club, however, fire tore through and destroyed the building. Without a job Oliver was forced to return to Johnson, mend fences, and ask for her old job back.

By the winter of 1949, marriage was in the air. Billy Rowe of the *Pittsburgh Courier* wrote that Ted Rhodes "is no longer amorous with glamorous. He's saving all his heart space for Claudia Rhodes."[29] The couple's dates included golf outings, from swing lessons to playing rounds. When Ted Rhodes held down fourth place after the first round of the All-American Open in Chicago, Claudia was in the gallery. Her beaming smile greeted him when he finished fourteenth to earn just under $400. The couple married and made Chicago their home. Both, however, continued to travel extensively—Ted to play in golf tournaments and Claudia to perform in shows.

Marriage brought added responsibilities if not pressures. Just as Joe Louis hammered home, and sportswriters reminded him, whenever Rhodes played in a golf tournament, he represented fifteen million Black Americans. Now he was also playing with greater incentive in his pursuit of prize money. He was playing for two.

7

Swinging at a Star

As Ted Rhodes traveled north along the California coast, he was a confident man. The 1950 golf season had begun in grand fashion. For two days Rhodes contested the lead at the Los Angeles Open. Midway through the event he held fourth place, two strokes behind Ben Hogan and Elly Vines. It was at that point that heavy rains wreaked havoc with the tournament. Still, Rhodes finished nineteenth to earn $160 in prize money. Particularly pleasing, he finished ahead of Butch Harrison, for whom he once caddied back in Nashville, and also Cary Middlecoff, the golfing luminary from his home state.

Finishing in the top twenty in Los Angeles earned Rhodes automatic entry into the event the following week, the Bing Crosby Invitational at Pebble Beach. It was an event golfers considered the glamour stop on the pro tour. Rhodes was far from alone navigating this windy swath of Highway 1. The allure of Crosby's event annually pulled the game's greatest golfers along with the biggest stars of the entertainment industry to the picturesque Central California coast. Its mixture of golfing greats and entertainment stars drew fans in droves, more than almost any other professional golf tournament.

Bing Crosby was far and away the most popular and the highest-paid entertainer in the world. *Life* magazine and the fan magazine *Photoplay* named Crosby America's number one star. As an actor he won the Academy Award for best actor in 1944 for his work in *Going My Way*. In that film he introduced the song "Swinging on a Star," which went on to top the bestseller list. It was one of forty-one number-one hit songs Crosby recorded. In the seven years after its release, Crosby's signature song, "White Christmas," sold six million copies. The *Los Angeles Daily News* trumpeted Crosby's income from acting in motion pictures at $410,000. Decca Records' report to the government tax agency showed Crosby earned $298,846 in royalties from sales of his records. He was also the highest-paid host on radio, pulling down $1,500 a week for hosting the popular one-hour radio show, the *Kraft Music Hall*, on CBS.

When not in a recording studio or sound stage, Bing Crosby was on a golf course. For him, the sport was far more than just a hobby. It bordered on obsession. Crosby played at least four days a week, generally shot in the low- to mid-70s, but had a best round of 69. He was champion of Lakeside Golf Club in Burbank, where he was a member. Almost everyone in the entertainment industry knew when you wanted to reach Bing Crosby, you telephoned his golf club.

In 1937, at the prodding of his brother Larry, Crosby invited friends and top golfers together for a weekend of fun. The idea was a two-day golf tournament with foursomes made up of entertainers, sports stars, friends, and professional golfers. Crosby put up the prize money, $3,000. He held the event at Rancho Santa Fe Golf Club near San Diego, then invited all 166 players as well as the officials who worked the event to join him for a barbeque at his ranch not far from the course.

Aside from rains that cut the inaugural tournament to just one day, Crosby's golf frolic went over so well it became an annual affair. By 1940 interest among prospective players had swelled. The field more than doubled to 324. Success of the event was noted by the PGA. In a rare gesture the organization presented Crosby with a gold lifetime membership card in appreciation for his interest in the sport. *Los Angeles Times* columnist Dick Hyland suggested Crosby "pow wow with some of the golfing gentry concerning the future of the tournament," a veiled prodding to turn his event into one sanctioned by the PGA.[1] When the organization released its 1942 calendar of tournaments, the Bing Crosby Pro-Am was on the list.

During World War II Crosby put the event on hiatus. In 1946 the sports editor of the *Monterey Herald*, Ted Durein, wrote to Crosby to suggest he move his tournament to Pebble Beach on the Central California coast. Crosby knew the course well. He had a house on the thirteenth fairway. Samuel F. B. Morse, who owned the course, offered Crosby use of it for his event. The idea appealed to the entertainer, and the switch was made. When the event resumed in 1947, Crosby changed more than just the location. He expanded the event from a weekend to a three-day, fifty-four-hole tournament. In order to accommodate even more players, the tournament would be spread over three courses: Pebble Beach Golf Links, Monterey Peninsula Country Club, and Cypress Point Golf Course. Crosby put up half of the PGA-required $10,000 prize money out of his own pocket. One thing that did not change was the unique Crosby flavor. The tournament had a party atmosphere. The format of celebrities and sports stars paired with pros remained in place. It was so popular with the spectators in the event's new area, they turned up to the tune of twelve thousand a day.

When Ted Rhodes arrived to check in for the 1950 Bing Crosby Pro-Am, the event's entry list was filled with big names from sports and entertainment. Baseball stars such as Leo Durocher, Lefty O'Doul, Ralph Kiner, and Jimmy Dykes were eager to play. The movie star contingent included Johnny Weissmuller, Randolph Scott, and Forrest Tucker. The buzz around the course was that Crosby's silver-screen cohort, Bob Hope, was a scratch. An auto accident on a rain-slicked Southern California road left him with a dislocated right shoulder and his arm in a sling.

There was, however, one expected name that did not appear on the list, Ted Rhodes. It was the PGA that turned Rhodes away. When Crosby learned the news, he was incensed. His brother Larry sought after Rhodes. It was in the parking lot where he found him, ready to return to Los Angeles. Larry Crosby apologized. He promised he would work things out and invite Rhodes to play in their 1951 event.

When word got out that Rhodes had been barred from Crosby's event, fury erupted. Joe Louis sprang into action. He sent a cordial yet biting letter to the entertainer he considered a friend. The men had golfed together on several occasions, and Louis was beyond disappointed by the discriminatory decision. Louis urged Crosby to reconsider the exclusion of Blacks from his tournament, adding that the "PGA must not be allowed to stand behind your good name."[2]

Crosby did not respond. Instead, his tournament manager, Maurie Luxford, replied with a letter dripping in both dismissiveness and condescension. Luxford took issue with the claim that Rhodes' place in the Los Angeles Open earned an invitation to the Crosby Pro-Am. Though widely publicized in several Los Angeles newspapers that the top thirty finishers in the Los Angeles Open received automatic entry into the 1950 Bing Crosby Pro-Am, Luxford insisted no such arrangement was ever made. "Basically, the tournament is a gathering of eighty-four of Bing's personal friends among the thousands of amateur golfers he knows, and eighty-four professionals selected by the National PGA and approved by Crosby," Luxford wrote.[3] It was abundantly clear that despite the declaration by the PGA following the resolution of the 1948 lawsuit, its "Caucasian-only" clause was still firmly in place.

Outrage at the exclusion of Rhodes from Crosby's tournament was for the most part muted, likely due to the small community and somewhat isolated part of the state in which the event was held. A week later that would not be the case. Following Crosby's tournament, golf's best migrated back to Southern California for the Long Beach Open. Only a year earlier the beach community was abuzz over its ability to step from the shadow of nearby Los Angeles and host its very own professional sporting event. The local Lions Club raised the money to fund the tournament. The Montana Land Company, owner of a local country club, provided the venue at no cost.

Promotion for the second Long Beach Invitational involved newspaper ads with names of top professional golf stars scheduled to play. During the days leading up to the tournament, newspaper write-ups touted Rhodes as not only a participant but a potential title contender. Yet when players arrived to play a practice round at Lakewood Country Club, Rhodes was blocked from doing so. The PGA declared Rhodes did not meet eligibility requirements and could not participate in the tournament. Immediately, Joe Louis sent telegrams to the mayor of Long Beach and the head of the sponsoring Lions Club. "Prejudice and discrimination have no place in sports," he wrote and urged that Rhodes' banishment be reversed.[4]

Los Angeles media joined the chorus of outrage. Al Jarvis on his KLAC radio program lambasted both the Long Beach mayor and the Lions Club. When the PGA's Schneiter explained that Rhodes was not qualified to play in a PGA event, NBC radio sportscaster Sam Balter decried, "Does being qualified mean that he has to be White?"[5] *Pittsburgh Courier* sportswriter Ches Washington pressed the new president of the PGA, Horton Smith, on what the qualification was to play in his organization's tournaments. Smith answered that to be an approved golfer one must be at least eighteen years of age and Caucasian.

If the Lions Club and the mayor were expecting sympathy from their local newspaper, they didn't get it. Frank Blair, sports editor of the *Long Beach Press-Telegram*, excoriated all involved. Blair called the matter an embarrassment and railed, "The PGA will have to face the fact that it will encounter a similar situation frequently in some cities and a move to liberalize the rules of the organization should be made."[6] Then, with a message to the Lions Club, Blair added, "If enough pressure is put on the PGA, if more co-sponsoring groups refuse to risk criticism and embarrassment maybe there'll be some changes made in those PGA rules and contracts."[7]

The *New York Age* gave Louis a platform to unleash more punches at professional golf. In a special column Louis declared, "We were slapped in the face." He urged,

We should be banded together, work conscientiously, and make this nation an inseparable one. We can do it by doing away with nationalities and color bars. Do away with segregation in sports, business, educational institutions, and elsewhere. We should act like Americans. Every tree is known by its own fruit. Segregation must vanish, the fight must continue until victory is won.[8]

For nine years Rhodes was on the payroll of boxing great Joe Louis as his valet and instructor. The men played frequently and often in the company of celebrities and sports stars. Left to right, Louis, boxer "Sugar Ray" Robinson, Rhodes, and South Florida golf standout Joe Roach. Courtesy of Deborah Rhodes

The subject of race-based denial and opportunity permeated sports throughout 1950. In the four years since Jackie Robinson joined the Brooklyn Dodgers, four more ball clubs integrated. By the time National Football League pioneer Kenny Washington retired following the 1949 season, four more Black players had joined the league, and four teams integrated. In August of 1950 Althea Gibson became the first African American invited to play in America's premier tennis event, the United States National Championship. Yet the PGA dug in its heels and remained an all-White organization.

Days after the calendar turned from 1950 to 1951, opportunity was given an exclamation mark. It occurred at the Los Angeles Open. When Ted Rhodes stepped to the first tee to begin his round, the kilt-wearing tournament starter, Scottie Chisolm, bellowed, "There is no discrimination here. Ted Rhodes is a gentleman of color!"[9] A loud cheer went up from the gallery.

Earlier in the week during the practice round, Rhodes gained notice. He turned in the lowest score, shooting 4 under par. The 1951 Los Angeles Open was Rhodes' best of the six he had participated in. With two rounds below par, a 70 on the final day, he finished ninth. Then, like the rest of the field, he set out for Pebble Beach. Rhodes traveled to Pebble Beach on a promise. Weeks after his 1950 tournament, Joe Louis had a conversation with Bing Crosby. According to Louis, Crosby made a promise that Rhodes could play in his tournament in 1951. With each mile covered on his trek to Pebble Beach, Rhodes became more anxious to learn whether Bing and Larry Crosby were men of their word.

During the second week of January 1951, the entertainment industry celebrated Bing Crosby's twentieth anniversary in show business. The format for Crosby's weekly CBS radio show was altered, and instead, the network broadcast Crosby songs and well wishes for twenty-four hours. Acclaim and celebration for the star of song and silver screen was cut short, however, by another ugly outburst at his golf tournament. For a second consecutive year, Ted Rhodes was denied the opportunity to play.

On being told he was barred, Rhodes became angry. It was rare for him to lose his composure, but a promise had been broken, and he wanted to know why. Rhodes scanned a nearby gathering of people searching for Crosby. He saw him among the group, smoking a pipe, a fedora perched atop his head. Rhodes started in his direction. When Crosby saw the golfer walking in his direction, he stopped what he was doing, made a 180-degree pivot, and hurriedly walked the other way. Rhodes' anger escalated, but now it was mixed with hurt. The idol of millions was now a pariah to one.

Unlike the year before, the eyes of the press, particularly the Black press, were on Rhodes' treatment at the Bing Crosby Pro-Am. When it was learned that Rhodes was again barred, Crosby went from celebrated nationally one week to vilified in the Black press the next. Words were harsh, accusations damning. *Pittsburgh Courier* columnist Billy Rowe declared, "It's kinda odd to come across a man in such an important position and find him so lacking in integrity he fails to stand on his word."[10] Halley Harding, sports editor of the *Los Angeles Sentinel*, noted "that a lot of his (Crosby's) cash came from our people going to see him, listening to him on the air and buying his records," and that Crosby should "give the tournament up or act like a real American."[11] In an editorial, the *Chicago Defender* said the PGA had "sunk lower than a snake's belly."[12]

The *Courier*'s Rowe received a letter from a reader, Alyce Key of Los Angeles. Upset at Crosby's treatment of Rhodes, she suggested a national boycott of an upcoming movie, *Follow the Sun*, the story of PGA star Ben Hogan. Rowe agreed with the idea and took it a step farther. He urged his readers to also boycott Crosby's movies, records, and any products endorsed by the entertainer that were sold in their local stores.

In Hollywood few if any would put Bing Crosby's name in the same sentence with bigotry. He was well known for being an advocate of Black actors. When he launched his own production company, he cast Ben Carter in the company's first project, *John L.*, a biopic about boxing great John L. Sullivan. Crosby fought studio executives who forbade him to put jazz artist Louis Armstrong in the 1936 film *Pennies from Heaven*. But the entertainer's sterling reputation was now tarnished as controversy swelled. Special committees formed around the country to promote the boycott of Crosby. Executives in Hollywood became particularly alarmed when popular singer-songwriter George Jessel joined the cause.

In the summer of 1951, tabulations from the third annual Long Beach Open showed a financial loss. Stung by both the controversy and financial losses, the Long Beach Lions Club and owners of the Lakewood Country Club declined to continue their support for the tournament. George Lake, the event's general manager, lined up new backers, but the withdrawal of the Lakewood owners meant a new host course had to be found. Because the city's municipal course, Recreation Park, was deemed most accessible for fans, it was chosen to be the tournament's new home. There was one obstacle, and it would prove insurmountable. Per a Long Beach city ordinance, any tournament held at Recreation Park could not exclude golfers based on race. When the PGA would not budge from its membership position, organizers of the Long Beach Open were left with no option but to discontinue their tournament. The PGA gave the spot on the 1952 schedule to organizers who sought a tournament for San Diego.

At the conclusion of his season, Rhodes hurried home. A momentous event waited. Claudia was expecting. The couple spent the holidays preparing for the baby's arrival. As January and the string of winter golf tournaments in Southern California drew near, Rhodes faced a dilemma. Claudia's doctor projected a February due date for the baby's arrival. Ted thought he could play in a few tournaments, make some money, then be back in time for the birth. No sooner had he hit the road for Los Angeles when, on New Year's Eve, Claudia went into labor early. Once in Los Angeles Rhodes learned he was a father. Claudia had delivered a healthy baby girl whom the couple named Deborah.

Claudia was none too happy that Ted was away. But within a few days he phoned with news that eased her frustration. He had finished sixteenth in the Los Angeles Open and was coming home with $220 in his pocket.

Four months after the hubbub at his golf tournament, Bing Crosby and a friend spent several days fishing streams in the mountains of Canada's British Columbia province. Upon completing their excursion, the men journeyed to Vancouver. Somewhat disheveled, wearing outdoor clothes of leather jackets, dungarees, cowboy boots, and with scruffy facial hair as evidence of their time removed from civilization, the men entered one of the city's larger hotels and asked for rooms. Without batting an eye or pausing to check his registry, the desk clerk muttered, "We're booked solid for days," and sent Crosby and his friend on their way.[13] Told later one of the men was Bing Crosby, the desk clerk gasped, "I thought they were a couple of bums, or Indians from up north." Columnists for several Black newspapers had a field day with the item. Wrote one, reflecting on Crosby's treatment of Ted Rhodes, "This ought to be a lesson for Bing."[14]

8

The Bomber's Battle

In living rooms and kitchen nooks, barrooms and bedrooms, fingers twisted knobs on radios as ears strained to hear static give way to the sound of a sought-after station. This was a Sunday-night staple. Curiosity mixed with anxiousness. Eagerness grew until, at 8:00 p.m., the unmistakable voice tinged with a New York accent declared, "Good evening, Mr. and Mrs. North America, and all the ships at sea."[1] When Walter Winchell's voice blared from radios, America listened.

Brash, brusque, with a rapid-fire staccato delivery, the pause between phrases filled with the sound of a clattering telegraph key, Walter Winchell delivered a unique brand of insight. His was a show filled with exclusive news reports, dotted with salaciousness, biting opinions, and invoked with distinct candor.

No radio program in America drew as many listeners as did Winchell's on a Sunday night. Throughout the 1930s, 1940s, and into the 1950s, he was a fixture on big-city stations like KECA in Los Angeles, WENR in Chicago, KXOK in St. Louis, as well as those in smaller towns and burghs, such as KRMD in Shreveport, KYJC in Medford, WROV in Roanoke. In all, 291 stations across America aired Winchell's show every Sunday night.

It was on Sunday, January 13, 1952, that Walter Winchell delivered to the PGA its most stinging rebuke to date. He informed his almost thirty million listeners that the great Joe Louis, America's revered boxing champion, had been barred by the PGA from playing in the San Diego Open solely because the organization did not want Black golfers to play in its tournaments. "A more contemptible, arrogant, and un-American attitude hasn't appeared since Harriet Beecher Stowe created Simon Legree," Winchell railed.[2]

Winchell's program cast far more illumination than ever before on the PGA's position toward Black golfers. The influence of Winchell combined with the conviction carried by the popular Louis would intensify pressure on the organization to a point where its previously unyielding resistance to integration began to fracture.

The latter weeks of summer in 1951 brought heartache for golf enthusiasts in one Southern California town and joy to those of another. With Long Beach Open organizers unable to find a course where the PGA could invoke its Caucasian-only policy, the decision was made to give the dates instead to a group that sought a tournament for San Diego.

Having worked for months to try to land an event, tournament organizers in San Diego were quick to assemble their operation. Anderson Borthwick, one of the area's best amateur golfers, was made chairman of the tournament. The San Diego Country Club, a fifty-year-old venue 10 miles south of San Diego in Chula Vista, was secured as the host site. An agreement was struck to make the San Diego Society for Crippled Children and its campaign to build a new children's hospital the benefactor and receive proceeds from the tournament. Then, Borthwick made a deal that would give a boost to his fledgling event but even more so have a profound impact on the future direction of professional golf.

When Lou Reneau Jr. agreed for his organization to be the sponsor of the inaugural San Diego Open, he stressed that what his members wanted most from the deal was publicity. Reneau had no idea the kind of publicity his group was to receive. President of the Chevrolet Dealers Association of San Diego County, Reneau oversaw a group of men who owned automobile dealerships that sold Chevrolet vehicles. He himself was owner of South Bay Chevrolet, an avid golfer, and a member of San Diego Country Club. Not long after agreeing to sponsor the fledgling pro-am, Reneau and members of his group proposed an idea they felt would generate publicity for the tournament and their product—to have Joe Louis participate in the amateur section of the San Diego Open.

None of the men was aware of the exclusionary PGA membership policy when they extended the invitation to Louis, one which the boxing champ was quick to accept. The possibility that he could be barred from playing came up when Louis told his golfing compatriots about the invitation. Nevertheless, Bill Spiller and Eural Clark decided they would accompany Louis and sent entry forms and fees to the tournament committee.

Horton Smith, two months into the presidency of the PGA, was participating in the Bing Crosby Open when informed of the invitation made to Louis. He sent word to the San Diego Open staff that under PGA policy, Louis could not play. Angry at the decision, Louis pondered a response. He knew if Ted Rhodes or Bill Spiller pressed the matter publicly, they would get the runaround from the PGA. Louis decided it was time he led the fight.

First, Louis phoned Winchell. He managed to reach him in time to get the news added to the content of his Sunday-night program. Then, Louis alerted several newspaper reporters. Before Smith could arrive in San Diego to confer with tournament leaders, his organization was being lambasted from several sides. Influential sports columnist Jimmy Cannon of *Newsday* in New York wrote, "I'm burned up good about Louis getting humiliated out in San Diego. The pros should be ashamed of themselves and apologize publicly because it's not the whim of some dirty bum but written down in the tournament rules."[3] *New York Daily News* columnist Ed Sullivan went a step farther and resigned his membership in the PGA. "There is no place in sports for that kind of discrimination," he wrote in a telegram to Horton Smith.[4] Newspapers from Honolulu to North Carolina blared bold headlines. "JOE LOUIS BARRED FROM GOLF MEET,"[5] and "JOE LOUIS DECLARES WAR ON PGA RULE BANNING NEGRO GOLFERS."[6] In Kansas City, the local Black newspaper *The Call* headlined the fight by the boxer nicknamed the "Brown Bomber," "BOMBER BATTLES BIGOTS."[7]

News of the PGA ruling provoked an array of reactions. Jonathan Rowell was perplexed. "We finally settled it in open court when the attorneys for the PGA made the statement that they didn't and wouldn't discriminate," said the man who represented Rhodes and Spiller in their 1948 lawsuit against the organization.[8] The San Diego County Chevrolet Dealers were furious. The tournament sponsors urged tournament organizers to sever their agreement with the PGA. "We are most anxious that Joe, one of America's true sportsmen, plays in our event," a spokesperson for the dealers said.[9]

As hopefuls played the Monday qualifying event at La Jolla Country Club, Smith and Louis were beseeched by reporters. Smith steadfastly hid behind the PGA membership policy. The organization's national secretary told reporters Louis and Spiller couldn't play because they hadn't signed the required player agreement, one which Louis pointed out Rhodes and Spiller had applied for three years earlier and still had not received an answer. Louis, on the other hand, moved from an incendiary approach to one far more explosive. "Horton Smith," he said, "believes in the White race like Hitler believed in the super race."[10] It was an assertion that made sportswriters hyperventilate and Smith burn with rage.

Horton Smith was considered golf's first wonder boy, a sensation of the late 1920s. Eight years before the PGA tour was organized, Smith began a spree of tournament successes. By 1941 he had earned title trophies from thirty tournaments, including the very first Masters Tournament ever held. Smith represented the United States five times in Ryder Cup competition. Known by the nickname the "Joplin Ghost," Smith was a Missourian, born and raised in the Jim Crow state. He was regarded as being fiercely supportive of the organization's Caucasian-only policy. As Smith fought to stem a wave of adverse publicity, he was, as one columnist suggested, "sitting on a giant firecracker that threatens to explode at any instant."[11]

Fueled by news of anger among members of the San Diego Chevrolet Dealers, Louis increased his assault. He asked what the San Diego Open expected to donate to the proposed children's hospital fund. When told $2,000 he told reporters, "I'll give them double that amount if they'll cancel the tournament."[12]

Newspapers went from presenters to proselytizers. Influential *New York Herald Tribune* columnist "Red" Smith chastised the PGA. "There can, of course, be no excuse or defense for any policy of qualification-by-pigmentation. It could not exist on the books of any sporting organization that didn't have the PGA's long and enviable record of stupidity."[13] Bill Corum of William Randolph Hearst's *International News Service* wrote, "If there is discrimination in the PGA, then this column is against the PGA until it rids itself of the taint."[14] Sid Ziff in the *Los Angeles Mirror* called out the PGA:

> More power to Joe Louis. The PGA seems to be attempting the neat trick of avoiding a showdown on its policy of Jim Crowism by turning Joe Louis's attack into a mere case of whether Louis, the person, should play in the San Diego Open golf tournament. But that is NOT the issue. Louis, through his great reputation, is only seeking to be the means of breaking through the racial barrier set up by the PGA. Let us hope that he is successful in smashing this last frontier of bigotry in national sports.[15]

International News Service offered both men the opportunity to share their side. Each wrote a column that was distributed to hundreds of newspapers across the country, many of which ran them side by side. "This is the biggest fight in my life," Louis opened. "This is the first time in my professional career that I've run into discrimination in sports, and I hope it's the last time."[16] Smith chose to explain the PGA policy stating, "We do not make the rules just to be tough but to control play in the tournaments and protect the sponsoring organizations." He added, "If at any time these rules seem unjust or outdated the membership of the PGA, composed of professional golfers has the right and obligation to change them."[17]

Buried under the onslaught of negative publicity, and with less than forty-eight hours before the San Diego Open was to begin, Smith scrambled to convene a meeting of his seven-man PGA tournament committee. Only two members were in San Diego. Four agreed to join by telephone. The seventh could not be reached. Louis and Eural Clark were invited to participate as were a handful of PGA member players. Smith intentionally chose not to invite Spiller even though he was at the course. Smith was concerned about what effect the man's temper and acerbic tongue might have on the meeting. But Jimmy Demaret, fresh off winning the Bing Crosby Pro-Am, saw Spiller in the hallway outside the meeting. Not a fan of Smith, Demaret urged Spiller to go inside and join in.

Ideas were discussed. Proposals kicked around. When it was pointed out that it was the USGA and not the PGA that governed amateur play, it was conceded that Louis could participate in the tournament. Members of the tournament committee suggested Louis and Smith play together with Leland Gibson, a member of the PGA national committee, as the third member of their threesome. Where Spiller was concerned, the PGA held firm. He was a professional and not on the organization's approved participant list. Therefore, he could not play. Spiller erupted at the edict. Threats were made. Two members of the committee urged Spiller to let them work it out. The golfer snapped, "You ran over me the last time and aren't going to this time."[18] He made threats to sue.

Discussions led to the formation of a five-member committee, one that Louis and Ted Rhodes would lead. Spiller, Eural Clark, and Howard Wheeler would complete the group. Tournaments held in cities and states not bound by Jim Crow laws were given the discretion to allow Black golfers to either try to qualify for their event or receive one of the ten slots exempted from PGA standards that every tournament was allotted. In the way the PGA gave tournaments a list of approved players who were eligible to receive invitations to play, the committee Rhodes and Louis were to lead would provide tournaments with a list of Black golfers of "recognized ability and standing."[19]

When the meeting broke up, Spiller vented his anger to Louis. He pleaded with the boxing great to boycott the tournament. Louis and his personal secretary, Louis Reed, worked to calm Spiller. The men explained that more could be accomplished by playing eighteen holes of golf a day with the president of the PGA and a member of the organization's national committee than through any boycott.

On Thursday, January 17, the inaugural San Diego Open was to begin. Rain held up play for close to an hour before a storm of a different kind struck the first tee. Bill Spiller arrived and refused to move unless he was permitted to play. He criticized Louis. "I play for money," Spiller said. "Joe, here, he plays for fun."[20] Frank Caywood, the tournament supervisor for the PGA, calmly reminded Spiller of the reason he could not play. Louis appeared and convinced Spiller to abandon his fight and give Smith's plan a chance. He finally relented and left.

When called to the first tee by the starter, Louis and Smith shook hands and posed for photographers. Then, just before 10:30 a.m., Louis sent his tee shot streaking down the fairway on the first hole and with it made history as the first Black man to play in a PGA event. The gathering of fans who followed the men was large, the biggest of any at the course. They watched as Smith took penalties on each of the first two holes and was 3 over par through four holes. Louis's scorecard showed two bogeys and a birdie over his first four. In the press room Black waitresses and servers at the club crowded by the window for a view of the tenth tee. Applause broke out when Louis appeared. "He's doing real good!" one exclaimed.[21] By the end of the day, Louis was 4 over par, to Smith's 1 over. The following day Louis struggled. He shot 82 and missed the cut by two strokes.

Later that night Smith accepted Louis's recommendation for the special committee to screen Black golfers. The PGA president promised to put his proposal to amend the tournament eligibility rules before the tournament

Louis shakes hands with PGA President Horton Smith moments before the men teed off in the historic 1952 San Diego Open. Courtesy of the author.

committee the following day. When he did, and it gained approval, the announcement of the plan brought criticism from all sides. Mainstream media, like *United Press*, felt the agreement fell short of what should have been done. "Actually the PGA has dumped its so called 'racial problem' into the laps of the sponsoring organizations."[22] Columnists with Black newspapers vented displeasure too. *California Eagle* columnist Brad Pye labeled the agreement "appeasement."[23] Marion Jackson of the *Alabama Tribune* called Louis's effort a "puny victory."[24] Some were far more caustic and questioned Louis's motivation. "Joe Louis crawled on his hands and knees before the lily-White Professional Golfers Association to be able to play in the $10,000 San Diego Open," seared the *California Eagle*.[25] Louis shirked the slings and arrows. He understood the reasoning of his attackers. Never did he consider the agreement to be a final resolution but merely a positive starting point "until something better is done."[26]

Louis received telephone calls from sportswriters in Phoenix who urged him to play the following week in the Phoenix Open. Unsure if the calls represented a formal invitation, he telephoned Allen Matthews. The man was head of the Thunderbirds, the special events committee of the Phoenix-area chamber of commerce, which put on the tournament. Matthews eagerly invited him to play. By the end of their conversation, Louis had assurances that he and other Black golfers could attempt to qualify for the 1952 Phoenix Open.

By the time they arrived in Phoenix, the group planning to play numbered six. Rhodes, Spiller, and Charley Sifford would contest for spots in the pro section. Louis, Reed, and Clark would compete for places in the amateur division. Almost immediately trouble arose. On checking in at Phoenix Country Club, the men received a list of rules. At no time could they enter the locker room or dining facilities, nor would they be permitted to take showers at the club. Spiller became angry. He threatened to force his way in and take a shower. Louis and Reed interceded. They calmed Spiller and explained that defiance could only hurt their cause. The group was told a member of the club would make his locker available. Though the member wished to remain anonymous, it was hinted the offer came from a local politician and department store magnate, Barry Goldwater. Before the golfers could take advantage, other members raised objections. Club management was forced to affirm the six could not use the locker room.

Pairings for qualifying divided the six Black golfers into two threesomes. The professionals Rhodes, Sifford, and Spiller would make up one group and begin play as the first threesome to tee off. Following would be the three Black amateur players: Louis, Clark, and Reed. Out first, all three of the professionals sent their chip shots onto the green for relatively short putts on the long par-5 first hole. Sifford strode toward the hole to remove the flagstick. As he reached it, Sifford recoiled in disgust. Anger surged. Someone well versed in the day's pairings and tee times left the men an odious welcome to the PGA circuit. The cup was filled with human feces.

In sharp contrast to the feelings of a worker at the course was the general public. A large turnout, rare for qualifying day, turned up. While more than 160 golfers played to try to earn one of forty available spots in the Phoenix Open, the primary interest of the spectators was Joe Louis and his golfing cohorts. Louis's long drives drew gasps and applause. His hooks, slices, and missed putts produced groans. Accepting nods and friendly smiles from White golfers were received by the six. Sportswriters who queried White golfers about the inclusion of Blacks in the tournament were told those able to qualify should be allowed to play.

By the end of the day, the faces of tournament organizers were painted with frowns. Despite delighting fans with a spectacular chip shot over a bunker and within inches of the hole on eighteen, Joe Louis failed to qualify. His score, 81, was not good enough to put him into the field. On the other hand, the third-lowest score among the 160 competitors was posted by Ted Rhodes, a 71. Bill Spiller and Eural Clark each shot 72 and also made it into the tournament field. For the first time, Black professional golfers would compete in a PGA event.

For Phoenicians, particularly those with an affinity for sports, the Open was the city's annual brush with big-time professional sports. This yearly arrival of the biggest names in professional golf was a source of civic pride. The 1952 Phoenix Open saw that feeling rise to a new level. "The national spotlight will be on Phoenix this week," trumpeted W. Jay Burk in the *Arizona Republic*.[27] The same newspaper's editorial page pointed out that more than just a golf tournament was taking place. Phoenix was part of historic change. "This year's Phoenix Open Golf Tournament will be memorable if only for one thing: For the first time the Professional Golfers' Association modified its rule barring negro players."[28]

At the first tee, Rhodes' competitiveness overwhelmed any appreciation for the historic significance of the moment. This Phoenix Open represented a rare opportunity to compete against the best PGA professionals, White golfers. More importantly for Rhodes, significant money was up for grabs—$2,000 to the winner, prize money to the top twenty-five finishers, and an automatic place in the upcoming Tucson Open to the top sixty. Rhodes had drawn an early tee time, 8:28 a.m. His would be the fifth of the forty-seven threesomes that would go off every seven minutes. Beyond making him the first Black professional golfer to play in a PGA tournament, the morning time slot involved strategizing for distinct course conditions. Dew was still on the grass. Balls wouldn't roll quite as fast, particularly on the greens.

A large percentage of the three thousand fans who turned out followed Rhodes around the Phoenix Country Club course. Part of the attraction was Joe Louis, who followed Rhodes as well. The more ardent among the gallery marveled at Rhodes' iron play. The accuracy of his chip shots brought applause. When he retrieved his ball and walked off the eighteenth green, wire-service reporters were sent scurrying to the pressroom teletype machines. Birdies on two of the final three holes gave Rhodes a 1-under-par score. When he turned in his scorecard, the first Black professional ever to do so in a PGA event, his score was good enough for the early first-round lead. Sportswriters clamored for comment. They found Rhodes humble and surprised. "I haven't been playing too much lately to score too well," he said.[29]

Rhodes' distinct spot on the leader board would last for another two hours. That's when Julius Boros became the big story of the day, shooting 66. By the time the first round ended, Rhodes was fifth, holding court with some of the most successful of all PGA competitors, Lloyd Mangrum, Cary Middlecoff, and Bob Toski, who held the spots between him and Boros.

When not at the course Rhodes and the other Black golfers spent almost all of their time at the Hotel Rice. It was an all-Black accommodation that was more boarding house than hotel, with small rooms, a communal bath, and looking as though it had seen better days. That night after the first round, they were informed Louis had been invited to play the following week in the Tucson Open. The event's general chairman expanded the invitation to include the group of Rhodes, Clark, Reed, Sifford, and Spiller.

In the early hours of Friday morning, Phoenix was soaked by an unexpected rain shower. When the field of golfers arrived at Phoenix Country Club, they discovered a course with conditions far different than in the first round. The biggest impact was going to be to putting. New bent grass had been planted on the greens just for the tournament. Now, rain made the greens soft, which meant balls would pick up dirt and roll much more slowly.

Rhodes, like many, struggled with his short game. "My boy couldn't sink a putt," Joe Louis said to a sportswriter.[30] But his 77 was good enough to be among the top sixty who would advance into the final thirty-six holes over the weekend. Eural Clark and Bill Spiller failed to make the cut. Optimism, if not enthusiasm, waned over the weekend as Rhodes faded from contention. He shot 75 on Saturday, then 79 over the final round to finish with a score of 302, well behind the tournament winner, Lloyd Mangrum.

Rhodes complimented the event's organizers. He told sportswriters he was treated well. Later, and away from the course, Sifford and Spiller shared opposing experiences. Both said they were mocked and targeted with slurs by fans. While Rhodes left Phoenix without monetary rewards, what he did take was worth far more than money. "I think I've contributed a little something to the struggle to have my people given a fair break in golf," he said.[31] For that he was well satisfied.

The following week Rhodes played in the Tucson Open. By finishing in the top sixty of the Phoenix Open, he was exempt from having to qualify for entry into the tournament. Rhodes played well in each of the first two rounds. He shot 70 both days, held eighth at the tournament's midway point, and easily made the cut to play the final two rounds. But a windy Saturday afternoon took a toll. With 30-mile-an-hour winds blowing sand across the course, Rhodes shot his worst round of the tournament, 78. A 77 the following day knocked him out of the money.

With the final putt on eighteen on that last day in Tucson, Rhodes and his traveling golf companions received the sort of slap in the face that served as a reminder there was still much work to be done. The PGA circuit was headed south. Rhodes and company would not be. The next three tournaments would be in Texas, a state with a decades-long practice of banning co-mixing of races on the field of play. While the ban had been fractured in the January 1948 Cotton Bowl game by a defiant Penn State football team, then again eight months later by the Los Angeles Rams, who played Kenny Washington in their exhibition game with the Philadelphia Eagles in Dallas, by February 1952 no minor-league baseball team in Texas or any college athletic team in the state had yet to suit up a Black player. Promoters of the impending tournaments in El Paso, San Antonio, and Houston made it clear no invitation would be forthcoming for Rhodes or any other Black golfer.

For the next four months, Rhodes was a golfer on the outside looking in. After its Texas tournaments the PGA circuit moved to Louisiana and then Georgia. Once spring became summer its events were held in North Carolina and Florida. It was the Fourth of July weekend when the PGA emerged from below the Mason-Dixon Line. By that time Rhodes was the recipient of good fortune—four PGA tournaments had extended invitations to play in their event. The Sioux City Open in Iowa acknowledged their decision to invite Rhodes "was based on excellence of performance and even temperament."[32] Rhodes took maximum advantage of the opportunities to generate headlines and impress both fans and fellow golfers.

At the Sioux City Open, during the official practice round the day prior to the tournament Rhodes astonished the gallery with a near-record score. A missed 5-foot putt on the final hole kept him from recording a 63, which would have equaled the lowest round ever shot at the course. "The best round of golf I've ever seen," marveled his playing partner, Earl Wilde.[33] Rhodes was among the early leaders in the Canadian Open. At the All-American Open he knocked in two 30-foot putts and curled in a 6-foot birdie putt on eighteen to grab the first-round lead, with a 67. "The mule turned into a racehorse today," Rhodes said to reporters.[34] His 70 put him three shots off the lead after the first round of the Fort Wayne Open. In each event Rhodes finished the tournament in the middle of the pack. His season concluded on an even higher note when he won the Negro National Open for the fourth consecutive year. His score, 280, was six strokes better than his closest pursuer.

As he reviewed the opportunities received by Rhodes, Joe Louis was pleased. He admitted the victory was small, and more work had to be done to achieve equality. But the deal struck with Horton Smith had the potential to give Black golfers greater future opportunities. As one sports columnist observed, "The Negro who stands to benefit most from the deal is Ted Rhodes."[35]

9

He's Too Good

Breaths stopped as the small white dimpled ball rolled swiftly across the finely trimmed grass. When it found its mark, the sound of the ball rattling inside the cup was muffled by applause from dozens of spectators perched from vantage points behind the green. The adulation was not just for sinking the putt, but for giving Ted Rhodes a 6-under-par score, which was good enough to make him the first of his race to win the annual pro-am tournament in St. Louis, Missouri.

By May of 1953 praise abounded for Rhodes. Harry Grayson, sports editor of the syndication service *Newspaper Enterprise Association*, called Rhodes "the best Negro golfer in the world."[1] Bill Matney of the *Michigan Chronicle* said Rhodes "stands far above all other Negro swingers." Bill Spiller took regard for Rhodes even higher when he rated his golfing rival as "among the top five in the country."[2]

Those who followed the UGA didn't need anyone to tell them of Rhodes' greatness. His record spoke for itself. Since joining the circuit in 1946, Rhodes had amassed a seven-year record unmatched by anyone in the history of professional golf. During his first two seasons, Rhodes entered fourteen tournaments and won twelve of them. The two tournaments he failed to win both happened to be the Negro National Open. In each case the event was played on the home course of the eventual winner, a veteran of the UGA, Howard Wheeler.

During the 1948 season Rhodes' mastery was interrupted only by the elements that were unique to the UGA. After winning the Houston Open in June to begin the season, Rhodes drove 1,300 miles to Cleveland for the next event on the schedule, the Sixth City Open. Such drives were not uncommon to UGA golfers. While the PGA tour bunched its thirty-five-tournament schedule by geographic proximity, which made travel easier, the UGA circuit was considerably different. Its season involved less than half the events of the PGA. In many cases, promoter wants and course availability played a large part in the date of a tournament. Thus, the circuit could be in Houston one week and Cleveland the next before moving 750 miles west to Minneapolis and then shifting 650 miles east to Dayton.

Travel not only put an added financial burden on golfers, it also took a toll physically. Hours of sitting either on a train or, in the case of Rhodes, in a car made muscles stiff and sore. Every golfer set out with the plan to get in a practice round or two in order to learn the nuances of the course before a tournament began. A missed or canceled train, difficulty navigating a city by car, or being unable to find a course would thwart such plans and rob a golfer of valuable practice time. In one such instance Rhodes drove around a city for two hours, unable to find the course. By the time he found it, he had just enough time to get in a couple of practice swings before he was called to tee off. On being asked by a reporter how he felt, Rhodes replied, "Not too good. I swung at a football this morning and missed it."[3]

Driving from tournament to tournament brought its share of hazards and even peril. On one particularly long drive, Rhodes became drowsy and did what for him was previously unthinkable. He picked up a hitchhiker and asked the man to drive so he could grab some shuteye. "Usually, I never stop for a hitchhiker," he said. Of the long drives Rhodes would often say, "I'll never do that again," only he would.[4] "I'm just a glutton for punishment," he liked to joke.[5] A perilous part of such city-to-city travel was law enforcement. Not unlike many of his race, Rhodes feared being pulled over. It galled him that he had no way to convince a police officer he was a professional golfer should he be questioned about his travel. Police were likely to view the PGA as the only professional golf in the land and find it doubtful that a Black man truly was a member. Such was his level of fear, Rhodes was always careful not to exceed the speed limit and was known to berate any travel partner who did.

During the first week of July in 1948, after his marathon drive from Houston, Rhodes found himself in a two-man duel for the title at the Sixth City Open. With Joe Louis, boxing champ "Sugar Ray" Robinson, and musician Lionel Hampton all part of the gallery, Rhodes finished tied for first with Charley Sifford at the end of regulation. A nine-hole playoff was used to decide the tournament champion. Sifford prevailed by two strokes.

One week later Rhodes returned to top form. He ran away with the Midwestern Elks tournament in Minneapolis. His performance at Superior Country Club made observers marvel. "Some of the shots Rhodes made at Superior were worthy of a national open," Dick Cullum wrote in the *Minneapolis Tribune*.[6] "I was pro out here for thirteen years, and I never played that kind of golf," praised Elmer Carlson.[7] Rhodes replied, "This was my best game of the season."[8]

Only a second-place finish in Dayton, Ohio, interrupted a streak of four tournament titles. During his streak Rhodes' wins in Toledo, New York, Chicago, and in the Joe Louis Open weren't simply assertive, they bordered on demoralizing. In New York, at the inaugural "Sugar Ray" Robinson Open, Rhodes ran away from the field winning by ten strokes. When he won his third consecutive Joe Louis Open title, Rhodes shot a course record 62 on the final day. While the general-circulation newspapers in Chicago ignored the inaugural Windy City Open in favor of covering the women's city golf championship, newspapers that served Black readership noted Rhodes finished 18 under par to take home top prize.

Rhodes' quest to cap his season by ending Howard Wheeler's run of supremacy in the Negro National Open came short by 1 inch, literally. On the final hole of the tournament, Rhodes trailed Wheeler by one stroke. He faced a 10-foot putt. His tap set the ball rolling over the short verdure only to stop 1 inch short of the hole and for the second time in three years leave him second to Wheeler. Rhodes returned home at the end of the season, possessor of six new title trophies from the nine UGA tournaments he played in.

Financial problems plagued several tournaments on the UGA calendar. As a result, the 1949 schedule was 30 percent lighter than it had been during the previous two seasons. In five of the six events that made up the season, the only hands to hoist winner's trophies were those of Ted Rhodes. And in most of the events, there was little doubt about the outcome. Rhodes won the season-opening Houston Open by eight strokes. In Cleveland he shot 8 under par to once again win the Sixth City Open. A course record, 10 under par, on the second day helped him come from behind and best the field in Sugar Ray Robinson's Gotham Open by six shots. The only trophy he did not capture during the 1949 season was that of the Miami View Open in Dayton, Ohio, where he came up a single stroke short of equaling the winning score posted by Bill Spiller. In 1949 the UGA held its championship event, the National Negro Open, in Detroit. The tournament was staged on the same Rackham Golf Course where Rhodes held the course record. He breezed past the competition to win by ten strokes. It would be the first of four Opens he would win in succession.

One week later Rhodes drew headlines for pulling off a Detroit double. Fresh from his triumph in the Open, he won the Joe Louis Open for a third consecutive year. This time he won it by nine strokes. The feat made him the first to win both the Open and the Louis tournament in the same year. Louis's event had gained such popularity that a Detroit television station, WXYZ, carried the final round live. As Rhodes approached the ninth hole, one of the commentators remarked, "Here comes Ted Rhodes folks . . . undoubtedly one of the finest golfers in the United States. In fact, he's among the first 20 in the country."[9]

Rhodes chose to celebrate his success with family. He journeyed to Nashville and showed off his trophies to his mother. It was an impressive collection. In four years as a professional, he had won twenty-five of the thirty-one UGA tournaments he entered. Of the six tournaments he didn't win, Rhodes was the runner-up in four of them.

Yet despite the voluminous publicity Rhodes' success generated for the UGA, there grew a negative opinion, one which seeped through the circuit. It

During the early 1950s Rhodes was heralded as the best African American golfer in the country. Fellow golfer Bill Spiller considered him to be one of the five best regardless of race. Courtesy of the United States Golf Association.

was first given amplitude in a column by Bill Matney in the *Michigan Chronicle* headlined, "Has terrible Teddy Rhodes outgrown Negro golf?"[10] On the surface the piece referenced what had been repeatedly stated; Rhodes deserved a place among the best golfers in the country, regardless of race. It was, however, the subtlety of the headline that people within the UGA ranks talked about. Was Ted Rhodes' success more hindrance than help to the growth of Black golf? Did Rhodes' monopoly on winner's checks and trophies discourage young upstarts from pursuing a career in professional golf?

In the years that followed the end of World War II, the UGA grew at an impressive rate. In 1947 the organization staged ten professional tournaments. It was remarkable growth for an organization that began relegated to playing its tournaments on nine-hole courses with a talent pool made up of players from cities that denied Blacks access to golf courses. Over the ensuing twenty years, UGA events graduated to full eighteen-hole municipal courses. In some seasons the organization even gained access to stage a tournament or two at a country club. Players improved too. Slowly opportunity materialized, particularly below the Mason-Dixon Line. Legal challenges seized upon the so-called separate-but-equal Jim Crow laws to force some cities to either make their public courses available to Black players or construct a course strictly for Black users. In other cases, Blacks constructed their own courses. Newspaper columnists such as Cal Jacox of the Norfolk, Virginia, *New Journal and Guide* and Bill Matney of the *Michigan Chronicle* credited the success of Ted Rhodes and the interest of Joe Louis to a rise of Black participation in the game. Unfortunately, the ten-event 1947 season would prove to be a zenith campaign for the UGA, after which the schedule would slowly dwindle.

By 1950, a year in which Rhodes entered just four UGA events and won three of them, the season consisted of eight tournaments. That summer Rhodes' stretch of four consecutive wins at the Joe Louis Open was snapped. It was stopped by, of all people, a White golfer. Not wanting to be cast as a hypocrite after his scathing criticism of Bing Crosby, Louis accepted the entry of Al Besselink, the assistant pro at the all-White, private Red Run Golf Club in Royal Oak, north of Detroit. Besselink had been a collegiate standout at the University of Miami in Florida and was working to escape the mandatory apprenticeship phase and move into full-fledged membership with the PGA. As Besselink, a tall, gregarious, long hitter put together four rounds below par, spectators were heard to grumble about his inclusion in the event. When Louis heard golfers complain, he snapped, "How do you fellows expect to play in anybody's tournament with attitude like that?"[11] After he defeated Rhodes by six shots to claim the $500 first prize, Besselink praised Louis for running one of the best tournaments he had ever played in. "The golfers with whom I've played for the last three days are definitely of sufficient caliber to play in any PGA tourney," he said.[12]

As Howard Anderson, the national tournament director for the UGA, assembled the 1951 schedule, he was faced with a dilemma. In a bulletin to members, he shared that a record number of tournaments was assembled. There was concern, though. Of the sixteen events, promoters of twelve wanted their tournament to be for amateur golfers only. Only four tournaments were willing to stage a professional section. Gone from the schedule were the Houston Open, Sugar Ray Robinson's Gotham Open, and the Windy City Open. Bill Seawright, the affable president of the Sixth City Open, was as enthusiastic as ever to put on a tournament, just not one with pros in it. Even Joe Louis was pondering how much longer he could continue to host his event. Not once had the Joe Louis Open managed to make money.

Michigan Chronicle sports editor Bill Matney sounded the alarm. "The future of Negro golf is imperiled," he wrote.[13] The *Chicago Defender* queried promoters. Many said the money they paid pros for prize earnings was the difference between breaking even and losing money. Equally frustrating, they said, was a yearly decline in the numbers of professionals who played while amateur entries grew. From a high point, years in which some tournaments saw as many as two hundred enter, that number was now forty or less.

Money certainly had a lot to do with the dwindling numbers. Not only was Rhodes taking home the bulk of the trophies but a large amount of the prize money as well. Aside from the Joe Louis Open, the average pot of prize money at a UGA tournament was between $1,000 and $2,000, a mere fraction of what PGA events offered. For a tournament promoter, prize money represented a sizeable outlay. Their sources of income were limited. Some cities prohibited charging admission at their municipal course. The more successful tournaments had a benefactor like Joe Louis in Detroit, or Sugar Ray Robinson in New York, or an underwriting sponsor like Cleveland's Sixth City Open enjoyed with Pilsener Brewing Company and its signature beer brand, P.O.C. From the pot of prize money, one-third to, in some cases, half was set aside for the winner of the tournament. A significant chunk of the remainder was designated for the runner-up. What money was left was divided among the third-place finisher and those after. Beyond the first- and second-place finishers, few left a tournament with enough money to cover their travel expenses.

A shrinking schedule and smaller pots of prize money gave golfers reason to think twice about a career in the sport. Only a small number of Black golfers could afford the cost to travel the circuit. A few of those were able to do so because of the help of backers. One—a golfer from Muncie, Indiana, Rube Poole—convinced his local bowling league, the Willard Street Bowling Association, to provide financial support. To cut costs, UGA golfers shared rides in cars and often slept four to a room in hotels. It was not uncommon for many in a tournament field to be unable to eat. It showed in their results. "You can't play golf when you're hungry," Charley Sifford said.[14]

From the 1946 through 1950 seasons, Rhodes walked away with first-place money in twenty-eight of the thirty-five UGA events he entered. His success was not only competitively demoralizing to other Black professional golfers but financially defeatist to career ambitions as well. By 1951 the decline in the number of professional tournaments offered by the UGA along with a reduction in prize money were catastrophic to the series.

The economic decline of Black professional golf was in sharp contrast to the financial health of Blacks in general throughout America. The National Negro Business League reported Blacks enjoyed higher incomes, their numbers in the middle class were larger, and they had more disposable income than ever before. In the years that followed World War II, the numbers of Black doctors, dentists, and lawyers grew. Labor unions opened their membership, and more than a million and a half Blacks joined, thus receiving higher wages for their work. The organization touted a 50 percent increase in the number of Black business executives. Black-owned businesses in America topped fifty thousand. Among them were fifty Black-owned insurance companies and fourteen Black-owned banks.

Yet while economic improvement swelled, it failed to translate to growth in professional golf. When the *Michigan Chronicle*'s Matney surveyed Detroit-area golf courses to find out why, he was surprised to learn the game had enjoyed a steady increase in popularity among Blacks over a ten-year span. But those in charge of the local Public Links tournament said few Black golfers ever signed up to participate. Matney examined the trend further and found younger Black golfers were not interested in competing in tournaments. Instead, they preferred playing skins—a game in which each hole comes with a prize, one that gets progressively larger—or outright gambling.

For Rhodes, the 1951 season took an inauspicious turn. His trouble with kidney stones flared up. It was the same issue that led to his medical discharge from the navy during World War II. Six weeks before the UGA season was to begin, he suffered an attack so severe he wound up in the Veterans Hospital. Surgery was needed to alleviate the pain. While his recovery prevented Rhodes from qualifying for the US Open, he was confident enough about his game to pursue the summer tournament schedule he planned.

The UGA's silver-anniversary season offered pros a paltry four events. Rhodes made plans to play in three. The first was a relatively new tournament in Atlanta, the Southern Open. Soon after Rhodes teed off, it was clear he was not in top form. For the first time, he failed to finish in the money in a UGA tournament. Two weeks later, golfers arrived in Detroit to find a city awash in festiveness. The city was celebrating the 250th anniversary of its founding by Antoine de La Mothe Cadillac, a French trader and military man, along with one hundred Native American members of the Algonquian tribe. They established what was then called Fort Pontchartrain du Detroit. On July 26, the city's Birthday Festival included a concert on Belle Isle by popular singer Margaret Whiting, a luncheon to commemorate the founding of St. Anne Church, and at 8:00 a.m., the first golfers teeing off in the Joe Louis Open.

Many were surprised that the host was not at his own event. Louis was away in San Francisco training for a fight that loomed with Cesar Brion. Al Besselink again entered and by the halfway point led Rhodes by two strokes with Howard Wheeler sandwiched in between. The third round saw Wheeler surpass Besselink and take the lead, while Rhodes was unable to improve his third-place position. On the tournament's final day, Wheeler added a stroke to his lead. Rhodes, with a 71, wound up third and Besselink second.

More festiveness abounded one month later, on August 27, when the UGA celebrated its fiftieth anniversary in Cleveland. Bill Seawright and his Sixth City Golf Association were selected not only to host the Negro National Open but to create an event befitting a silver-anniversary celebration. What Seawright constructed drew fans like no previous Open had before. Interested spectators flocked by trains, buses, boats, and cars from all over the country. Every room at the city's Black hotels was filled. Seawright's staff recruited hundreds of private homes to house fans from out of town. The number of out-of-towners was put at four thousand.

Ted Rhodes arrived in Cleveland holding a rare position, that of tournament underdog. Even though he was the two-time defending champion, his play over the summer and nagging back pains made bettors put their money on others. As the tournament was to begin, a crush descended upon the starters' tent at Seneca Golf Course. A record number of golfers registered to play. "Never anything like this before," said Howard Anderson, the tournament director.[15] The total would hit 400, a figure far exceeding the previous record of 267 from 1946. As golfers registered, A. D. V. Crosby, president of the UGA, beamed at the turnout. What went unspoken, though, was of the record number of entrants only twenty-eight were professionals.

Throughout the four rounds, Rhodes was in top form. He won the event, defeating Wheeler by six strokes. The drama came in the men's amateur division, where Joe Louis and a seventeen-year-old caddy from Dallas, Texas, Lee Elder, battled into sudden death before Louis claimed the title.

Later that night, Rhodes was feted at a cabaret party at Cleveland Arena. It was a combination anniversary party for the UGA and a victory celebration for the Open winner. A throng filled five hundred tables to enjoy entertainment from singers Corettea Greene and Paul Breckenridge, dancers Takela and Pepe, and comedian George Williams. During a pause in the entertainment, Rhodes was cheered when Crosby handed him the large winner's trophy and a check for $700.

The gala night in Cleveland would be a pinnacle both for the UGA and for Ted Rhodes. The 1952 season would bring further decline. Only three UGA tournaments offered sections for professionals. Joe Louis joined the list of promoters whose tournament ceased to offer a pro division. Rhodes entered two of the three events and won both—the Windy City Open and, for the fourth consecutive year, the Negro National Open. Entries for the signature UGA event held in Pittsburgh fell from 400 the year before in Cleveland to 284. Prize money for the winner fell, too, from $700 in 1951 to $650.

The decline would also include Ted Rhodes. The 1953 season would take him in a new direction. But before leaving full-time participation with the UGA, Rhodes amassed a remarkable seven-year tournament record. Of the thirty-nine UGA tournaments he entered, Rhodes won thirty-one of them. His winning percentage, 79 percent, far exceeded those of Ben Hogan (21 percent), Sam Snead (14 percent), and Gene Sarazen (12 percent) on the PGA tour. But new doors were opening and with it a journey of greater significance. A goal, a dream once believed unreachable, had manifested. Rhodes had no option but to pursue it. After all, he was now forty-two. Peak playing years were at a premium. But an equal factor in his decision was the end to a challenge. It was there for all to see; Ted Rhodes had outgrown the UGA.

10

Get That Champagne Ready

The telegram was unlike any Ted Rhodes had received before. While the invitation it brought—to play in a golf tournament—was nothing out of the ordinary, it was the sender who made this both unique and special. The telegram was not sent by just any tournament organizer. It came from Adolfo Ruiz Cortines, the president of Mexico. His country's capital was to host a unique event, a golf tournament made up of 138 of the best golfers from all over the world. Among those whom the president sought to participate in the Mexico City Open at Club de Golf Mexico was Ted Rhodes.

In the early weeks of 1953, new doors opened for Ted Rhodes—and not just to exalted events in foreign countries. Surprisingly, the majority of his invitations came from golf tournaments sanctioned by the PGA. These doors first opened ever so slightly in the summer of 1949. On the heels of the lawsuit filed by Rhodes, Bill Spiller, and Madison Gunter, organizers of the Iowa Open invited Rhodes to Cedar Rapids to play in their tournament. The seventh year of the tournament was also its first sanctioned by the PGA. "I told Teddy he should accept the invitation," Joe Louis explained to a sportswriter. "It will mean more chances for Negro golfers to enter these White tournaments."[1] Rhodes was conflicted. Louis's words resonated. The layout of the Cedar Rapids Country Club favored strong iron play, which was the strongest part of Rhodes' game. But the Iowa Open was scheduled to take place on the same days as the

Joe Louis Open and three days after the Negro National Open, which would also be held in Detroit at the same course Louis used for his tournament.

Rhodes stayed in Detroit. He played in and won both the Negro National Open and the Joe Louis Open. His share of the prize money was $750 for winning the Negro National Open and $1,100 for winning the Joe Louis Open, from which he bought a brand-new Buick Special.

Playing in tournaments made up almost exclusively of White golfers was not new to Rhodes. Since he first arrived in Southern California during the winter of 1946 and learned about the myriad local Opens held in the small towns that surrounded Los Angeles, he became a fixture in the El Centro Open, Fox Hills Open, Montebello Open, Pomona Open, Santa Anita Open, Southern California Open, Tijuana Open, and the Yorba Linda Open. In fields with top PGA and area amateur standouts, Rhodes finished in the top five numerous times. In 1948 Rhodes set the Montebello Open single-round scoring record, shooting 65. One year later he led the event at the halfway point, then finished second. In 1950 he was the first-round leader in the Fox Hills tournament before he finished third.

Later, during spring, Rhodes regularly traveled north to compete in the California Open. The May tournament was a sort of state championship. It offered the kind of prize money and a level of prestige which annually lured three hundred of California's best golfers. Pro entrants included US Open champion Lloyd Mangrum and PGA champion Paul Runyan, while Walker Cup star Charley Seaver and the comedic entertainer Bob Hope headlined the amateurs.

The 1948 event was played at Pebble Beach. Rhodes finished fourth. A year later the tournament was held in Fresno. During the pre-tournament pro-am, Rhodes shot 66, then in the seventy-two-hole main event, earned $250 with a fifth-place finish. When the final round teed off in the 1950 California Open, many among the four thousand spectators who turned out in Fresno thought this might be Rhodes' breakthrough event, the one in which he prevailed over a predominantly White field for the first time. Rhodes began the final day two shots behind the leader. He was poised to grab the lead on the back nine only for misfortune to bite. On the fifteenth hole Rhodes' putt rolled to a dead stop on the lip of the cup. On sixteen it happened again. He finished with a 70 for the round, 283 for the tournament.

Playing in a group that teed off almost an hour after Rhodes, "Dutch" Harrison shot the low round of the tournament, 66. His total score eclipsed Rhodes' by one stroke and tied Elly Vines. Harrison captured the playoff to determine the tournament winner. Later, when asked if he had recorded a lower nine-hole score than the 31 he shot in his Sunday round, Harrison acknowledged he had. It was a 29, accomplished at Belle Meade Country Club in Nashville. On that day Ted Rhodes was his caddy.

From Rhodes' play in the Phoenix and Tucson PGA events during the spring of 1952, favorable reviews spread. A playing partner's comments were picked up by newspapers. "Rhodes," the man said, "is a very fine player, has a fine temperament, is very cool and calm—the type who doesn't let a bad shot bother him. And he has a beautiful short game."[2] From both his play and the favorable opinions of observers and opponents, Rhodes received invitations from tournaments the likes of which he had never received before. In addition to the president of Mexico, several PGA events let Rhodes know he was welcome to play.

Rhodes began his season winning two local pro-am events. He became the first African American to play in and win the Public Links Association tournament in St. Louis. Rhodes then shot 64 on the final day to win the Lone Star Open in Houston. With two tournament wins under his belt, Rhodes pointed his car north and began a long-coveted summer aspiration—playing on the PGA circuit. For Rhodes, it was a chance to prove not only that he belonged but also that Black golfers belonged.

Winds of change accompanied Rhodes to St. Paul, Minnesota, for the Keller Open. This was the tournament that banned him five years earlier. Now, on July

16, 1953, he was welcomed. Newspapers featured his photo in pre-tournament stories. Tidbits about his game and success in the UGA dotted columns. During the previous week, Rhodes caused a stir at the Canadian Open. He joined Alan Morrison, a Torontonian, and Zeke Hartsfield as the first Blacks to play in the event. "If someone hadn't mentioned that they were the first negro pros to be around and about," wrote one columnist, "no one else would have noticed it. Which is the way it should be."[3] It was Rhodes' play and not his skin color that stunned the Toronto gallery. At the tournament's halfway mark, Rhodes' name was at the top of the leader board. An even-par third-round score and a 3-over-par final round saw him topple down the leader board. Rhodes did manage to leave Canada with prize money in his pocket.

It was just after noon when Rhodes teed off to begin his first round in the Keller Open. A total of $15,000 in prize money was at stake, ten times what was normally offered at a UGA event. Rhodes' start was an inauspicious one. He came up short on his drive and bogeyed the first hole. From that point on, however, his iron play and accuracy proved nothing short of scintillating. Before he finished the front nine, Rhodes had made four birdie putts.

While on the back nine, news came that Jimmy Clark had set the standard. He circulated Keller Golf Course in 6 under par. His 66 was low score and put him in the lead. With each hole completed, enthusiasm for Rhodes grew. Giddiness ebbed from his caddy, Mike Olson, a bespectacled high school sophomore and lineman on his football team. Rhodes' iron play consistently set him up for short putts. While he squandered a small handful of birdie opportunities, he remained within striking distance of Clark's score. Hope erupted on sixteen when Rhodes curled in a long 30-foot putt for birdie, much to the delight of spectators. Then on his final hole of the day, the 462-yard, par-5 eighteenth, Rhodes produced the shot of the day. It was a case of marvel erupting from despair and came after Rhodes' second shot went awry. His ball wound up in the white sand of a bunker, 30 feet from the hole. A birdie would equal Clark's score but seemed an impossibility. Par, which would leave

Rhodes in second place or a bogey, which would put him no worse than third, appeared the most likely outcome. When Rhodes reached his ball, he surveyed the situation. For more than a minute he stood silently eyeing the topography of the green. He took a club, a wedge, from Olson, hitched his red trousers, then ground the soles of his shoes into the sand to gain firm traction. When Rhodes' shot wound up in the cup, the gallery became frenzied. His score on the hole, an eagle, gave him 66 for the round. It was the best round Rhodes had ever recorded in a PGA event. For the first time, a Black man was in first place at the conclusion of a round in a PGA tournament.

While sportswriters like Jim Klobuchar of the *Winona Daily News* lavished praise, "a superb iron game which kept him within easy reach of the pin all day,"[4] Rhodes was critical. "I should have shot a better score than I did," he said.[5] Sportswriter Glen Gaff pointed out in the *Minneapolis Tribune* that great could have been sensational. "If Rhodes' putts had been dropping, he might have been four shots in front."[6] Rhodes' caddy explained, "He missed four- or five-foot putts for birdies on four holes. The only bad drive he had all day was off seventeen. Then he laid the ball two inches from the pin with a chip shot."[7]

Rhodes spent the evening at the Fourth Avenue home of a fellow golfer, Solomon Hughes. He enjoyed a home-cooked meal prepared by his friend's wife, Bessie, and played with their three young children. Through much of the night the men dissected Rhodes' round. Shots were lamented, strategies dissected, and plans plotted for the next round of play.

On day two Rhodes' game was again outstanding. He was among the early starters and maintained his 6-under-par score through the first three holes. Then, on the fourth hole came a brush with the phenomenal. Rhodes narrowly missed a hole in one. Number four was one of the shortest holes at Keller, just 134 yards from tee to hole. It was straight, with a bunker at the left front corner of the green. Rhodes' tee shot flew straight for the green. It landed inches shy of the cup, bounced, then began to roll swiftly in the direction of the hole. Onlookers gasped as the ball caught the edge of the cup. But the speed of the roll propelled it aside rather than in. When Rhodes tapped in his short putt, he recorded the only birdie he would score on the front nine during the round.

On fourteen, Rhodes sank a 40-foot putt for birdie, then added another when he bumped in a 10-foot putt on seventeen. Upon completion of the round, he had a score of 68 to remain in the lead. As he drew near the clubhouse, Rhodes spied a friend and hollered, "Get that champagne ready!"[8] When the press gathered for comment, Rhodes said, "I hit better than Thursday. I just birdied the wrong holes, that's all. I didn't beat the easy ones."[9] When a reporter suggested winning the tournament would be the upset of the season, Rhodes replied, "You never can predict in golf. One little slip and you are out of things. I feel every time I go out there that I'm going to shoot a 60."[10]

But Rhodes' enthusiasm, like his name on top of the leader board, would last just two more hours. While he conducted interviews, a player who teed off late, Freddie Haas, a driving range operator from New Orleans, was on a blistering round. Using a self-made mahogany putter, Haas put together a sterling afternoon of golf—one eagle, seven birdies, and a bogey—for an 8-under-par score to vault past Rhodes and take the lead at the tournament's halfway mark.

On the third day of the tournament, Rhodes was once again below par. He shot 69, but it was a round that left many wondering what could have been. A short putt on fourteen lipped out, as did another on eighteen. "I thought they were both in," Rhodes remarked.[11] His score for the round kept Rhodes in second place, though, one shot behind Haas.

It was midmorning on Sunday, July 19, when Rhodes arrived at Keller Golf Course for the final round. He retreated to the practice range to hit balls. Around the course, workers noted a larger number of Black spectators than in previous years and attributed it to the possibility of a Black man winning a PGA tournament for the very first time. The *Baltimore Afro American* primed its readers that Rhodes was on the cusp of winning "the first important prize ever won by a colored player under PGA sanction."[12] As the *Minneapolis*

Spectator noted, Rhodes was "carrying the hopes of Negroes and Whites who believe in fair play."[13]

A check of the sky brought concern. Dark clouds loomed. The morning paper forecast thunderstorms during the day. Rhodes fretted. Wet bent grass on the fairways could become a problem. "I need a fast track," he said to a friend. "I can't drive with these big fellows on the wet fairways. I need a roll."[14] While weather gave Rhodes cause to stew, something far greater drove him to the cusp of torment—the makeup of a threesome he would play in. It consisted of the top three names on the leaderboard. It was a featured threesome that would tee off at 2:00 p.m., after all the others had begun their round. In addition to Rhodes, the grouping included the leader of the tournament, Freddie Haas. But it was the third member who raised Rhodes angst, the man who held third place in the tournament—Sam Snead.

Sam Snead was by far the best player in the PGA. His supremacy was akin to the dominance Rhodes enjoyed in the UGA. In 1950 Snead won a record eleven tournaments. He won ten in 1952, including The Masters. Like Rhodes, Snead was a self-taught southerner; in his case home was Virginia. While the same height as Rhodes, he was almost 30 pounds heavier. When Snead whipped his stiff-shafted, 14½-ounce persimmon driver, he sent golf balls farther than anyone else in the game. His prowess evoked nicknames such as "The Slammer," which he didn't particularly like, and "Slammin' Sam," which he only tolerated. Snead had a gruff side and loved to tweak opponents. His mere presence along with his strength could intimidate foes without intent. But Snead loved to throw out an innocent comment, an implied tip, or a veiled critique, then watch an opponent react, alter their stroke, or make a last-second change of strategy and flub.

At tournaments, Snead regularly drew the largest following. On the first day of the Keller Open, he shot 72 to Rhodes' 66, and many thought he might not be a factor in the pursuit for the tournament title. But earlier in the week, Snead broke his favorite driver. After downing a hot dog and a soft drink, he made a beeline for the course pro shop, where he proceeded to take apart his new driver, remove a slight amount of weight from the head, then add just a bit more to the handle. Snead came back the next day to record a 66. When he equaled the feat a day later, the result saw him soar into third, one shot behind Rhodes.

Organizers were pleased to see more than eight thousand fans turn out for the final round of play. A large percentage of that crowd congregated around the first tee at two o'clock, when the threesome of Rhodes, Haas, and Snead prepared to play. The crowd was larger than any Rhodes had ever played in front of. Once the threesome teed off, it was Snead who set an early pace. He birdied the first and third holes, then parred the fourth to surpass both Rhodes and Haas on the leader board. Thirty minutes into their round, hindrances arose which disrupted the rhythm of the three golfers. The first involved overzealous fans who thought nothing of traipsing onto the fairway or even the greens during play to ask Snead for an autograph. The second was rain. Umbrellas popped open throughout the gallery. Caddies hurriedly rushed umbrellas to their golfer. Those fast fairways Rhodes so desperately needed in order to come close to Snead's length off the tee disappeared.

Jimmy Griffin, a sportswriter with the *St. Paul Recorder*, was among those who followed Rhodes. He could tell soon into the round that Rhodes appeared to be nervous. He seemed tentative with his shots. Rhodes' short game wasn't as good as it had been the previous three days. His putting was off. Still, Griffin bristled when he heard people in the crowd criticize Rhodes. The next day he called them out in print. "Bush league duffers," he wrote, adding they "have a lot of nerve second guessing Rhodes."[15]

The threesome neared the end of the front nine when Stew MacPherson went on the air with his first live report on WCCO radio. By that point Snead had birdied two more holes to take the lead. For Rhodes and Haas, birdies became elusive. Both began to fade from contention. On the back nine the men learned that an upstart playing ahead of them had posted the lowest round of the tournament. Shelley Mayfield's 65 gave him a total score that nobody was going to beat. Dutch Harrison managed to grab second, while Snead finished with a 68 to take third. Rhodes' final round was his worst of the tournament. It left him sixth and frustrated. "I kicked in a 73 and blew myself out of the big money," he groused. Rhodes admitted he was nervous playing with Snead. He admitted it affected his game. "Everybody was watching Snead. I didn't have a chance."[16]

Rhodes took home $700, sixth-place money that was more than many tournaments in the UGA paid their winner. He drew praise. The *Pittsburgh Courier* called him magnificent. The *Minneapolis Spokesman* called Rhodes "second only to the winner Mayfield as a tournament sensation."[17] In the days that followed, Rhodes expressed frustration that he was made unnerved by Snead. "I cried all night after that," he told a friend. "I kept waking up with nightmares. All I could hear was 'whack' 'whack' 'whack'—that man hitting that ball. I didn't sleep for a week hearing those 'whacks.'"[18]

Four more PGA-sanctioned tournaments extended invitations to Rhodes. Two weeks after the St. Paul Open, organizers of the Fort Wayne Open welcomed him. Over the four days of the tournament, he amassed a 14-under-par score to finish tenth out of an initial field of 147 entries. In Montreal, one week later, Rhodes was called the surprise of the tournament. The Labatt Open offered $25,000 in prize money, the third most of any tournament in North America. Playing in ideal weather and on a relatively flat Summerlea Golf Course, Rhodes recovered from a 1-over-par first day that left him in thirtieth place to shoot 4 under par for the second round and climb to twelfth. A 2-under-par third-round score and 3-under-par round on the final day earned Rhodes a fourth-place finish and a sizeable paycheck to take home to the United States.

Rhodes remained on the East Coast to play in two PGA events during late summer. In both cases a severe heatwave wreaked havoc with many a golfer's round. In Hartford, Connecticut, for the Insurance City Open, Rhodes endured 97-degree heat through his first round and recorded the worst score of his professional career, a 7-over-par 79. Even scoring 69 and 67 the next two days and a 73 on the final day wasn't enough to net any prize money. Two weeks later in Baltimore, oppressive heat and humidity made eleven golfers withdraw from the Eastern Open. Rhodes never put together a round under par and finished deep in the pack.

Throughout the summer Rhodes found PGA players accepting. He already knew many from the Southern California winter golf circuit. He made friends. Surprisingly, some of his closest were players from the South, one in particular was his fellow Tennessean, Cary Middlecoff. Clubs afforded Rhodes locker-room privileges. He often chose instead to dress with the caddies. When he was permitted to eat in the club dining facilities, more often than not Rhodes declined, saying he didn't want to upset or make anyone feel uncomfortable. Among the fans were a majority who were accepting, but there were those whose actions ranged from mischievous to malicious. From the galleries it was not uncommon to hear racial epithets. Along the fairways were the occasional fans who would kick Rhodes' ball to a worse lay, sometimes into the rough. There were times when Rhodes found his ball almost completely buried, ground into the earth by the heel of a pernicious fan's shoe. Once Rhodes and his caddy arrived where he was certain his tee shot wound up only to be unable to find the ball. A helpful fan solved the dilemma when he revealed that another fan made off with the ball.

As challenging as the weather made tournaments in Hartford and Baltimore, none of it could prepare Rhodes for Mexico City. Enticed by the presidential invitation, $12,000 in prize money, and reports from several golfers that Club de Golf Mexico was the best course they had ever played, Rhodes was eager for the event. Despite its prestige, the Mexico City Open was a tournament that had been a burr in PGA's saddle for several years. In 1951 several top PGA players ignored the organization's tournament in Texas to play in the Mexico City event. Horton Smith railed at their decision and charged the Mexican tournament with "making a wholesale raid on our players."[19] Despite Smith's threats of fines and suspensions, the players refused to back down. A year later the Mexico City event offered to cover Sam Snead's travel expenses and pay the PGA's marquee player a guaranteed $750 to play in their tournament. Snead sought Horton Smith's response. When he didn't receive one, he accepted the offer. Only then did Smith reply, forbidding Snead to compete in Mexico City.

The February 1954 Mexico City Open attracted a stellar field. Several countries were represented by a field of 138 golfers. Winners of some of the biggest titles in the sport—Gene Littler, winner of the US Amateur championship; Jimmy Demaret, with three Masters titles to his credit; and Lew Worsham, the 1947 US Open champion—headlined the golfers who journeyed from the United States. When play began, Rhodes got off to a strong start. He recorded a 69 for his first-round score, good for second place, one shot behind Johnny Palmer, a golfer with six PGA tournament wins to his credit.

Playing in previously Whites-only tournaments exposed Rhodes to a number of elements uncommon to the UGA circuit: large and at times ill-mannered crowds, tricky course layouts, and playing through severe weather. None of it would prepare him for Mexico City. The Mexican capital sat on a high plateau 7,350 feet above sea level. Its altitude was higher than that of any other major city in North America and more than 2,000 feet higher than Denver, known as "The Mile-High City" in the United States. High altitude meant air had less density. Struck balls traveled farther. A reduction in density also meant less force against the ball, which made balls travel straighter and hook or slice less. But altitude didn't just affect the flight of golf balls. It also had a significant effect on the human body. Headaches and nausea were common among visitors. For those participating in athletic endeavors, the body fatigued faster.

On the second day of the 1954 Mexico City Open, Rhodes and many other golfers from the United States faltered. As they did, Roberto De Vicenzo, an Argentinian and two-time winner of the tournament, jumped out in front.

Rhodes finished the second round with a 76 and fell far back in the field. Lew Worsham, who trailed Rhodes by a shot after the first round, recorded a 5-over-par score and quit the tournament in disgust. Rhodes struggled to come even close to par for the remainder of the tournament. He returned home without having earned a single peso of prize money.

While Rhodes arrived in Los Angeles frustrated by the results in Mexico City, he carried respect from fellow players. "Teddy's a great golfer," said Cary Middlecoff.[20] Bob Seymour, a Michigan pro, said, "There's no finer iron player around today." But both men were quick to point out that one thing held Rhodes' game back: experience on country club courses. "If Ted Rhodes could play the entire circuit for one year, he'd be in the top ten in the country," said Seymour.[21] Middlecoff explained, "You have to play those difficult courses all the time to keep in practice on shots where you deliberately have to hook and slice around dog leg holes. If it weren't for that he'd be murder." [22]

Whatever frustration Rhodes carried was in sharp contrast to that which was no longer felt by a legion of Black golfers. To them, Rhodes forged opportunity. The *Chicago Defender* called Rhodes' participation in PGA events one of the Black sports highlights of 1953. The *Michigan Chronicle* praised, "It was truly thrilling to see one of our great golfers getting a chance and making such a fine showing with the top golfers in the country."[23]

While full PGA membership had yet to be achieved, and the organization still refused to exorcise its discriminatory membership policy, a door had been opened. Rhodes' character, work ethic, and skills brought acceptance among quarters of the PGA. Hope for Black golfers was realized. Opportunity for more was closer than ever before.

11

The Money Dries Up

The men had hit their tee shots. As the last of the group scooped up his small wooden golf tee, his playing partner moved in the direction of the fairway. It was not many steps into the trek to find their ball when they noticed a man walking across the course in their direction. It was an unusual sight, but this was not an ordinary situation. When the man drew near, he asked the taller of the two if he was Joseph Louis Barrow. A nod made the man thrust a piece of paper at him. He was not after an autograph. On the contrary. He was a process server. Joe Louis was being sued.

In the spring of 1954, Joe Louis was a man in serious financial trouble. He had lived on the fringes of financial catastrophe for five years. Louis owed the Internal Revenue Service $544,954 in back taxes. The agency now sought the money in trust funds for Louis's two young children to pay down the debt. The root of Louis's trouble depended upon whom you asked. His first manager, John Roxborough, pointed a finger at Louis's promoter, Mike Jacobs, who he said gave the boxer pay advances anytime he asked. Jacobs admitted he advanced Louis $100,000 during the three years he was in the army during World War II. Jacobs blamed Louis. "I've seen some pretty fast men with a dollar in my time," he said. "What he doesn't manage to spend he gives away."[1] There was no denying Louis was quick to pick up tabs and was generous with friends. He was quick to deny accusations that those close to him were parasites. "It wasn't that I was a soft touch. It was just that I enjoyed having them around," he said.[2] Louis claimed it was disallowed tax deductions and a costly divorce in which he had to give his ex-wife 25 percent of his pay from several fights that put him in a bind. While newspapers reported that Louis earned more than $3 million during his boxing career, in actuality the amount he took home was 30 percent of that total. Of that he sank thousands into investment and business opportunities. Louis bought apartment houses in Detroit and Chicago, an insurance business in Detroit, and a 400-acre farm in Utica, New York. He invested in a home construction company in California, opened the Joe Louis restaurant in New York, and spent $12,000 to buy Rhumboogie Café in Chicago, which he turned over to his brother to run. He created an auto mechanic school in Chicago that contracted with the government to train soldiers home from the war. Louis put money into a beverage company that featured a grape-flavored drink called Joe Louis Punch. He invested in a line of men's grooming products that included The Champ hair pomade for men. But one by one and for differing reasons, all of the companies Louis invested in failed.

And then there was golf. Fueled by his passion for the game, Louis spent generously on golf. His tournament, the Joe Louis Open, offered the most prize money of any UGA event. At the height of his enthusiasm, Louis subsidized, in one fashion or another, eight golfers. Rhodes was on the payroll. Others such as Bill Spiller, Charley Sifford, Eural Clark, and Leonard Reed saw Louis cover their tournament entry fees, green fees at outings, meals, and, on occasion, travel expenses. But as Louis spiraled deeper in his financial morass, his tournament was canceled, and the financial support provided to his golf friends ended too.

For Rhodes, the friendship and assistance afforded by Joe Louis had been life-changing. He never hesitated to express gratitude publicly for all Louis had done. "It would be hard to put in words how good Joe has been to me," he told a writer for *Golf Magazine*. Rhodes added that while serving as Louis's full-time golf instructor had come to an end, a friendship between the two would

"I sincerely hope last forever."[3] The loss of Louis's financial support placed additional pressure on Rhodes.

By the early-1950s Ted and Claudia made St. Louis their home. Ted's lengthy absences put child-rearing in Claudia's domain. She was also a working parent who toiled at multiple jobs to help pay the bills. She transitioned from performing to producing and choreography and was also head of the usherettes at the Ambassador Theatre. Though the money was tight, Claudia Rhodes was an enthusiastic and gracious host. The family apartment included a fold-out bed to accommodate overnight guests. Golfers who received an invitation rarely said no, especially when they knew a home-cooked meal would include Claudia's fried chicken and candied yams.

Ted Rhodes' decision in 1953 to eschew UGA events for PGA tournaments brought a change to the household income. During the summer of 1953, not only was Ted Rhodes away from home for long stretches, but the gap between paydays was far longer too. In July, when he traveled to Minnesota for the St. Paul Open, Claudia's patience was pushed to the brink. Her husband had won just $250 on the year. A telegram was waiting when Ted arrived at the course.

THEODORE YOU AREN'T MAKING MUCH MONEY. IF YOU CAN'T DO ANY BETTER THAN THAT YOU BETTER COME HOME AND GET A JOB.[4]

Rhodes flashed the telegram to his caddy and chuckled, "Orders from headquarters."[5] That weekend he broke his dry spell, winning $700.

Always a fashion plate, Rhodes curtailed his spending. Berman's Men's Store on West Ninth Street in downtown Los Angeles saw far less of the golfer, and Irving Berman, the owner, received only a fraction of the money he had become accustomed to getting from Rhodes. Still, when Claudia Rhodes read in *Jet Magazine* that her husband was protecting his golf clubs with covers made of mink that cost fifteen dollars each, she hit the ceiling and fired off a letter:

SUGGEST YOU SELL THE SOCKS AND SEND ME SOME MONEY SO I CAN GET ME A NEW PAIR OF "PUMPS." I'M TIRED OF WEARING THESE "GYM" SHOES.[6]

For the Black professional golfer, the quest to earn a decent living from the game was frustrating if not futile. While it wasn't easy for White professional golfers either, UGA events offered considerably less prize money than did events in the PGA. During the summer of 1953, PGA sensation Ben Hogan entered six tournaments, won five of them, and earned $25,000. While his earnings were five times that of the average American household income, Hogan was quick to point out that 75 percent of the money he won went to cover expenses—hotels, meals, train tickets, or if he drove, gas and wear and tear on his car.

In his best year, Rhodes earned one-fifth of Hogan's 1953 prize earnings, $4,800. He earned additional money playing in winter tournaments around Southern California. Then there was contest money. At many UGA tournaments tests of skill were staged. These often paid fifty to one hundred dollars to the winner. Rhodes captured his share of long-drive contests. When it came to tests of accuracy, it was a rare occurrence when anybody chipped better than Rhodes.

Rhodes further supplemented his tournament winnings in a way that wasn't widely spoken of. It was done discreetly on back courses in Michigan, Illinois, Ohio, and Indiana. He earned it through gambling. Joe Louis had a voracious appetite for wagering. In Rhodes, he had a willing partner. Not only did Louis enjoy playing with money on the line, but he also liked to arrange matches with much more than just simple bragging rights going to the winner. He constructed match-play challenges in which he and Rhodes would take on local course pros and area professional players. Sometimes he put Rhodes together with another UGA professional. A day after a 1948 tournament in Minneapolis, Rhodes was paired with Howard Wheeler in a match put together by Louis. Their opponents were Pat Sawyer, called the "Boy Wonder of Minnesota Golf," and a PGA tour player, Wally Ulrich. A 2-and-1 victory by Rhodes and Wheeler earned Louis $4,500. He happily shared a percentage of the prize with the winning duo.

What Louis particularly liked to set up were challenges. Seizing on someone's bluster, Louis would press to settle the boasts with an eighteen-hole challenge against a player of his choosing. In most cases that player was Rhodes. The challenge would be staged in some out-of-the-way town and appear to onlookers to be just a friendly game. Few, if any, ever knew that big money was at stake. Nobody ever realized the player Louis put up was one of the best golfers in the country. More often than not, Rhodes reported back to Louis that he was victorious, and the boxing great was always generous with his winnings. There was one occasion when things went awry. During the summer of 1950, Louis arranged for Rhodes to play a local pro in Flint, Michigan. A total of $1,000 was wagered on the outcome. When Rhodes arrived at the course, he was met by a friend of the pro. "That guy's gone, but I'll play you some skin for a quarter."[7] Rhodes waved the man off, turned around, and drove back to Detroit. On hearing the story Louis howled with laughter.

Successful golfers on the PGA circuit were able to supplement their earnings with an array of commercial deals. Success enabled Ben Hogan to use his name to earn more than $100,000 per year. MacGregor paid Hogan $30,000 to use their golf clubs. He received $5,000 to put his name on a syndicated newspaper column that was ghostwritten by a sportswriter. Chesterfield paid him $10,000 to appear in ads for their cigarettes. He was paid $10,000 to appear in ads for 7 Up and another $10,000 for doing Pabst Blue Ribbon beer ads. Hogan did ads for pain reliever Ben-Gay and upset-stomach settler Bromo-seltzer. He earned substantial money from writing a book, *Ben Hogan Power Golf*. Hogan was also paid handsomely for radio and television appearances and to play in golf exhibitions. Black golfers had no such opportunities.

When Sam Lacy, a columnist for the *Afro-American*, asked a representative of MacGregor why the company wouldn't sponsor Rhodes, he was told, "Don't think golf is ready for sponsorship of a colored pro."[8] When the man pointed out that PGA players sponsored by the company played twenty-five tournaments a year to Rhodes' ten, Lacy wrote, "It isn't their fault Texas, and Florida, and Louisiana, etc. won't let them in. What's fair about penalizing them for that?"[9] *Pittsburgh Courier* columnist Wendell Smith urged creation of a National Golf Fund and suggested Black golfers and golf enthusiasts contribute to provide financial support for Rhodes, Bill Spiller, Charley Sifford, and others. Rhodes and Sifford met with Ted McLaughlin, president of Gotham Promotions in New York. Together they crafted a plan to seek support from prominent companies to cover travel and living expenses for the men.

In the summer of 1954, Rhodes' hopes were realized. Chick Harbert, vice president of Burke Golf Manufacturing Company, signed Rhodes to a contract to serve as an advisor to the firm. The agreement made Rhodes the first African American to receive an endorsement deal with a golf equipment manufacturer. The arrangement called for the Ohio-based company to provide Rhodes with their clubs. Rather than compensating Rhodes with a set fee, Burke agreed to match whatever prize money Rhodes received from tournaments he played in. Upon learning of the agreement, Jackie Robinson placed an order for a set of Burke clubs "to express our loyalty to those people who look upon us as citizens."[10]

Many top players in the PGA earned a handsome second income serving as a resident teaching pro at a country club. When Tamarisk Country Club opened near Palm Springs, California, it boasted Ben Hogan as its resident pro. For doing so for four months out of the year, Hogan received a new $45,000 home on the course and was paid $95,000 over five years. When not traveling to play in PGA tournaments, Dutch Harrison was resident pro at Old Warson Country Club in St. Louis. Sam Snead was the pro at Greenbriar Resort in

West Virginia, Jack Burke Jr. was the pro at Metropolis Country Club in White Plains, New York, and George Fazio at Hillcrest Country Club in Los Angeles.

Through the early 1950s golf was booming. Golf course architects were unable to handle the demand for their work. The PGA declared 2,500 more pros would be needed to handle the demand from the many new country clubs and municipal courses being built. Opportunities to become a teaching pro were greater than ever before, but they remained beyond the reach of Black golfers. There were only a dozen golf courses in America owned and operated by Blacks. Most of the nation's courses and country clubs required their resident teaching pro to be a member of the PGA, something no Black player was yet able to attain.

Shut out of country club jobs, Rhodes and other Black golfers channeled their teaching skills to wealthy and celebrity Black clients. From his initial work with Billy Eckstine and Joe Louis, Rhodes later tutored baseball star Jackie Robinson and in the 1950s, Harry Mills, the baritone member of the Mills Brothers singing quartet. When Rhodes' schedule became too full to continue working with Eckstine, he introduced the singer to Charley Sifford, who in time became the benefactor of the man's financial support.

A group in Chicago offered to back Rhodes in a golf school. It took three years for the project to get off the ground. A year and a half after it opened, the school went out of business. When the board of directors of the Chicago-area Lincoln Golf and Country Club considered bids to operate its pro shop, one of the two proposals involved hiring Rhodes as manager of the pro shop and teaching pro. A rival bidder argued the club should operate as a private club free of for-profit operators and won the contract.

Travel was another area that separated the top PGA players from those in the UGA. Ben Hogan, for example, traveled with his wife, Valerie. The train was often their mode of transportation. The couple stayed in some of the finest hotels, like the Biltmore in Los Angeles, and dined in the best restaurants in tournament cities. Rhodes' primary means of transportation was his car. This involved drives of several hundred miles, drives that wrought back pains and worse, hemorrhoids, all of which brought more challenges to tournament play.

As Rhodes grew in stature, Black-owned establishments accorded him celebrity treatment. One such place was the Manhattan Tap Room in Cleveland. It was owned by the husband-and-wife duo Fleet and Beulah Slaughter and was praised as "The finest Negro owned and operated restaurant in the northern part of Ohio," by the *Cleveland Call and Post*.[11] Golf was Fleet Slaughter's game. When he returned home from serving in World War II, he helped found the Sixth City Golf Club. Whenever Ted Rhodes set foot in the Manhattan Tap Room, he was treated like royalty. But on one visit an unknowing waiter laid a bill on Rhodes' table. When Slaughter saw what had happened, he scolded his employee and explained that Rhodes was never to be charged.

Invitations to play and the lure of prize money made another summer of PGA events too good to pass up in 1954. Both the Los Angeles and Eastern Open tournaments offered $20,000. The Labatt's Open offered $26,500. In every PGA event, the top thirty finishers came away with prize money. Summer for Rhodes began, however, in a disconcerting fashion. He played in a pair of local tournaments, one in St. Louis and another in Atlantic City. In each event one bad round sent him on his way with very little to show for his efforts. His first PGA tournament of the summer was the Insurance City Open in Hartford, Connecticut. By the end of it, he was in a distressed state. Rhodes struggled to overcome a bad first round. He finished twenty-seventh and earned just $55. Expenses left him with only $6 in his pocket and forced him to pick up the phone and make a call he never wanted to make. He sought help from Joe Louis.

Rhodes wanted to play in the Motor City Open in Detroit, which was in four days. Louis wired funds to cover the demanding drive. For two days Rhodes drove almost nonstop, covering close to 900 miles before he arrived in Chicago. He visited Herb Fair at the Hotel Pershing barber shop for a haircut, then set out over the remaining 285 miles to Detroit. Rhodes was tired when he arrived. He had no time to get in a practice round, only to sign in at the registration booth and begin play.

Through the first three days, Rhodes hung on the fringe of contention. He'd jumped as high as third in the first round before falling back to eighth at the end of the third round. On Sunday, the final day, many of the golfers arrived at the course with trepidation. Overnight rains and morning wind brought trouble. Rhodes teed off just after noon. His round was fairly nondescript, that is, until he reached the next-to-the-last hole. Seventeen was among the longest holes at Meadowbrook Country Club, a par-5 hole that measured 507 yards. Rhodes reached the green with his second shot. Then, with a large gallery watching, he sank a 35-yard putt for an eagle. His score, 68, completed a fifth-place finish to earn $485.

As summer turned to fall, Ted Rhodes drew nearer to a professional fork in the road. For eight years he carried the weight of his race on his shoulder. Sportswriters and columnists predicted Rhodes would be the first of his race to win a PGA event. They drew parallels to Jackie Robinson's achievements in baseball, those of Kenny Washington in football, and even Joe Louis in the boxing ring. But Rhodes was now forty, an age when keen observers recognize the decline of body strength and reaction time, when one's peak golf skills begin to wane.

Rhodes was being tugged to transition from professional player to club pro. The result of court rulings meant opportunities were growing for Black players in the field. Beginning in 1952, Federal and District Courts ruled that cities such as Atlanta, Dallas, and Louisville must permit Black golfers to play on city-owned golf courses. To circumvent a legal fight the city of Fort Worth, Texas, built a nine-hole course just for Black players. In 1953 Nashville did the same. By July of 1954, Cumberland Golf Course was completed. It was a nine-hole course built on the banks of the Cumberland River east of Bordeaux Bridge.

As the course was in development, interests in Nashville sought to persuade Rhodes to become its resident teaching pro and also manage the pro shop.

Rhodes agreed to meet and traveled to Nashville. But rather than arrive equipped to listen to an offer, he brought with him Bill Spiller. Spiller, Rhodes told his hosts, was the man they should consider for the job.

In Ted Rhodes' mind, the fork in the road was still many miles off. He was confident there were more tournaments to be won.

12

Breaking the Barrier

The strings of twinkling lights in the shape of evergreen trees that hung from light poles along Hollywood Boulevard served as a reminder that Christmas was mere days away. The Christmas Day dinner plan to serve Swordfish Steak Almondine, baked Hubbard squash, and fruit cake had long been decided upon by the chef of the Los Angeles Athletic Club, whose menu was now in the hands of the printer. Parents led wide-eyed children through Santa's Village in the town of Lake Arrowhead, east of Los Angeles. While Los Angeles was where the much-heralded song "White Christmas" was written and recorded in 1942, the city at this time of year was a far cry from any image conjured by Bing Crosby's crooning. Rather than snowflakes, Southern California in the week leading up to Christmas in 1957 was bathed in 70-degree temperatures, warm enough weather for a golf tournament.

East of Los Angeles, in the early afternoon of December 22, a poignant scene caught the eye of many among the gallery at the Pomona Valley Open golf tournament. Schools in the area let out at noon to begin Christmas break. The family of one of the golfers joined him at the course. Ted Rhodes enjoyed days when this was possible and particularly relished walking hand in hand with his daughter as he played. On this day Rhodes was especially happy as he prepared to hit his tee shot on the tenth hole at Los Serranos Country Club. With birdies on his first three holes of play on this the final day of the tournament, he had surpassed Billy Casper and Gene Littler to take over first place. Just nine holes were left to play. Many in the crowd were convinced Ted Rhodes would win the tournament.

After hitting his tee shot, Rhodes began to march in the direction of his ball. He had not walked far when the voice of his daughter made him pause. Deborah Rhodes declared she was cold. The girl wanted to retreat to the clubhouse and, with her father's permission, scampered away.

The Pomona Valley Open represented the final professional golf tournament of the 1957 calendar year. For Rhodes, it was a place to launch an entirely new scheduling strategy. He planned to enter every tournament he could from local pro-am events to the UGA circuit. Once he made $500, he would then play in whichever PGA events would accept his application.

After missing out by a single stroke of finishing in the money at the first tournament of the year, the Los Angeles Open, Rhodes traveled east to Florida. Ray Mitchell, a golf instructor at the Harlem branch of the YMCA in New York City, had turned promoter with a goal to increase Black participation in golf. In Miami, Mitchell put together the new glamor event of the UGA circuit. Mitchell's North-South Open drew not only the top Black golfers in the country but also baseball stars such as Jackie Robinson, Jim Gilliam, and Don Newcombe, as well as entertainers like Billy Eckstine and Arthur Prysock. Singer-actor Sammy Davis Jr. put up prize money. Mitchell's spectacle included a ladies' swimsuit contest and a gala awards ball.

The North-South Open drew more than two hundred golfers to Miami Springs Golf Course. All manner came—professionals and amateurs, men and women. Rhodes quickly established himself as the player to beat. By the end of the first day, he led the field by five strokes. When rain shortened the tournament to thirty-six holes, Rhodes held a ten-stroke lead and was declared the winner. At the awards ball in the Fiesta Room of the Mary Elizabeth Hotel, Rhodes was presented his winner's trophy, a 2-foot-high cup topped by a golfer swinging his club. The gleaming trophy was handed to Rhodes by entertainer Nat King Cole.

When Rhodes put $300 more in his pocket with a second-place finish at a UGA event in Houston, he had the funds needed to turn his attention to playing in PGA events. From Houston he drove to Detroit only to learn on arriving at Plum Hollow Golf Club for the Western Open that his entry, along with those of four other golfers, did not arrive in time, and he was not permitted to play. Rhodes' luck didn't change over the next three weeks. The Labatt Open near Montreal brought horrendous luck in previous attempts. On the seventh hole during the second day of the 1954 event, neither Rhodes nor his caddy could find his tee shot. The men searched for the ball for several minutes until the caddy happened to look upward. There, stuck in the fork of a branch was Rhodes' ball. A year later, during the first round of the tournament, Rhodes hit a shot on eighteen that wound up on the edge of a creek in front of the green. He removed his shoes and socks, waded into the water, and smashed a shot that wound up 3 feet short of the hole. But during this year's event, the spectacular was missing from his game. Rhodes shot a 3-over-par round on the second day, toppled far behind the leaders, and left without earning any money.

A week later in the Canadian Open, Rhodes finished the first round only three shots behind the leader. A 3-under-par round on day two put Rhodes in a tie with Arnold Palmer, four shots off the lead. A 2-under-par score for the third round kept Rhodes in a seventh-place tie with Palmer heading to the final day. Despite high hopes Rhodes could not maintain his pace over the final eighteen holes. He faltered and finished out of the money.

In the St. Paul Open, Rhodes' fortunes did not change. Not even a 2-under-par third-round score could offset a 2-over-par first round and help Rhodes make the cut. Once eliminated, Rhodes made a snap decision. He learned of a pro-am tournament in Waterloo, Iowa, where the field was made up of mostly local players. Seeing a chance to earn some prize money, Rhodes hastily left St. Paul, drove all night, and arrived at the course in Waterloo, tired and with no time to practice. The Waterloo Open was a thirty-six-hole, single-day tournament, a grueling test of endurance as much as golf skills. Over the first eighteen holes, Rhodes shot 74. By the time he finished, darkness shrouded the course. Rhodes' afternoon round was a 70. His total score of 144 was ten strokes behind the winner.

Rhodes' run of bad luck pushed his attention back toward the UGA and, specifically, the Negro National Open. Since he last participated, much had changed. The UGA worked hard to recruit sponsors. The involvement of firms such as Coca Cola, Seagram's, and Shaefer Brewing Company helped to offset costs. The UGA awarded its 1957 Open to Washington, DC, and the influential Wake Robin Golf Club as host.

Named for the purplish wildflower, Wake Robin Golf Club was a Maryland-based, all-Black golf organization made up entirely of women. Its originators were so-called "golf widows," women whose husbands spent a great deal of time golfing. Created in 1937, the club's goal was to encourage more Black women to take up the game. Their mission also grew to include the fight for integration. They marched onto segregated golf courses and demanded to play, an effort that in some instances saw them chased away by rock-throwing White golfers.

Prior to the Open, golfers congregated at another area course for a pro-am event. Langston Golf Course held historic significance to Black golfers. First proposed in 1927 by Black architect John Langston, the ultimate construction of the course came after strong efforts to persuade the government to build a course for Blacks. When it opened in 1939, it was one of only twenty golf courses in the United States open to Black players. The Royal Golf club, an all-Black group of male golfers, staged the Langston Pro-Am, a fifty-four-hole tournament that offered $500 to the winner.

Rhodes and his protégé and travel partner, Charley Sifford, engaged in a spirited duel. Over the first eighteen holes, Rhodes recorded a 69 to lead the tournament. The second eighteen holes saw Sifford leapfrog Rhodes and hold a one-stroke lead. Upon the event's conclusion, it was Rhodes who prevailed.

Though he shot a 73, he managed to defeat Sifford and Zeke Hartsfield by the narrowest of margins, a single stroke.

A mixture of freneticism and glee abounded on the first day of the 1957 Open. As workers hurriedly registered and gave instructions to entrants, members of the UGA were ecstatic that a record 476 golfers were on hand to play. Sportswriters throughout the country were unanimous in their prediction that Charley Sifford would win the tournament. After all, since Rhodes had shifted his emphasis to PGA events, it was Sifford who prevailed in the Open. His four consecutive Open titles equaled that of Rhodes, yet both men trailed Howard Wheeler's record of six Open titles.

When play began, the large number of golfers traversed one of the more historically significant courses in the country. East Potomac Golf Course was a municipal course constructed by the Capital National Parks in 1921. US President Warren G. Harding, an avid golfer, played a round to inaugurate the course. Shortly after its opening, the course was made off-limits to Black golfers with the exception of Tuesdays, after 3:00 p.m. On and off for twenty years that decision was protested. Finally, in July 1941, Secretary of the Interior Harold L. Ickes ordered the course open to all. On the first day of the new mandate, three Black golfers were denied access to the course. When they persisted, police were called, but rather than escort them away, they forced the attendant to let the men play. To guard against trouble, the officers accompanied the golfers throughout their round. At the tenth hole, which was close to the clubhouse, a somewhat hostile crowd gathered but was dispersed by police.

East Potomac Golf Course witnessed one of the greatest duels in the history of the Negro National Open. The tournament was a two-day event with a grueling format that called for playing thirty-six holes each day. Rhodes and Sifford engaged in a classic battle throughout a long first day. By nightfall, Sifford was in front by a single stroke. The next day, Friday, several hundred spectators followed every shot the two men took. They saw Rhodes exhibit peak form. He grabbed the lead by shooting 3 under par to Sifford's even-par round. After a short break, the men embarked on the deciding eighteen holes of the tournament. With each afternoon hole Rhodes' play grew from better to exceptional. As the *Afro-American* described, "Rhodes exhibited a brilliant approach game and putted even better. Taking to the greens as though manufactured to his own personal satisfaction, Ted sank long and short putts with an accuracy that was uncanny."[1] The result, a 7-under-par 65 score brought Rhodes his fifth Negro National Open title. The margin of victory was a commanding seven strokes. As Rhodes was handed the Seagram's trophy, observers were buzzing over one of the more overwhelming performances in the thirty-one-year history of the Negro National Open.

After celebrating, Rhodes spent time in the Midwest, where he played in several local tournaments. Once the leaves had changed color and temperatures dropped, Rhodes' attention turned to the winter circuit in Southern California. He arranged for his wife and children to join him. As the family was in transit, play began in a PGA-sanctioned tournament in their destination region. The Long Beach Open had not been played in five years. With stronger backing from the Long Beach Chamber of Commerce and its events arm, the Century Club, the tournament returned to the PGA calendar. It differed from its predecessor in two areas. It employed a fifty-four-hole format rather than the usual seventy-two. Unlike in its previous existence, Black golfers were permitted to play, and Charley Sifford entered.

Playing in ideal 70-degree weather, Gene Littler shot 66 to lead at the end of the first day. Sifford recorded a 69 and was part of a group of golfers bunched together in fourth place. A day later, a local product, Dale Andreason, surprised everyone by shooting 66 to take over first place. Sifford fell to sixth after recording a 70. But on the final day, everything changed. Dramatics moved into the spotlight. Sifford, a short, stocky, quiet, 34-year-old, whose love of golf began as a nine-year-old caddy in North Carolina, opened his round with a birdie binge. He recorded four over the first five holes. They were holes that were considered the toughest at the course. Sifford finished the front nine with a 31.

With an ever-present cigar in his mouth and lucky rabbit's foot in his pocket, Sifford began the back nine as impressively as the front. Using a putter borrowed from Joe Louis, Sifford sank superb putts to record birdies on twelve, thirteen, and fourteen. Then, on eighteen, with first place on the line and a large crowd watching, Sifford sank an 8-foot birdie putt. As the ball fell into the cup, Sifford ran to the hole. He pulled out the ball and kissed it. He had recorded a 64 to tie Eric Monte for first place. The tournament champion would be decided in a sudden-death playoff.

By the time the men reached the third extra hole, darkness was beginning to blanket the course. Harvey Raynor, the PGA tournament coordinator, became fearful he may have to call a halt to the competition and declare an eighteen-hole Monday playoff. Before he could, Sifford sank a 6-foot putt, then watched to see what Monte would do. The man's ball was farther away, 20 feet from the hole. The flat side of his blade putter tapped the dimpled white ball to send it rolling. Just as it drew near the hole, it stopped, a fraction of an inch short. Charley Sifford was the Long Beach Open champion. For the first time, a Black man was the winner of a PGA tournament.

Sifford was filled as much with jubilation as relief. "Man it's tough to win when you gotta win, when you need that dough and when you've got every Negro on your back pulling for you," he said.[2] Sportswriters such as Jerry Wynn of the local *Long Beach Independent* heralded Sifford, "joining Jackie Robinson of baseball and Althea Gibson of tennis fame as trail-blazers of their race in the world of sports."[3] Hank Hollingworth, columnist and executive sports editor for the *Independent*, wrote of Sifford, "His win gave this city the distinction of being the one where the last color line in sports was broken."[4]

Around the country, Sifford's milestone received bold headlines. "SIFFORD IS GOLF'S ANSWER TO ROBINSON AND GIBSON," boasted *Newsday* in New York.[5] "NEGRO PRO WINS OPEN GOLF," touted *The Boston Globe*.[6] In Detroit the *Free*

Press blared, "A FIRST: NEGRO WINS GOLF MEET."[7] In Black newspapers hope was expressed that Sifford's breakthrough win sent a message. Marion Jackson wrote in the *Alabama Tribune*, "I hope the segregationists who pass racist laws will read this. What the Negro wants is merely a chance. He wants to be a man not a pawn or ward."[8]

But several miles from the course, the message was not heard. In the afterglow of Sifford's celebration, the PGA began its annual convention. In the luxurious Lafayette Hotel, flagship of the Hilton Hotel chain, golf's leaders met to forge future plans and policies. Bill Spiller turned up. He sought a meeting with executives in the hope they could finally be persuaded to remove the Caucasian-only policy from membership requirements. He was wrong.

There had been progress. Many midwestern, northern, and East Coast tournaments now welcomed Black golfers. But membership in the PGA remained unattainable. Events such as Bing Crosby's annual pro-am tournament remained off-limits. For all his effort, Spiller received the brush-off. When he did manage to speak to someone, he was told that procedural matters prohibited discussion of his request. Proposals to amend policy, it was explained, had to be received seventy-five days in advance of the convention in order to become part of the agenda. Spiller was then sent on his way.

In eleven years of professional golf, Ted Rhodes had never missed out on the winter circuit in Southern California. In the winter of 1957, he arrived in the area later than usual but keen to share the warm-weather experience with his family. In the week that followed his groundbreaking triumph, Sifford met Rhodes at a tournament in Gardena, a small community south of Los Angeles known for its legal cardrooms and vast strawberry fields. At Western Avenue Golf Course, a favored socializing spot where he relished dropping nickels in the juke box and doing a dance he called The Sand, Rhodes put together three under-par rounds to finish fifth, one shot ahead of Sifford, and six behind the winner, Tommy Jacobs.

At the Indian Wells Country Club near Palm Springs a week later, a single over-par round spoiled his pursuit of prize money in the Southern California Open. Rhodes remedied that at the next event when he shot 5 under par on the final round to place seventh in the Montebello Open.

The Montebello Open was delayed two days by heavy rain. The weather threw a wrench in the area golf schedule. By the time the rain let up and the Montebello Open finally concluded, golfers had to hurry to Chino Hills for the Pomona Valley Open, which was scheduled to tee off the very next day. Rhodes carried his streak of strong play into the event's first round. He vaulted through a field of ninety-six professionals, shooting 5 under par over the Los Serranos Country Club course to share the first-round lead with Sifford and Jerry Barber. Twenty-four hours later Billy Casper celebrated a 6-under-par round that propelled him into first. Rhodes shot 69 to hold third place, two shots back.

It was when Rhodes made the turn to begin the back nine on the final day of the tournament that optimism soared. He had taken the lead earlier in the round on the third hole. Now having shot 33 on the front nine, he led Casper by one stroke. When Deborah Rhodes left her father's side and went to the clubhouse, the expectation among fans in the gallery was that Ted Rhodes was destined to win the tournament. By the time the girl returned, things had changed. "Your daddy didn't play too good when you left," her mother said.[9] In her absence her father was plagued by a string of bogeys, four in total, and had fallen from first.

Playing in a threesome that included Casper and one group behind Sifford, Rhodes fought to stay in the title chase. At times it appeared mistakes and stray shots by Casper and Sifford would return the lead to Rhodes. But at the end of eighteen holes, Casper and Sifford were tied for the lead and headed to a playoff. Rhodes, who shot 37 on the back nine, finished with 70 for the round and in third place for the tournament, two strokes behind Casper and Sifford. In their playoff Casper defeated Sifford to win the tournament.

The conclusion of Rhodes' season was one of missed opportunities and frustrations. It conjured a truism, once articulated by the legendary amateur golfer Bobby Jones and oft repeated over the ensuing years. "Golf," Jones said, "is the closest game to the game we call life. You get bad breaks from good shots; you get good breaks from bad shots—but you have to play the ball where it lies."[10] While Ted Rhodes had overcome tremendous adversity to achieve success, there were tribulations brewing, the kind he could do nothing about.

13

Fighting for His Life

The end of summer and early weeks during the fall in 1961 had been taxing. Ted Rhodes pushed himself through a grueling schedule. It became evident in his play. Favored to win once play teed off in the Negro National Open, Rhodes failed to break par and for the first time finished out of contention at the Negro National Open. Determined to play in and earn money from another event, Rhodes drove all night from the tournament site near Boston to Rochester, New York, and without sleep entered and played in a local pro-am. When he shot 2 over par, he told a sportswriter the fans would see a better Ted Rhodes after he'd had a night's sleep, but they didn't. His score the next day was even worse.

By the end of the 1961 summer golf season, Ted Rhodes' body was breaking down. He was forty-nine. Results on the golf course belied the name and reputation that had been built over more than a decade. Pain was now a constant companion. Convinced it was a product of the road, long drives, and little sleep, Rhodes persevered until, in October, it became too much. With the change in weather bringing East Coast golf to an end, Rhodes set out for Nashville, where convinced his excruciating pain was from a case of hemorrhoids, he checked into the local VA hospital. Doctors performed a series of tests that concluded Rhodes' problem to be far worse. They found heart trouble, but much more serious, Rhodes' kidneys were failing.

Surgery was performed to remove the more seriously damaged of his two kidneys while doctors fought through other means to try to save the remaining organ. Claudia, with the couple's daughter, caught the first train from St. Louis to be by Ted's side. Treatment stretched from days to weeks, then, ultimately, months. Rhodes spent the holidays in the hospital, first Thanksgiving, then Christmas, and he ultimately welcomed 1962 while still ailing.

In January, Rhodes was again wheeled into the operating room. This time a portion of his remaining kidney was removed. A grim prognosis spread. When news reached the media, alarm sounded. Les Matthews with the *New York Amsterdam News* reported Rhodes' condition was serious. Marion E. Jackson of the *Atlanta Daily World* brought deeper insight when he wrote that Rhodes was in a fight for his life. Shock rippled through the sport of golf. Quickly, that shock evolved into compassion from which a desire to help Rhodes and his family was born.

Throughout the ordeal Maxi Barber, a golfing friend from Chicago, was in constant contact with Rhodes. Barber was a member of a golfing organization, the Linksmen, and he suggested the group stage a benefit to raise money for the Rhodes family. While members solicited auction items from Chicago sporting goods stores, the Starz Club was secured to host the event. Eugene Porter, president of the Linksmen, was taken aback at the overwhelming show of support. "It seemed the more people heard the more they wanted to contribute," he said.[1] The group set a goal to raise $900 and was surprised when their effort topped $1,200.

Porter made plans to surprise Rhodes. He phoned to tell him he and two club members were coming to Nashville for a visit but revealed nothing else. Four days after the benefit, Porter, Judson Mitchell, and Jimmy Taylor arrived at the VA hospital in Nashville. Rhodes' attending physician, Dr. C. J. Walker, took the men to their friend. Rhodes' demeanor brightened when he saw the men and even more so when they surprised him with an explanation of what they had done and presented him with a check for $1,205.75. Overwhelmed,

Rhodes told the men he was undeserving of such generosity and motivated to get well again to justify the faith and respect shown.

In Los Angeles, Bill Watkins, owner of the Watkins Hotel and Jazz Club, along with Harry Mills of the singing Mills Brothers, organized Ted Rhodes Week. They assembled a series of events to raise funds for their ailing friend. Together with the Rubaiyat Golf Club, the men made plans for a benefit golf tournament at the Fox Hills Golf Club, a fundraising dinner at Watkins' hotel, and a dinner auction. Their events raised more than $2,000.

Assistance came in a variety of ways. In Nashville, fast-rising rhythm and blues singer "Little Willie" John agreed to perform at a benefit dance arranged at the Club Baron to raise funds for the Rhodes family. In Los Angeles, *Sentinel* columnist A. S. "Doc" Young received a letter from an advertising executive in Minneapolis. Robert B. Pile of Campbell-Mithun, Inc., the agency which handled the Hamm's Beer account, wrote the following:

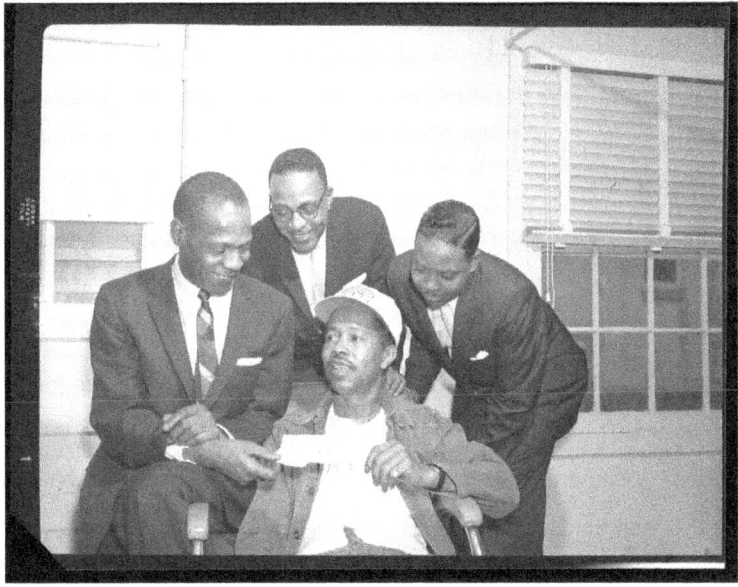

Members of the Linksmen present Rhodes with a check as he recovers from life-threatening surgery. Courtesy of the Nashville Public Library Special Collections.

I was enormously moved by your account of the troubles of Ted Rhodes. I am attaching a check to help out in a small way. I saw Ted play golf only once but that was in the St. Paul Open 10 or 12 years ago. I recall that he led after the first and second rounds, and he gave me and the rest of the gallery a heck of a thrill.[2]

Charley Sifford pledged to send Claudia Rhodes a portion of what he earned in upcoming tournaments. At Wethersfield Country Club in Hartford, Connecticut, host to the PGA Insurance City Open, members took up a collection for Rhodes and his family. In Novato, north of San Francisco, members of Count Basie's Orchestra paused from their West Coast tour to play in a benefit tournament for Rhodes held at Indian Valley Golf Course. Freddie Green, Basie's guitarist, came away a trophy winner. Wealthy golf enthusiasts such as Chicago attorney Peter Short offered Rhodes large sums of money in exchange for future golf lessons.

As Ted Rhodes lay in a hospital bed, significant change came to professional golf. During Rhodes' second month in the Nashville VA Hospital, the PGA held its annual convention at the Diplomat Hotel in Hollywood, Florida. Paramount was a motion put forth by the Southern California, Georgia-Alabama, and four New York chapters of the organization. It was a resolution to remove the Caucasian-only clause once and for all from the PGA membership policy.

The seeds for the move were planted on a Los Angeles-area golf course several months before. Bill Spiller was caddying for an influential Southern California businessman, Harry Braverman. During his round the man asked why Spiller wasn't working as a golf instructor or playing professionally. When told of the PGA's membership policy and the restrictions it imposed on Black golfers, the man pledged to connect Spiller with California's attorney general, Stanley Mosk.

It was at that time Mosk received a handwritten letter from Charley Sifford. In it Sifford complained that despite winning a PGA tournament, his applications for membership in the organization had been rejected or ignored. Mosk traveled to Los Angeles, where he played a round of golf with Sifford. He then decided to build a case around Sifford as a California resident whose civil rights were being violated by the PGA. Mosk informed the PGA their constitution violated public policies and state laws in California. He gave the PGA a choice, either remove the Caucasian-only clause from its membership policy or be barred from doing business in California. Mosk's ultimatum sparked a firestorm. The PGA had awarded Brentwood Country Club and the Los Angeles Junior Chamber of Commerce the right to host the 1962 PGA championship, an event the organization liked to call "golf's greatest prize."[3] Some among the PGA hierarchy bristled at Mosk's demand. They accused him of playing politics. "He wants to become governor," said Ed Carter, the PGA's tournament director.[4]

As the furor grew, prominent business leaders in the Los Angeles area made it known they would not sign on as sponsors of the tournament unless the PGA changed its membership policy. The Los Angeles Junior Chamber of Commerce wanted no involvement in the controversy. Faced with the prospect of staging a money-losing tournament, the group told the PGA they wanted out of their contract to host the event. No opposition came from the PGA's local chapter. Willie Hunter, pro at Riviera Country Club and head of the Southern California chapter of the PGA, urged the national body to remove the Caucasian-only clause. Rather than fight Mosk, the PGA scrambled to find a new host site. As they did, Mosk heightened his attack. He contacted attorneys general in other states and urged them to block the PGA from doing business unless their segregationist practice ended. New York's attorney general, Louis J. Lefkowitz, agreed. He went a step further and threatened to sue the PGA unless it did away with the Caucasian-only clause. The PGA turned to Dallas. The Dallas Salesmanship Club and Oak Cliff Country Club felt it was too short notice and turned down the offer to take over as host of the event. After a hastily arranged meeting of its executive committee, the PGA offered the event to the Aronimink Golf Club in Philadelphia, which agreed to become host venue. But in doing so, the PGA conceded it would take up the matter to change its membership policy at the annual convention in November.

Announcement of the players who qualified to play in the 1961 PGA championship sparked further controversy. The National Association for the Advancement of Colored People (NAACP) offered sharp criticism of the PGA for not including Charley Sifford on the list. "Charley simply didn't make the grade this year on the basis of his playing record," said Lou Strong, president of the PGA. He added Sifford's exclusion had nothing to do with race.[5] But the NAACP countered that it did. To play in the PGA Championship, a golfer was required to be among the top twenty in points earned or the top twenty in money earned over the prior season or be one of the twenty-four lowest scorers in the previous PGA championship. The requirements were made almost impossible to meet by a schedule of tournaments in which 35 percent were played in states with Jim Crow laws that barred Blacks from participation.

On November 9, Ted Rhodes lay in a hospital bed; his professional golf career, and possibly his life, hung in the balance. At the same time, in a meeting room in South Florida, the very thing Rhodes longed for his entire adult life, membership in the PGA, was the topic for discussion. Delegates from eighty-five PGA chapters were read the agenda item. When they were asked to vote, each held the same position. By their 85-0 vote, the Caucasian-only clause was removed from the PGA membership policy. The thirteen-year fight dating back to the lawsuit first filed on behalf of Rhodes, Bill Spiller, and Madison Gunter over their exclusion from the Richmond Open had ended. "The unanimous approval of the change in membership requirements speaks for itself and for the representatives of the PGA," said PGA president Strong.[6]

Charley Sifford learned of the vote when he walked off the eighteenth green at Western Avenue Golf Course. He had just shot 3 under par on day one of the Gardena Open. Sifford told reporters he was grateful to Mosk and to the Southern California chapter of the PGA, which introduced the resolution to remove the Caucasian-only clause. "It's been a long hard road," he said. "It's been tough."[7] A pleased Bill Spiller viewed the news with more in mind than tournament golf. "Well, it's a fine start," Spiller said, then added he hoped it could lead to PGA Class A membership and the ability to own a golf shop. "Then we can call it success."[8]

It was generally accepted both in the press and among fans that Charley Sifford was the golfer most likely to benefit from the PGA's action. Few would argue that the 38-year-old Sifford had supplanted the now 49-year-old Rhodes as the preeminent Black golfer in the sport. Still, publications such as the *Pittsburgh Courier* reminded readers that while Sifford might be the golfer most likely to gain from the change, Rhodes should be remembered as the Jackie Robinson of the sport. In his Detroit newspaper column, Ziggy Johnson lamented that Ted Rhodes was a golfer born ten years too early.

While the PGA decision was celebrated, Rhodes remained in serious condition in the Nashville VA Hospital. Friends visited regularly and found him in good spirits. Newspaper columnists gave out the hospital's White Bridge Road address and urged readers to send letters to Rhodes. So touching was the response that Claudia and Deborah Rhodes devoted time to pen thank-you notes to the newspapermen.

In Rhodes' fourth month in the hospital, his doctors decided a second operation was needed. This one removed a part of his remaining kidney. The procedure went well, and the resulting prognosis was positive. As Rhodes recovered, his physician, Dr. C. J. Walker, phoned some of the golfer's friends as well as a few of his own contacts with ties to the sport. Concerned that the stress and exertion of tournament golf might be too much for Rhodes, the physician sought to arrange a soft job, one with little stress, perhaps that of a golf instructor.

Only the previous summer Rhodes received a unique offer of just such a job. It came from the new prime minister of Cuba, Fidel Castro. The offer was for the job of head pro at Biltmore Yacht and Country Club, a frequent fishing spot of writer Ernest Hemingway. Rhodes along with a golfer from South Florida, Joe Roach, was invited to the island by the Cuban Tourism Commission. They played a round at Villareal Golf Club, a club off-limits to Blacks before Castro seized power. It was an exhibition intended to showcase changes Castro was bringing to the island. As had been the case with previous offers to become a teaching pro, Rhodes wanted to continue playing competitive golf and turned the offer down.

During the final week of May, Rhodes was deemed sufficiently recovered to venture from the hospital for a few hours. He traveled to Belle Meade Country Club, where local golfers were playing in a qualifying event for the US Open. Still thin and frail, Rhodes was greeted warmly by old friends. His smile beamed. The usual twinkle in his eyes was hidden by dark glasses, now a regular requirement to protect retinas damaged by kidney disease. He told well-wishers he expected to be released from the hospital in a few days and detailed plans to continue his recovery in Chicago.

After seven months in the Nashville VA Hospital, Rhodes was finally discharged. He ventured to Chicago carrying with him strict instructions from his doctor not to overexert himself. Dr. Walker told the golfer's friends he could not predict whether Rhodes would ever play again. What he was certain of was that Rhodes' remaining kidney and heart were fragile and could not tolerate a great deal of stress.

Soon after Rhodes arrived in Chicago, the PGA circuit did as well. Rhodes was part of the gallery at Medina Country Club to watch old friends play in the Western Open. He stood among the throng at the eighteenth green as Charley Sifford lined up a 12-foot putt with a chance to finish the first round one shot out of first place. Once Sifford's ball had fallen into the cup, the golfer turned and made a beeline for his friend. The two men enthusiastically shook hands and exchanged compliments before Sifford retreated to the scorer's tent to turn in his scorecard.

As late spring turned to summer, Rhodes' weight returned, so much so that his friends jokingly called him fat. As his strength grew, he found his way back to the golf course. Swinging a driver on the range ebbed into playing nine holes, then as his stamina allowed, a full eighteen.

In Chicago, the Chicago Women's Golf Club, one of the many organizations to engage in fundraisers for Rhodes and his family, was putting the final touches on their annual showpiece event—the Midwestern and Walter Speedy Memorial Tournament. It was a staple of the region's golfing calendar and regularly attracted both a large number of professional and amateur golfers as well as a big turnout of spectators. Such was the magnitude of the event, area politicians jockeyed to present trophies. The New York-based dairy company Borden signed on to sponsor the tournament. As popular as the tournament itself was, access to the post-tournament party, known as the 19th Hole, was even more sought after. For their 1962 event, the entertainment committee had real floral leis flown in from Hawaii. Miniature orchids were to be passed out to all of the ladies. The bartenders at Roberts Lounge, the awards dinner venue, were schooled on how to create The Sand Trap, a drink designed to help the imbiber forget all of the bad shots they hit during the tournament.

During the planning of the tournament, one idea that was enthusiastically adopted was to name the plaque that would go to the men's professional division winner the "Ted Rhodes Plaque." Rhodes agreed to the idea. But when the committee asked if he would attend and present the plaque at the 19th Hole party, Rhodes surprised them with his answer. Not only would he present the plaque, but he planned to win it. Rhodes was going to play.

Umbrellas and caps were staples of the thousands that streamed into Burnham Woods Golf Course south of Chicago, close to the Illinois-Indiana border. The first Saturday in July 1962 was painted by a bright sun, muggy humid air, and temperatures in the low 90s. Still, the 24th Annual Midwestern and Walter Speedy Memorial Tournament attracted more than two thousand to watch 237 men and women compete in pro and amateur divisions.

Prior to teeing off, Rhodes was applauded as the tournament committee saluted him for his contribution to the sport. Wonder at how Rhodes' body would hold up over the scheduled thirty-six-hole tournament was quickly answered. He blazed through the first eighteen holes in 1 under par. The score put Rhodes in second place, one shot behind Wally Kolodziej, the pro at Gleason Park in nearby Gary, Indiana. The syndicated news service, *Associated Negro Press*, called Rhodes' play amazing. The *Chicago Defender* gave special praise to a recovery shot Rhodes made with one knee positioned on a pedestrian bridge and the foot of the opposite leg in a ditch.

The next day an even larger crowd of more than two thousand fans followed the golfers over the final eighteen holes. Rhodes' game was not quite as sharp as it had been the day before. He finished with a 4-over-par score to conclude the tournament in fourth place. When, at the 19th Hole dinner, Rhodes presented his namesake plaque to Booker Blair, there were few who would disagree with the *Chicago Defender* when it called Rhodes' play the highlight of the tournament. Marion E. Jackson writing in the *Atlanta Daily World* called Rhodes' performance "both amazing and impressive."[9] That Ted Rhodes had gone from fighting for his life to fighting for a tournament title, Jackson suggested, was "one of the comeback stories of the year."[10]

14

Mentor to the Next Wave

Heads turned all about the course. A chilly morning on the banks of the Cumberland River was not exactly synonymous with a vision of greatness. But even those tempted to do a doubletake found that it was indeed one of the most iconic athletes in the world who walked to the practice tee at Cumberland Golf Course. Doubts were allayed by the newspaper reporter and photographer who trailed her. Althea Gibson needed help with her game. One of the greatest tennis players in the world, now turned professional golfer, made this trip to Nashville for a specific purpose. "No one," she said, "has made golf as emphatic and clear to me as Teddy Rhodes."[1]

It was in Florida that Rhodes and Gibson first met. Rhodes was sent to spend time in warm weather and sunshine during his recovery from another health crisis. In the two years that followed his major kidney surgeries and buoyed by his play in the 1962 Midwestern Open, Rhodes ignored his doctor's orders and returned to play in competitive tournament golf. "The doctor didn't exactly suggest that I play in this tournament," Rhodes explained to a sportswriter before a charity event in Maryland. "But he didn't ban me from it."[2]

Invited to give a clinic prior to a UGA tournament in New Jersey, Rhodes wound up entering and finished fourth, nine strokes behind the winner, Charley Sifford. He made ambitious plans for the 1963 season and quickly saw it produce dividends. After being honored and presented with a plaque for contributions to golf, Rhodes finished fourth in the North-South tournament in Miami. A week later, he rallied from six shots behind to win the inaugural Mid-Winter Classic in Tampa. Weeks later, golf writer Jimmie Bowman saw Rhodes play in Chicago. He wrote that Rhodes "was swinging as of old and looking like his former self again."[3]

Rhodes' play in the fall of 1964 confirmed Bowman's observation. At the UGA's Gate City Open in Greensboro, North Carolina, Rhodes led the tournament with two holes to play. On seventeen he ran into trouble, recording a triple bogey 8. The tally left Rhodes in fourth place, four strokes behind the tournament winner, Lee Elder. Rhodes began his 1965 schedule in Florida, attracted by a plethora of tournaments which filled the February page of the calendar. But it was after playing in the North-South tournament in Miami, then the Mid-Winter tournament in Tampa, when another health crisis struck. Ted Rhodes suffered a heart attack.

As Rhodes recovered in Florida, a wealthy friend paid him for golf lessons. The men got together regularly at the Airco Golf Course in Clearwater. It was one morning while in the midst of a session when Althea Gibson turned up at the course. A golfer in a quandary, she knew help could only come from one person, Ted Rhodes.

Althea Gibson was a phenomenon, the biggest female sports sensation in the world. The daughter of South Carolina sharecroppers, Gibson moved with her parents to New York at the age of three. By her early teens the tall, gangly African American girl was more interested in physical fighting than befriending. Neighbors raised money to send Gibson to a tennis club in Harlem for lessons. Three years later, at the age of seventeen, she won the American Tennis Association national championship. Her rise was mercurial, and by the latter half of the 1950s, there was no greater female tennis player in the world. Gibson won both Wimbledon and the US Open twice. She won the French Open and Australian Open as well. They were achievements never before accomplished by a Black woman. Her first Wimbledon triumph was celebrated with a ticker-tape parade in New York City. The only other time an African

American received the honor was when Jesse Owens returned home with four gold medals from the 1936 Olympic games. Twice, once in 1957 and again in 1958, Gibson was named Female Athlete of the Year by the *Associated Press*.

By the end of the 1950s, having won just about every trophy there was to win in the sport, Gibson grew bored. She shocked the sport with the announcement that she was finished with tennis and would instead pursue a career in professional golf. "No competition left in tennis," she said. "I love sports and want to stay in them as long as possible. Golf seemed like a good place to go."[4] In actuality, it was Joe Louis who prodded Gibson to swap her tennis racket for a golf club. She had confessed her boredom with tennis. At first, Gibson was reluctant to take up golf, but it wasn't long before the game enthralled her.

In 1964 Gibson joined the Ladies Professional Golf Association (LPGA). As the first Black to play on the LPGA circuit, she encountered many of the same problems that curtailed Ted Rhodes' career ten years before. Jim Crow laws prevented her from playing in tournaments in Georgia, Louisiana, Oklahoma, South Carolina, Tennessee, and Texas. From some galleries came hostility. Fellow players scoffed at her game. "She started too late in life... can't compete with the rest of us," one LPGA veteran said to a wire-service reporter.[5] Gibson's first season of professional golf produced results that were a far cry from those of her tennis career. In seventeen tournaments she won a paltry $561.50. It was that lack of success that made her seek Rhodes' help.

Their initial meeting at the course in Clearwater began a mentor-pupil relationship. Over a period of several days, Rhodes broke down Gibson's game. She was strong and very long off the tee, but her iron play and putting were badly in need of work. Rhodes attacked every facet of Gibson's game. By the time she left Florida to join the LPGA tour, her play had improved and her confidence risen.

At the Waterloo Open in Iowa, Gibson flashed impressive results. In the second round of the tournament, she shot 68, both her lowest round as a professional and the low round of the event. Gibson finished sixth and earned $255. A week later at the Milwaukee Open, she began the tournament with a 71, a score that put her one stroke behind the leader.

The mentor role was not new to Rhodes. He was often sought out for help. Just as Gibson approached Rhodes in Florida, Jackie Robinson requested his help as well. So, too, did a young Charley Sifford. Their meeting took place at Cobbs Creek Golf Course near Philadelphia during the 1947 Negro National Open. Sifford was frustrated and approached Rhodes. He confessed he saw little potential for financial success in professional golf and told Rhodes he had abandoned his dream. Rhodes quickly gave him a subtle scolding.

A native of the South, Sifford became a caddy at the age of thirteen in his home state of North Carolina. Four years later, he fled his hometown for Philadelphia. It was an altercation that sparked the move. A man who was likely drunk spewed slurs and insulted Sifford's mother. The teen struck the man over the head with a bottle. Fearful of repercussions, Sifford quickly hopped a freight train and rode it to Philadelphia. There he found a different world. Unlike in North Carolina the golf courses allowed him to play. His skills developed. But when he told Rhodes he was discouraged and had abandoned plans to play professionally, Rhodes wouldn't hear of it. He implored Sifford to pursue his goals and offered support. Unable to make time to give Billy Eckstine the golf instruction he sought, Rhodes introduced Sifford to the popular singer, who hired the young golfer and gave Sifford the financial support he needed to play on the UGA circuit. Rhodes invited Sifford to be his travel partner, and the two shared driving and hotel rooms while on the road.

Sifford followed Rhodes' lead and relocated to Los Angeles to take advantage of the winter weather and tournament calendar to further polish his game. As age and health issues made Rhodes' skills begin to wane, it was Sifford who supplanted him in the eyes of sportswriters as the country's premier Black golfer. Goals long harbored by the mentor were realized instead through the pupil. Predicted for ten years to be the one who would be the first Black golfer to win a PGA tournament, Rhodes was elated and filled with pride when it was Sifford who achieved the milestone. While Rhodes became the first Black golfer to receive a contract to represent a golf club manufacturer, his was a contingency arrangement that matched the money he earned. Sifford's success brought a deal in 1959 with Kroydon Golf to produce a signature line of clubs. He was also paid to use US Rubber brand golf balls and to be a part of a sports advisory panel for Ballantine Beer.

While Rhodes was part of the first effort to try to force the PGA to remove the Caucasian-only clause from its membership policy, Sifford was at the center of the 1961 effort that succeeded in doing so and was the first Black golfer to receive an accredited player card from the PGA, none of which would have been possible were it not for Rhodes' support. "I have a very special reason for loving this man," Sifford said.[6]

Four years after Rhodes first met Sifford, another young golfer fell under his mentorship. At the UGA's 1951 National Amateur Championship, Joe Louis became locked in a thrilling battle for the amateur division title with a seventeen-year-old golfer from Texas. The teenager endeared himself to spectators with a semifinal triumph that required a sudden-death playoff to settle. Play raged so late into the night that cars were brought to the ninth green so their headlights could illuminate the hole. After defeating the young upstart in their thirty-six-hole title match, an enthralled Louis urged Rhodes to work with the teen, whose name was Lee Elder.

What Rhodes saw was a young man in need of direction. Elder was brimming in natural talent, but his game was riddled with bad habits. The youngest of ten children, Lee Elder's life went awry after the death of his father, an infantryman in Germany during World War II. Three months later his mother also died. Elder was sent to Los Angeles to live with an aunt and soon found himself under the spell of a street hustler. Elder dropped out of school in the tenth grade and followed the hustler back to Dallas. Smitten by the game of golf, Elder got a job as a caddy at Tennison Park Golf Course. It wasn't long before he partnered with a gambler known as "Titanic" Thompson. Using Elder's golf skills, the duo fleeced wealthy oilmen on public golf courses around Texas and Oklahoma with elaborate ruses.

Elder entered and won the Black section of the Texas State Amateur championship, then decided to test his skills against the best Black golfers in the country. He joined six other Dallas golfers who journeyed to Cleveland to play in the Negro National Open. It was there that Elder was introduced to Rhodes. One of the first things Rhodes noticed about Elder's game was his unorthodox cross-handed grip. He sent Elder back to Los Angeles, where he arranged for him to work in Lloyd Mangrum's golf shop in Apple Valley cleaning clubs. Mangrum changed Elder's club grip to a more conventional Vardon grip, in which the pinkie of the right hand rests on top of or in some cases is intertwined with the index finger of the left hand.

In the mid-1950s, Rhodes invited Elder to move in with his family. In 1954 the Rhodes had moved to Claudia's hometown of St. Louis. Ted spent hours in the shade of the large trees at the golf course in Forest Park tutoring Elder on his game. When Rhodes went on the road to play in tournaments, Elder came along and caddied. Rhodes introduced Elder to Jackie Robinson, and whenever the Brooklyn Dodgers came to St. Louis, the three men would get together. "Lee," Rhodes said one day, "if you ever get a chance, you're gonna make a lot of money playing golf."[7] In 1959 Elder left St. Louis to join the army. While stationed at Fort Lewis in Washington, he won the Sixth Army golf championship. Upon completing his two-year military hitch, Elder joined the UGA circuit. By this time Charley Sifford had moved on to play primarily in PGA tournaments, and Elder established himself as the best golfer in the series. Over a span of twenty-two tournaments, Elder won eighteen of them. By 1967 he was considered the best Black golfer in the sport. "He never had a slump," Rhodes said of his pupil. "He always has the ball in play."[8]

While celebrities and potential up-and-comers received the benefit of Rhodes' teaching talents and encouragement, so too did his family. Since being taught the game while the couple was dating, Claudia Rhodes made golf a form of recreation. She often signed up for and played in amateur events in and around the St. Louis area. When his daughter Deborah turned three, Ted asked his club supplier if they would make a set sized for her. He meticulously taught her the proper grip, saying "A good grip is the most important part of the swing."[9] Once old enough, Deborah Rhodes entered amateur tournaments. She and her mother kept a locker at Forest Park and frequently hit balls at the St. Louis park. In summers during her teenaged years, Deborah traveled with her father. She competed in the youth section of UGA tournaments her father played in. The trips brought special father-daughter times. Especially memorable were trips to the East Coast that would include a day at the beach in Atlanta City highlighted by frolicking in the ocean.

As Rhodes continued his Florida recovery, temptation lured him back to the golf course. He accepted an invitation to play eighteen holes at one of the tougher courses in the Tampa–St. Petersburg area with Dave Rush, a retired Western Union press chief. Rush was astounded when Rhodes, still striving to regain his strength, shot 67.

Once sufficiently recovered, Rhodes traveled to Nashville. His physician advised that he be close to the VA hospital there. Rhodes made a room at the Eldorado Motel his new home. The motel was a short walk to Cumberland Golf Course, where Rhodes gave lessons. When the competitive itch returned, Rhodes' physician gave him the green light to play in tournaments just as long as they weren't too far from Nashville. He found one at Fort Campbell, Kentucky, which was sixty-three miles away, and won the Commanding General's Invitational. Away from the course, the UGA added him to its board of directors.

Instruction, however, was the focal point of his work in golf. Althea Gibson evolved into a primary pupil. When the 1967 LPGA season began, Gibson set as her goal to finish among the top ten in points at the end of the season. A

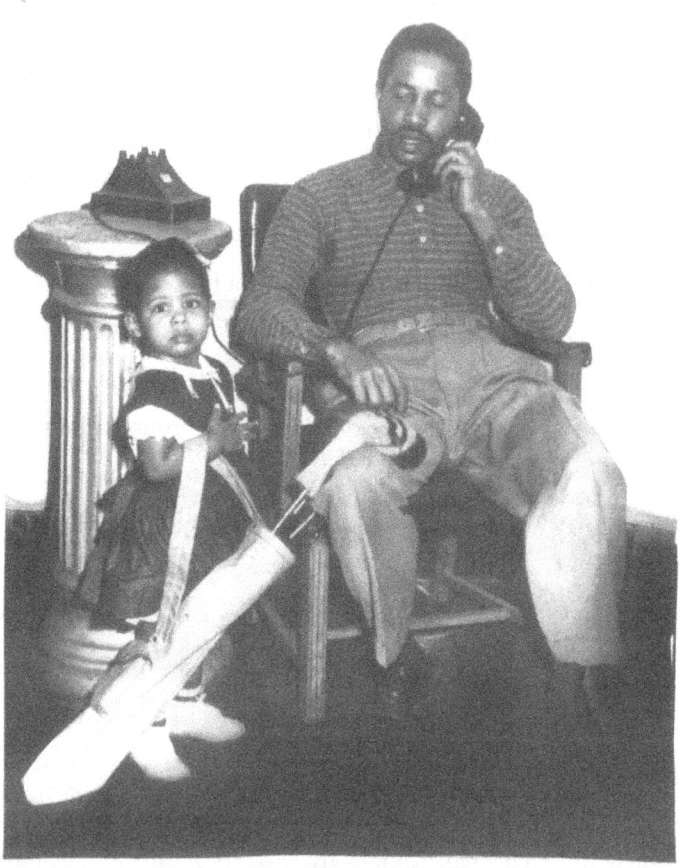

Rhodes had a special set of clubs made for his three-year-old daughter Deborah. He began lessons by teaching her the proper grip. Courtesy of Deborah Rhodes.

dismal first tournament made that goal appear unlikely. For four rounds in the St. Pete Open in Florida, Gibson shot 79-79-79-77. Dick Young, the acerbic columnist in the *New York Daily News*, wrote, "Althea Gibson shot consistent golf. She was consistently horrible."[10] In a field of fifty golfers, Gibson finished thirty-fourth.

Before the next event Gibson sought Rhodes' help, and he agreed to travel to Florida. As Gibson played in the Venice Open, Rhodes walked the course and studied his pupil. But after she shot 79 in the third round and hovered in fourteenth place, Rhodes sprang into action. He ordered Gibson to be at the course practice range at sunup the morning of the final round. There, as darkness gave way to morning light, he instructed his pupil to take a swing. When she did, he shook his head, then barked instruction. Early arrivals heard the voice of Ted Rhodes echo about the course. "Get that big butt around! Get your hips pointed to where you want the ball to go."[11] When Gibson's tee time arrived, and she embarked upon her round, fans in the gallery could hardly believe the improvement. Drives that one day earlier were cringeworthy and inconsistent flew high and straight. Gibson finished with an astounding 68, a women's record at Lake Venice Golf Club. Her final-round score helped her vault all the way to fifth place, for which she received $570, her biggest paycheck as a professional. "What happened?" asked columnist Dick Young. "Teddy Rhodes happened."[12]

After the Florida tournaments Gibson traveled to Nashville for further work with Rhodes. The mentor found his pupil's strength to be a problem. Gibson's large hands and strong arms and shoulders could produce fierce forehands and backhands on the tennis court, but they made a mockery of finesse play on a golf course. Gibson could drive the ball off the tee more than 300 yards. Her short game was a shambles. Rhodes put his emphasis on polishing Gibson's iron play. Golfers, workers, and onlookers at Cumberland Golf Course couldn't help but laugh when they heard Rhodes bark at Gibson, "Quit gorilla-ing the ball!"[13]

The instruction paid dividends. Once back on the LPGA tour, Gibson ran off a string of top-ten finishes. At the Milwaukee Open she had her best tournament yet, finishing in sixth place. Her game continued to improve, and in September she challenged for the lead in the Pacific Open before finishing third.

Around Cumberland Golf Course it was not uncommon to hear Rhodes recite Gibson's LPGA accomplishments. When he did so, his voice was tinged with enthusiasm. Teaching brought Rhodes joy. His own ability to play was sorely limited by his health. On occasion he would play nine holes. On a rare

Crowds would gather to watch whenever Rhodes played at Cumberland Golf Club in Nashville. Courtesy of the Nashville Public Library Special Collections.

day, if he was feeling strong, he might stay on the course and play eighteen. Whenever Rhodes broke out the clubs, there was still an awe about him. Children and fellow golfers at Cumberland would gather to watch. They gawked when he asked a teenaged boy to catch his chip shots and made ball after ball land so close to the youth he barely had to move to pick up the ball and drop it into a shag bag. Admirers would follow him from hole to hole, all the while riveted. At the end of his round, Rhodes would chortle that he was going back out on tour. But everyone within earshot knew the truth. He couldn't and wouldn't. In teaching he had a gift, and that was where his place in the sport lay. For Ted Rhodes, the competitive playing days were over.

15

So Long, Old Pro

Reporters and photographers scrambled at the sight of Lee Elder emerging from the scorer's room. At least half the field was still scattered about Warwick Hills Country Club in Grand Blanc, Michigan, 50 miles north of Detroit, where only twenty-four hours earlier heavy rain and even hail drove everyone for cover and brought a halt to play in round two of the Buick Open. Among the assembled sportswriters, columnists, magazine writers, and radio reporters was an expectation that the personable Elder would be smiling and jubilant. After all he had just shot 67 to go with the 68 he shot on Thursday. The two sub-par rounds thrust his name to the top of the leaderboard. He was two rounds from potentially winning his first tournament on the PGA tour.

As Elder approached, the reporters began to assemble in the form of a half circle. Questions were quietly pondered. Some made a plan to ask about his bogeyless round, others about his eight one-putt holes. Some wondered if he encountered any of the hostility and slurs that angered him at recent tournaments in Pensacola, Florida, and Memphis, Tennessee. But as Elder drew near, members of the group were startled by an unmistakable sight. The golfer was fighting back tears. It was then that he shared the news that his mentor, Ted Rhodes, had died.

It was the morning of July 4, 1969, when curiosity among those in the clubhouse at Cumberland Golf Course was aroused. Rhodes had not followed his usual routine. The night before he had been out late with friends. A few among them had been drinking. Some in the group walked with Rhodes down Ed Temple Boulevard toward the Eldorado Motel, where he bid them good night and retired to his room. When a concerned friend went to the golfer's room to check on him the following morning, he found Rhodes dead, having suffered a fatal heart attack during the night.

"I shot that 67 for him," a teary-eyed Elder said.[1] Whatever insight reporters sought about the round that catapulted Elder into the tournament lead, they were unlikely to get. Elder wanted to talk about his friend. "Ted Rhodes was like a father to me," he explained.[2] "He taught me everything I know about golf."[3] What added to the shock Elder felt was that two weeks earlier Rhodes surprised him at the Kemper Open. A television producer flew Rhodes to Charlotte, North Carolina, to conduct an interview about Black golfers. Rhodes made it a point to go to Quail Hollow Country Club and watch Elder and Charley Sifford play. A sportswriter saw him and asked about his game. "I mostly just sit around the clubhouse and argue," he joked.[4]

Elder shared with reporters a little-known aside to his remarkable sudden-death duel with Jack Nicklaus the previous year at the American Golf Classic in Akron, Ohio. The inaugural Ted Rhodes golf classic was in progress that same day at Cumberland Golf Course in Nashville. When word reverberated through the course that Elder had taken Nicklaus to a sudden-death playoff, golfers abandoned their rounds and rushed to the clubhouse to watch the duel on television. Elder was well known at the course. He'd spent hours whacking balls on Cumberland's practice tees under Rhodes' tutelage. As each golfer entered the room, they found Rhodes, the focal point of their local tournament, seated front and center riveted to Elder's play.

Rhodes regaled the clubhouse gathering with tales about the similarity of what they were watching to the first time he ever saw Elder play—his battle with Joe Louis for the amateur title at the Negro National Open in Cleveland in 1951. "They had a rip snorting match all the way around," he said.[5] Like in that duel with Louis seventeen years before, Elder was again the producer of drama, this time for much bigger stakes. For an hour and a half, over four nerve-wracking holes, Rhodes watched as Elder and Nicklaus matched pars and birdies. Then, on the fifth hole of sudden death, Nicklaus knocked in a tricky 8-foot putt. Elder sent a 15-foot putt toward the hole. Expectations rose that the golfers would need a sixth hole of sudden death. But at the last instant Elder's ball curled and failed to go in. A loud groan filled the Cumberland clubhouse. Nicklaus had won. "I don't believe, after his display of courage in the playoff with Nicklaus, that we have to worry about his nerves," Rhodes said of Elder the next day to a sportswriter.[6]

Once Elder completed his post-round responsibilities at Warwick Hills, he retreated to his hotel room. He phoned Claudia Rhodes and, in their conversation, pledged to send her $10,000 from the $25,000 winner's purse if he won the tournament. Friday's rain had sent the Buick Open into disarray. Organizers decided that instead of the usual eighteen holes, they would make up for the lost day by playing thirty-six holes on Sunday, the final day of the tournament. At the end of his first eighteen, Elder shot 71 and was still in the thick of the title chase. But not long into his second eighteen, his game fell apart. Elder pulled shots. Drives faded. Wedge shots came up short. He pushed putts to the right. Over the final eighteen holes of the tournament, Elder's game collapsed. He finished with an 80 and tumbled down the leader board to fourteenth place and a $2,180 payday.

Critics unaware of Rhodes' death wondered aloud how Elder could have collapsed so dramatically. One questioned his club selection and stated that Elder played it too safe. Others felt certain Elder succumbed to the pressure that came with title contention. Still more said flawed shots were a sign of fatigue and suggested it was a product of having to play thirty-six holes in a single day. But Elder's caddy, Thomas Clark, muted the debate. He answered what unequivocally was behind Elder's poor final-round play. "There's no doubt the death of Teddy Rhodes had some effect on Lee. He didn't get much rest and he just got tired," Clark said.[7]

Claudia Rhodes was with her daughter Deborah in Los Angeles when she received the news that her husband had died. The women were shocked and grief-stricken. When Rose Sifford, Charley Sifford's wife, learned they hadn't the money to fly to Nashville, she provided funds to cover Claudia's and Deborah's plane tickets. Once in Nashville Deborah Rhodes went to the room where her father had lived at the Eldorado Motel and was shocked by what she discovered. All of his valuables were gone. Someone had made off with his treasured sapphire ring, a watch, wallet, and all of his clothes. The only thing that remained in the room was Rhodes' set of golf clubs. Claudia Rhodes felt relief the clubs weren't taken. They were a memento she badly wanted. As the women left the motel and scanned the parking lot, they noticed one more item of value missing—Rhodes' car. He never let anyone else use it. They informed the police it, too, had been stolen.

A similarly wicked callousness reared its ugly head in Southern California and Florida. In Chino, California, a man appeared at the Cosmopolitan Golf Club's tournament with an appeal for funds to buy and send flowers to Rhodes' funeral. The man left the course pleased at having collected $150. He was never seen or heard from again, nor were any flowers received. Similarly, a fundraising effort in Florida to support Rhodes' family also raised ire when it was found to be a financial scam.

It was just after one o'clock on Wednesday, July 9, when the Reverend D. L. Williams stood before mourners at T. T. Hockett & Sons funeral home. The chapel was filled beyond capacity. Television cameras captured the service, a previously unrealized occurrence for a Black man in Nashville, Tennessee. Those gathered included golfers from far and wide. Elder had hurried to Nashville from the Buick Open. Pete Brown, who reigned over the UGA in the early 1960s before moving to the PGA circuit, skipped a PGA tournament in Minnesota to instead mourn his friend. Joe Louis found words difficult to come by. "He was like a brother to me," he said of Rhodes.[8] Upon conclusion of Williams' eulogy Louis and Elder rose to take their place with the other pall bearers. Friends and golf associates stopped to express condolences to Claudia Rhodes and her daughter. As they shook hands, some pressed money into the women's palms.

A warm afternoon sun beat down on those gathered as a hearse carried Rhodes to his final resting place, National Cemetery, the military veteran's cemetery in Madison just north of Nashville.

Before and after the service, family members were surprised when Deborah Rhodes introduced them to a young woman. "This is my sister, Peggy," she said.[9] The woman, they would later learn, was the product of a relationship when Rhodes was stationed in Chicago during World War II.

Words of compassion flowed from news of Rhodes' death. Within forty-eight hours of the golfer's passing, newspapers throughout the United States and Canada carried the news. The two major American wire services, *Associated Press* and *United Press International*, immortalized Rhodes as "the first Negro to play the Professional Golfers Association tour."[10] The *Call and Post* in Cleveland praised Rhodes as "a well thought of man and pro golfer who sighted his goal, and through all kinds of handicaps . . . He stuck to his clubs . . . He never knew the word 'quit.'"[11] On the morning of Rhodes' funeral, John Bibb wrote in the hometown *Nashville Tennessean*, "It wasn't enough that Ted had the ability, desire, and dedication to overcome this challenge. He was trapped in the deepest hazard of all. In those days, Negroes weren't eligible to play the game, not in week-to-week, big time competition anyway."[12]

Thoughts of Rhodes weighed on many in the days following the funeral. Lee Elder struggled with his game. He fell from second place with one bad round to finish twelfth at the Flint Open in Michigan. At the American Golf Classic in Akron, Ohio, where he battled Jack Nicklaus the previous year in a sudden-death thriller, Elder failed to make the cut. When he arrived in New York for a tournament, he admitted he felt a void. "I always went to him [Rhodes] when my game went bad and he helped me immensely."[13]

In Los Angeles Maggie Hathaway was on a deadline. Her weekly golf column for the *Los Angeles Sentinel* was due. As she sat at a typewriter, she decided to fill the space with a tribute to Rhodes, who was a friend. "Goodbye to our beloved friend Ted Rhodes," she wrote. "Everybody loved Ted that loved golf." Hathaway closed her column with "So long old pro; hope you enjoy the heavenly courses where all golfers are equal and can join the PGA."[14]

Epilogue

In the days that followed Ted Rhodes' funeral, Nashville city councilman Bob Lillard was inspired to see his friend appropriately honored. A large man with a gravelly voice and an ever-present cigar, Lillard's previous involvement with golf, sixteen years earlier, put him on the receiving end of considerable criticism. Then Nashville was embroiled in controversy. Black golfers sought to open the city's three segregated municipal golf courses. When Lillard pushed his fellow city council members to instead set aside funds and land to create a golf course strictly for use by Nashville's Black citizens, it rankled those who fought fiercely for integration. But Lillard was both savvy and astute. He proposed the city issue $40,000 in bonds and set aside 109 acres of land it owned on the south banks of the Cumberland River in the Bordeaux section of Nashville and use it for a nine-hole golf course. Lillard's plan was approved by a 12–6 vote, and on July 10, 1954, the first of 108 golfers began play on the new Cumberland Golf Course.

Lillard's second foray into the golf realm provoked far less controversy. The plan he conceived in the late summer of 1969 poured from the heart and a long-standing friendship with Ted Rhodes. Lillard set the ball in motion with a letter to the Metropolitan Nashville Davidson County park board. In it he requested the board change the name of Cumberland Golf Course. When friends of Rhodes learned of Lillard's idea, many joined the campaign. Six weeks after the golfer's passing, the park board gave Lillard's idea its unanimous approval. The name Cumberland Golf Course was changed to Ted Rhodes Golf Course.

EPILOGUE

Six weeks after his death, Cumberland Golf Course was renamed in honor of Ted Rhodes. Courtesy of the author.

In the days, months, and years since Rhodes' passing, he has been remembered and immortalized with many touching and inspiring tributes. When the National Links Trust embarked upon a plan to rehabilitate historic Langston Golf Course, Rhodes became part of the project. The course, the second in the Washington, DC area, designated for Blacks, managed to survive several attempts at closure. Included in the rehabilitation plan was an idea to name each hole for a legendary figure in Black golf history. The first hole was named for John Shippen, while the names of Charley Sifford, Lee Elder, Althea

Gibson, and Tiger Woods were affixed to others. Hole number eight bears the name of Ted Rhodes.

For decades, the PGA's segregationist past continued to chafe at many. When Jim Remy was elected president of the organization in 2008, he wanted to do something about it. "They say that you can't turn back time," Remy said, "but you can do your very best to make it right."[1] In New Orleans at the PGA's annual meeting in November 2009, an item was placed on the agenda that called for righting a wrong of more than six decades. Members of the PGA board approved the idea in a unanimous vote. On November 10, 2009, PGA membership – forbidden during his life by the color of his skin – was awarded posthumously to Ted Rhodes. His daughter Deborah attended the ceremony. "It meant everything in the world to me," she said.[2]

Rhodes was not alone. Posthumous membership was also bestowed upon John Shippen and Bill Spiller, while Joe Louis received honorary PGA membership for his many contributions to golf. "The PGA of America believes these men, were it not for the color of their skin, would have been PGA members who play the game, teach the game and promote the game," Remy said.[3] Remy would later call the event the greatest experience of his tenure as president of the organization.

In 1970 a foundation was created to perpetuate the memory of Rhodes. An annual golf tournament is held at Ted Rhodes Golf Course. In its early years the tournament drew celebrity players such as Jackie Robinson and Don Newcombe and later welcomed such golf luminaries as Elder, Sifford, Pete Brown, and Calvin Peete. Moneys raised benefit several charities. The foundation is headed by Rhodes' daughter Peggy.

The prominence of Ted Rhodes and distinction for his skills have led to immortalization in several Halls of Fame. When the Black Golf Hall of Fame opened in 1986, Rhodes was made part of its inaugural class of inductees. Thirteen years later he was inducted into the Tennessee Golf Foundation Hall of Fame. "I am thrilled we are able to revive the memory of someone who had a really unique place in Tennessee golf history. The time was overdue to recognize his contribution to the game," said Dick Horton, president of the foundation.[4] Rhodes was a member of the inaugural class of the African American Golfers Hall of Fame. Three months after the PGA bestowed posthumous membership upon Rhodes, the Tennessee Sports Hall of Fame announced he had been chosen for induction as part of its class of 2010.

Of all the tributes paid Rhodes, one of the most unique came in 2017 from the fashion magazine, *GQ*. In an article titled "Golf's Fashion Masters," Rhodes was ranked third on the magazine's list of the best-dressed golfers of all time. "He had the look—a unique hipster jazz fest sense—and he was super cool," wrote Paul Henderson.[5]

During the late 1990s and through the 2000s, the remarkable rise of Tiger Woods to the pinnacle of his sport renewed interest in Black golfers from past eras. Woods himself held an appreciation for his pro golf predecessors. Much of it came from stories he was told by his father. But there was also gratitude that came from friendships forged with Black golf pioneers. One that drew a line from Woods to Ted Rhodes involved Lee Elder. In 1989 Earl Woods met Elder and asked him to take a look at his fourteen-year-old son. Elder agreed and played a round with the teenager at Fox Hills Golf Club in the Los Angeles area. That day launched a friendship that saw Elder become a mentor to Woods. It was a mentorship in which lessons and philosophies Elder had gleaned from Rhodes were passed along.

Each decade brings with it new stars whose achievements relegate those of their predecessors to the recesses of history. The depths of those recesses are often in direct correspondence to the numbers of remaining witnesses. In the case of Ted Rhodes, we are left with the words of those who saw him the most. Men like Bob Devine, who caddied for top Black and White golfers, held Rhodes in high regard. "Rhodes was probably one of the greatest players ever. He was fantastic," Devine said.[6] Few saw more of Rhodes than Lee Elder. "When I tell people about Teddy Rhodes' greatness," said Elder, they sometimes look at me like he couldn't have been that good. But he truly was great, a full notch up from me and the other Black players. It was Teddy who helped me when I was about eighteen, let me caddie for him and taught me how to play. I learned a lot by just watching Teddy. Only two men I was to see later compared to Teddy as a ball-striker: Ben Hogan, and Tommy Bolt in his prime. Teddy was good with every club in the bag, and he hit it flush every time. Only Hogan controlled the really small area through impact as well.[7]

Charley Sifford was much more succinct. When asked who he thought was the greatest Black golfer ever he replied, "Ain't no think in it. I know he was. Nobody could play as consistently as Teddy."[8]

But for Ted Rhodes his true measure of greatness was as a golf pioneer. It was Joe Louis who kicked the door open to create PGA opportunities for African American golfers. Rhodes was the man who took advantage. The invitations he received from PGA tournaments in the summer of 1952 and 1953 came about because of his combination of golf skills and demeanor. It was the character and acumen of Ted Rhodes that paved the way for Charley Sifford, Lee Elder, Pete Brown, Jim Dent, and Calvin Peete. They, in turn, helped to inspire and pave the way for Tiger Woods.

Said a golfer at the 1965 Eastern Open Invitational, "Anything that ever happens to a Negro golfer is due to the dedication of Ted Rhodes. He did for us what Jackie Robinson did in baseball, but it's a shame he's never gotten the public credit he deserves."[9]

NOTES

Introduction

1. Karen Crouse, "At Augusta National, Not Talking About Race Is Tradition," November 10, 2020, www.NewYorkTimes.com
2. Tiger Woods, "Interviewed by Jim Nantz, 1997 Masters Tournament Final Round Broadcast," April 13, 1997, YouTube.com.
3. Mike Tschappat, "To Elder, Nothing's Changed," *Daily Record*, August 10, 1980, 35.
4. Chip Alexander, "Elder Still Working on Behalf of Minorities," *Grand Island Independent*, June 4, 2008, 23.
5. Daniel K. Knapp, "Charlie Keeps His Cool," *Los Angeles Times*, June 22, 1969, 498.
6. Jim Gullo, "A Salute to Sweet Swinger," May 31, 1993, SI.com.
7. Dick Young, "Young Ideas," *New York Daily News*, April 16, 1967, 453.
8. Todd Graff, "The Clause That Closed a Rule in the PGA of America's Constitution Kept African Americans Out Of the Country's Top Tournaments From 1943 to 1961," April 21, 2001, Greensboro.com.
9. Bruce Berlet, "Woods' First Major Title a Sports Masterpiece," *Hartford Courant*, April 14, 1997, 128.
10. "A Time to Remember the All-Time Greats," *Philadelphia Tribune*, July 11, 1997, 9E.
11. Renee Graham, "k.d. Lang Dresses Up, Dumbs Down in *Vogue* Spread," *Commercial Appeal*, July 20, 1997, 56.

Chapter 1

1. Plessey vs Ferguson, 163 U.S. 537, (1896).
2. 1 John 4:7.
3. Ted Rhodes, "Tourney Near," *Metropolitan Weekly*, September 1–15, 1980, 19.
4. Will Grimsley, "Curry Ranked No. 1," *Tennessean (Nashville)*, July 9, 1939, 12.

5   John Bibb, "Sports Scope," *Tennessean (Nashville)*, July 9, 1969, 28.

6   Will Grimsley, "Bob York's Rally . . . " *Tennessean (Nashville)*, January 1, 1939, 19.

7   Will Grimsley, "Golf's Brown Bomber." *Tennessean (Nashville)*, August 10, 1941, 35.

8   Bob Rule, "Memphis State's Golf Capital? Nashville Just as Strong," *Nashville Banner*, July 14, 1941, 8.

9   Will Grimsley, "Middlecoff Beats Brothers 5 and 4, to Retain Title," *Tennessean (Nashville)*, July 13, 1941, 25.

10 Grimsley, "Golf's Brown Bomber."

11 Grimsley, "Golf's Brown Bomber."

Chapter 2

1   Wilfred Smith, "57,000 See Louis Stop Carnera in Sixth," *Chicago Tribune*, June 26, 1935, 1.

2   William G. Nunn, "I Feel That the Race's Prayers Were Answered," *Pittsburgh Courier*, June 29, 1935, 1.

3   Dean Gordon E. Hancock, "Joe Louis Idol of the Nation," *The Weekly Review (Birmingham)*, July 6, 1946, 4.

4   Heywood Broun, "It Seems to Me," *Pittsburgh Press*, June 28, 1935, 25.

5   Grantland Rice, "The Sportlight," *Pittsburgh Post-Gazette*, July 16, 1945, 16.

6   Curt Sylvester, "They Remember a Young Fighter," *Detroit Free Press*, April 13, 1981, 54.

7   Sylvester, "They Remember a Young Fighter."

8   Grantland Rice, "Louis Chills Paycheck in Two Rounds," *Des Moines Tribune*, March 30, 1940, 6.

9   Braven Dyer, "The Sports Parade," *Los Angeles Times*, April 13, 1939, 26.

10 Charles Johnson, "The Lowdown on Sports," *Minneapolis Star*, July 7, 1948, 33.

11 "Detroit Okays Rackham Course for Louis Tourney," *Chicago Defender*, March 29, 1941, 22.

12 "Biggest Golf Tourney Opens Here," *Detroit Tribune*, August 16, 1941, 7.

13 Art McMahon, "The Sportsman's Corner," *Herald-News*, September 30, 1941, 20.

14 Wendell Smith, "Louis Kayoes Nova in 6th," *Pittsburgh Courier*, October 4, 1941, 1.

15 "15th AAF in Italy," *The Macon News (Georgia)*, September 10, 1944, 29.

16 Bob Stedler, "Sport Comment," *Buffalo Evening News*, December 21, 1944, 29.

17 "Well, Whadya Ya Know?" *San Pedro News-Pilot*, July 4, 1944, 7.

18 Stedler, "Sport Comment."

19 Richard Bak, "The Brown Bomber Was No Average Joe," May 22, 2012, vintagedetroit.com.

20 Jack Hand, "Joe Louis Is Civilian Again and in Good Shape," *Casper Star-Tribune*, October 2, 1945, 7.

21 "Joe Louis Visits Coast, on Benny Show," *The Daily Herald (Provo, UT)*, October 22, 1945, 10.

22 Walt Jayroe, "Closed Opens," *The Arizona Republic (Phoenix)*, January 13, 1980, 65.

23 "Sepia Golfers Perform Well in Southern California Open," *California Eagle*, November 8, 1945, 17.

24 Bob Williams, "Bobbing Along," *Cleveland Call and Post*, July 13, 1946, 7N.

Chapter 3

1 "Rhodes Credits Brinke for Putting Accuracy," *Michigan Chronicle*, September 10, 1949, 12.

2 "Top Notch Golfers Are Entered in Chicago Tourney," *The Paterson Morning Call*, July 17, 1946, 19.

3 Forrest R. Kyle, "Once Over Lightly," *Herald Review (Decatur, IL)*, July 24, 1946, 5.

4 "Teddy Rhodes Wins Colored Golf Tourney," *New Castle News*, August 12, 1946, 14.

5 "Sentinel Sports Staff Selects Honor Roll of Outstanding Athletes for Negro History Week," *Los Angeles Sentinel*, February 13, 1947, 22.

6 Russ Cowans, "Sports Chatter," *Michigan Chronicle*, July 27, 1946, 14.

7 Don J. Davis, "Houston Open to Draw Top Golfers," *Pittsburgh Courier*, June 7, 1947, 11.

8 Russ Cowans, "Sports Chatter," *Michigan Chronicle*, August 7, 1947, 15.

9 Wendell Smith, "The Sports Beat," *Pittsburgh Courier*, August 16, 1947, 14.

10 "Rhodes Wins Wake Robin; Louis Quits," *Cleveland Call and Post*, September 13, 1947, 10B.

11 Ralph Trost, "Fore the Golfer," *Brooklyn Daily Eagle*, June 10, 1949, 19.

12 Peg Johnson, "Keller Fans Learn Golfers Believe Silence is Golden," *Minneapolis Star Tribune*, July 11, 1955, 1.

13 "Rhodes Credits Brike for Putting Accuracy."

14 Jack Saunders, "Wheeler Defeats Rhodes," *Pittsburgh Courier*, September 6, 1947, 15.

Chapter 4

1 Harold V. Ratliff, "PGA Took Step Toward Right Direction in Naming George," *Charlotte News*, March 2, 1948, 17.

2 Ratliff, "PGA Took Step Toward Right Direction in Naming George."

3 Robert Joseph Allen, "The Odyssey of Ted Rhodes," *Golf*, February 1961, 47.

4 Hannibal Coons, "Please Go Away, Says the PGA," *SPORT*, July 1949, 86.

5 Bill Spiller, "Spiller Gives Sentinel Exclusive Story of Golf Struggles," *Los Angeles Sentinel*, January 29, 1948, 23.

6 Herman Hill, "Barred From Meet, Spiller and Rhodes File Suits," *Pittsburgh Courier*, January 24, 1948, 17.

7 Alan Ward, "On Second Thought," *Oakland Tribune*, January 13, 1948, 18.

8 "PGA Rule Bars Star," *The San Francisco Examiner*, January 13, 1948, 18.

9 Louis Moore, "We Will Win the Day: The Civil Rights Movement, the Black Athlete, and the Quest for Equality," *Praeger Publishers*, September 21, 2017, 68.

10 Edwin B. Henderson, "Los Angeles Open Was Open to All," *Cleveland Call and Post*, January 19, 1952, 1D.

11 Henderson, "Los Angeles Open Was Open to All."

12 Joel W. Smith, "U. S. Open Golf Tourney 'Open' for First Time in Long History," *Atlanta Daily World*, June 15, 1949, 5.

13 Ed Schoenfeld, "Officials Shelve Richmond Open," *Oakland Tribune*, May 12, 1948, 25.

14 Conklin Bray, "Sports Round Up," *Detroit Tribune*, July 3, 1948, 7.

15 Jim Scott, "Scott's Sports Shop," *Berkeley Daily Gazette*, January 17, 1948, 9.

16 "St. Paul 'Open' Bars Top Golfers," *Minneapolis Spokesman*, August 13, 1948, 1.

17 Paul McCarthy, "Lookin 'em Over," *Redwood City Tribune*, January 14, 1952, 6.

18 "Report PGA Ban on Negroes Off," *Oakland Tribune*, September 21, 1948, 31.

19 "Bill Spiller, Rhodes, Win PGA Golf Suit," *Detroit Tribune*, September 25, 1948, 1.

20 Conklin Bray, "The Round-up," *Detroit Tribune*, October 2, 1948, 11.

21 "Jim Crow Rocked by 3 Stunning Blows," *Pittsburgh Courier*, October 2, 1948, 7.

22 A. S. "Doc" Young, Sportivanting," *Cleveland Call and Post*, October 2, 1948, 6B.

23 Hugh Fullerton Jr., "Sports Roundup," *The Leaf-Chronicle*, December 17, 1948, 5.

24 Coons, "Please Go Away, Says the PGA."

Chapter 5

1 Ward Gillilan, "Sportsward," *Pomona Progress Bulletin*, June 7, 1948, 10.

2 Maxwell Stiles, "Sarazen Tabs Hogan for U.S. Open Crown," *Long Beach Press-Telegram*, June 10, 1948, 35.

3 Herman Hill, "Rhodes Loses; Driving Thrills," *Pittsburgh Courier*, June 19, 1948, 10.

4 A. S. "Doc" Young, "Sportivanting," *Los Angeles Sentinel*, March 3, 1949, A6.

5 "Snead, Rhodes Shoot 67s on Riviera Course," *Los Angeles Times*, June 8, 1948, 31.

6 Stiles, "Sarazen Tabs Hogan for U.S. Open Crown."

7 Bill Matney, "Jumpin the Gun," *Michigan Chronicle*, August 15, 1953, 12.

8 Charles Bartlett, "Hogan, Worsham Tie at 67 for U.S. Open Lead," *Chicago Tribune*, June 11, 1948, 33.

9 Beth Hightower, "Sunday's Short Putts," *Sacramento Bee*, June 13, 1948, 19.

10 Ned Cronin, "Ned Cronin," *Los Angeles Daily News*, June 14, 1948, 25.

11 Charles Curtis, "Golfagraphs," *Los Angeles Times*, June 13, 1948, 18.

12 Hill, "Rhodes Loses; Driving Thrills."

13 Hill, "Rhodes Loses; Driving Thrills."

14 "Golfer Ted Rhodes, A Worthy Pioneer," *Pittsburgh Courier*, June 12, 1948, 20.

Chapter 6

1. "Teddy Rhodes Plans in L.A. Golf Tournament," *California Eagle*, January 9, 1947, 17.
2. Cal Jacox, "From the Press Box," *New Journal and Guide*, June 4, 1949, 13.
3. "Good Sportsmanship First Mr. Rhodes!" *Los Angeles Sentinel*, January 14, 1949, A6.
4. A.S. "Doc" Young, "Sportivanting," *Los Angeles Sentinel*, January 20, 1949, A6.
5. Young, "Sportivanting."
6. Young, "Sportivanting."
7. Young, "Sportivanting."
8. Peter Carlson, "An Ugly Test of Jackie Robinson's Will," June 7, 2017, Historynet.com.
9. Tommy Holmes, "Public Will Decide on Jackie Robinson," *Brooklyn Daily Eagle*, October 31, 1945, 17.
10. "Jackie Robinson," *Alabama Tribune*, April 18, 1947, 8.
11. Wendell Smith, "Sports Beat," *Pittsburgh Courier*, June 12, 1948, 13.
12. William Tucker, "Jackie Robinson Should Follow After Champion Joe Louis to be Successful," *Durham Morning Herald*, October 30, 1945, 10.
13. Peter Andrews, "The Prizefighter and the Press," *FIVE*, May/June 1986, 61.
14. "Louis Tells Eloquent Story of Fight Against Prejudice," *Pittsburgh Courier*, November 22, 1947, 13.
15. C. E. McBride, "Sporting Comment," *Kansas City Star*, October 6, 1946, 14.
16. Wendell Smith, "The Sports Beat," *Pittsburgh Courier*, March 22, 1947, 14.
17. Smith, "The Sports Beat."
18. Rube Samuelson, "Quiet Please!" *Pasadena Star-News*, April 16, 1947, 18.
19. Tommy Holmes, "Clinical Notes on Opening Day," *Brooklyn Daily Eagle*, April 16, 1947, 19.
20. "Jackie Has Painful Bone Spur Removed From Foot," *Los Angeles Tribune*, December 20, 1947, 13.
21. Hannibal Coons, "Please Go Away, Says the PGA," *SPORT*, July 1949, 68.
22. Russ Cowans, "Sports Chatter," *Michigan Chronicle*, July 10, 1948, 10.
23. Leon Snead, "Deadline Dust," *Afro-American*, July 10, 1948, 4.
24. Sam Lacy, "Ted Rhodes Hedges on Anti-Press Statement," *Afro-American*, July 17, 1948, 8.

25 Lacy, "Ted Rhodes Hedges on Anti-Press Statement."
26 Deborah Rhodes, telephone interview, January 17, 2024.
27 Ben Thomas, "Footlights," *St. Louis Argus*, July 24, 1936, 4.
28 "St. Louis Talent Used in 'Ziggie' Johnson's Windy City Revue," *Call*, September 13, 1940, 15.
29 Billy Rowe, "Billy Rowe's Notebook," *Pittsburgh Courier*, January 7, 1950.

Chapter 7

1 Dick Hyland, "Behind the Line," *Los Angeles Times*, January 30, 1940, 31.
2 Ches Washington, "Louis Queries Crosby on 'Igging' Ted Rhodes," *Pittsburgh Courier*, January 28, 1950, 21.
3 Washington, "Louis Queries Crosby on 'Igging' Ted Rhodes."
4 Bob Hall, "Half of Record Field Tees Off Tomorrow in Long Beach Open," *Long Beach Press-Telegram*, January 18, 1950, 18.
5 Washington, "Louis Helps Launch Attack on Link Bias."
6 Frank T. Blair, "Frankly Speaking," *Long Beach Press-Telegram*, January 20, 1950, 14.
7 Blair, "Frankly Speaking."
8 Joe Louis, "Joe's Write Hand," *New York Age*, January 28, 1950, 16.
9 "Topped Lawson Little," *The Pittsburgh Courier*, January 20, 1951, 15.
10 Billy Rowe, "Billy Rowe's Notebook," *Pittsburgh Courier*, January 20, 1951, 16.
11 Halley Harding, "Lily White Tournament," *Los Angeles Sentinel*, January 25, 1951, 5.
12 "A Loud Protest," *The Chicago Defender*, January 27, 1951, 16.
13 Marion Jackson, "Sports of the World," *Atlanta Daily World*, June 2, 1951, 5.
14 Jackson, "Sports of the World."

Chapter 8

1 "Walter Winchell: The Power of Gossip," September 15, 2020, PBS.org.
2 Walter Winchell, "The Walter Winchell Show," January 13, 1952. New York Public Library, Billy Rose Theatre Division, Walter Winchell Collection.

NOTES

3 Jimmy Cannon, "Jimmy Cannon Says," *Newsday*, January 15, 1952, 25.

4 "Ed Sullivan Quits PGA Over Race Ban," *Afro-American*, January 26, 1952, 17.

5 "Joe Louis Barred from Golfing in San Diego Over PGA Rules," *Eugene Guard*, January 14, 1952, 1.

6 "Joe Louis Declares War on PGA Rule Banning Negro Golfers," *Norfolk Ledger-Dispatch*, January 14, 1952, 1.

7 "Brown Bomber Battles Bigots," *The Call*, January 18, 1952, 10.

8 Paul McCarthy, "Lookin 'em Over," *Redwood City Tribune*, January 14, 1952, 6.

9 "Joe Louis Barred from Golfing in San Diego by PGA Rules."

10 "Joe Louis Declares War on PGA Rule Banning Negro Golfers," 16.

11 Ray McNally, "Sportingly Yours," *Tucson Daily Citizen*, January 30, 1952, 15.

12 "Joe Louis Declares War on PGA Rule Banning Negro Golfers."

13 Red Smith, "Views of Sport," *The Philadelphia Inquirer*, January 16, 1952, 49.

14 Bill Corum, "Corum Advises," *Urbana (Ohio) Daily Citizen*, January 15, 1952, 5.

15 Ches Washington, "Ches Says," *Pittsburgh Courier*, January 26, 1952, 15.

16 Joe Louis, "Louis to Fight Ban on Negro Golfers," *Bryan Times*, January 16, 1952, 4.

17 Horton Smith, "PGA Head Says Group Will Study Ban Rule," *Bryan Times*, January 16, 1952, 4.

18 Al Barkow, "Bill Spiller, Pioneer Forced PGA to Change Its Ways," Oklahoma Golf Hall of Fame.

19 "PGA Okays Louis in San Diego Golf," *Los Angeles Times*, January 16, 1952, 49.

20 Bob Myers, "Ted Kroll's 65 Leads San Diego as Louis Plays," *Morning Call (Allentown, PA)*, January 18, 1952, 29.

21 Jack Murphy, "So They Tell Me," *San Diego Union*, January 18, 1952, B3.

22 "Louis Says Seven Negroes to Enter Phoenix Tourney," *Santa Barbara News-Press*, January 21, 1952, 13.

23 Brad Pye Jr., "Prying Pye in Prep Sportdom," *California Eagle*, January 24, 1952, 6.

24 Marion E. Jackson, "Sports of the World," *Alabama Tribune*, January 25, 1952, 7.

25 "Joe Louis Deserts Golf Fight," *California Eagle*, January 17, 1852, 1.

26 Myers, "Ted Kroll's 65 Leads San Diego as Louis Plays."

27 W. Jay Burk, "Four Negroes Qualify for Phoenix Open Golf," *Arizona Republic (Phoenix)*, January 23, 1952, 9.

28 "Memorable Tournament," January 25, 1952, 6.

29 Jack Stevenson, "Boros Fires 66 to Lead Phoenix Open Meet," *Arizona Daily Star (Tucson)*, January 25, 1952, 25.

30 "Revolta Topped Phoenix Feat in '33," *Arizona Republic (Phoenix)*, January 26, 1952, 17.

31 Robert Joseph Allen, "The Odyssey of Ted Rhodes," *Golf*, February 1961, 18.

32 John Wood, "Rhodes Gets Near Record 64 in Tournament Tuneup." *Sioux City Journal*, July 23, 1952, 15.

33 Wood, "Rhodes Gets Near Record 64 in Tournament Tuneup."

34 Charles Bartlett, "Tam Go9lf Field Pursues Unknown," *Chicago Daily Tribune*, August 1, 1952, 45.

35 Arnott Duncan, "Dunkin' with Dunc," *The (Phoenix) Arizona Republic (Phoenix)*, January 26, 1952, 6.

Chapter 9

1 Harry Grayson, "Ted Rhodes Is Best; But Only Dozen Negroes Among Top Golfers," *Odessa American*, February 5, 1952, 7.

2 Walter Jayroe, "Closed Opens," *Arizona Republic (Phoenix)*, January 13, 1980, 59.

3 Will Robinson, "Pick-Ups Along The UGA Tourney Trail," *Pittsburgh Courier*, July 15, 1950, 24.

4 Russ J. Cowans, "Cowans Corner," *Chicago Defender*, June 17, 1950, 16.

5 "UGA Highlights," *The Pittsburgh Courier*, August 30, 1952, 26.

6 Dick Cullum, "Cullum's Column," *Minneapolis Tribune*, July 8, 1948, 16.

7 Tom Briere, "Louis' Tutor Paces Elk Golf," *Minneapolis Tribune*, July 7, 1948, 15.

8 "Joe Louis Calls Turn in Golf, Too," *Minneapolis Tribune*, July 7, 1948, 15.

9 Bill Matney, "Rhodes Cops Third Straight Tourney," *Michigan Chronicle*, September 10, 1949, 12.

10 Bill Matney, "Has Ted Rhodes "Outgrown" Negro Golf? Statistics Support Claim," *Michigan Chronicle*, June 18, 1949, 10.

11 Bill Matney, "Spotlight," *Michigan Chronicle*, January 19, 1952, 21.

12 Matney, "Spotlight."

13 Bill Matney, "Jumpin' the Gun," *Michigan Chronicle*, July 22, 1950, 12.

14 A.S. "Doc" Young, "Sports Show," *Los Angeles Sentinel*, February 14, 1957, C1.

15 John Fuster, "Tournament at Cleveland Proves Golf Is a Game for All the People," *Cleveland Call and Post*, September 8, 1951, 2.

Chapter 10

1 Russ J. Cowans, "Rhodes Will Not Defend Title in Louis Tourney," *Chicago Defender*, August 13, 1949, 15.

2 Robert Morrison, "Ted Rhodes, Louis's Golf Teacher, Wins Tourney With 66," *St. Louis Post-Dispatch*, May 4, 1953, 5B.

3 Ted Reeve, "Sporting Extras," *The Ottawa Citizen*, July 11, 1953, 34.

4 Jim Klobuchar, "Clark, Rhodes Card 66s in St. Paul' Ulrich at 68," *Winona Daily News*, July 17, 1953, 12.

5 Joe Hendrickson, "'Do Better or Come Home,' Wife Warns Ted—So He Did," *Minneapolis Tribune*, July 17, 1953, 18.

6 Glen Gaff, "Clark, Rhodes Fire 66s, Led Keller Open," *Minneapolis Tribune*, July 17, 1953, 18.

7 Jim Byrne, "His 68 Is Good but Ulrich Has Done Better," *Minneapolis Star*, July 17, 1953, 16.

8 Joe Hendrickson, "Haas Combined Putting, Irons for Keller 'Best,'" *Minneapolis Tribune*, July 18, 1953, 14.

9 Hendrickson, "Haas Combined Putting, Irons for Keller 'Best.'"

10 Hendrickson, "Haas Combined Putting, Irons for Keller 'Best.'"

11 Glen Gaff, "'Didn't Have It,' Says Haas After 70," *Minneapolis Tribune*, July 19, 1953, 33.

12 "Ted Rhodes Surprises St. Paul Golf Field," *Afro American*, July 25, 1953, 15.

13 "Hughes, Rhodes & St. Paul Open," *Minneapolis Spokesman*, July 24, 1953, 2.

14 Joe Hendrickson, "Mayfield Not an Upstart, Was 'Perfect' Says Burke," *Minneapolis Tribune*, July 20, 1953, 24.

15 Jimmy Griffin, "Griffin's Sports," *St. Paul Recorder*, July 24, 1953, 8.

16. "Old Story for Rhodes, 'and Then They Put Me With Snead,'" *Minneapolis Star*, August 25, 1956, 12.

17. "Hughes, Rhodes & St. Paul Open."

18. "Despite Open Failure, Rhodes A Top Prospect," *New Journal and Guide*, June 23, 1956, 17.

19. "Four Players Plan to Play Mexican Event," *News and Observer*, February 12, 1951, 11.

20. Edgar C. Greene, "Teddy Rhodes Only Needs More Competitive Action," *Pittsburgh Courier*, June 18, 1949, 23.

21. Bill Matney, "Jumpin' the Gun," *Michigan Chronicle*, August 15, 1953, 12.

22. Greene, "Teddy Rhodes Only Needs More Competitive Action."

23. Frank Lett Sr., "The 19th Hole," *Michigan Chronicle*, July 17, 1954, 11.

Chapter 11

1. "Joe Louis Broke; Just Spent All," *Santa Barbara News Press*, January 19, 1946, 3.

2. "Joe Louis Wouldn't Alter Life Except Divorce," *Detroit Tribune*, October 15, 1955, 5.

3. Robert Josephy Allen, "The Odyssey of Ted Rhodes." *Golf*, February 1961: 47.

4. Red O'Donnell, "Top O' the Mornin,'" *Tennessean (Nashville)*, July 21, 1953, 4.

5. O'Donnell, "Top O' the Mornin.'"

6. Ziggy Johnson, "Zagging With Ziggy," *Michigan Chronicle*, March 13, 1954, 9.

7. "Down the Fairway," *Chicago Defender*, July 29, 1950, 18.

8. Sam Lacy, "A to Z Sports," *Afro-American*, August 2, 1958, 13.

9. Lacy, "A to Z Sports."

10. Sam Lacy, "Jackie Joins Swing to Burke Golf Sets Because of Policy," *Afro-American*, April 7, 1956, 15.

11. "Manhattan Café One of Finest Dining Rooms in North Ohio," *Cleveland Call and Post*, June 20, 1953, 6.

Chapter 12

1. "Ted Rhodes Rallies to Take UGA Golf," *Afro-American*, September 7, 1957, 13.
2. "Sifford Elated Over Victory, Hopes to Break Down Color Barrier in PGA," *York Daily Record*, November 12, 1957, 27.
3. Jerry Wynn, "Sifford Wins Golf Playoff," *Long Beach Independent*, November 11, 1957, 1.
4. Hank Hollingworth, "Sports Merry Go Round," *Long Beach Independent*, November 14, 1957, 30.
5. "Sifford Is Golf's Answer to Robinson and Gibson," *Newsday*, November 11, 1957, 95.
6. "Negro Pro Wins Open Golf," *The Boston Globe*, November 11, 1957, 7.
7. "A First: Negro Wins Golf Meet," *Detroit Free Press*, November 11, 1957, 35.
8. Marion E. Jackson, "World of Sports," *Alabama Tribune*, November 15, 1957, 6.
9. Deborah Rhodes, telephone interview with author, June 21, 2024.
10. "Bobby Jones, The Game of Life," https://libraries.emory.edu/events-exhibits/exhibits/bobby-jones.

Chapter 13

1. Tommy Picou, "Tommy's Corner," *Chicago Daily Defender*, February 21, 1962, 23.
2. A.S. "Doc" Young, "Refreshing World of Sports," *Los Angeles Sentinel*, May 17, 1962, B11.
3. Frank Eck, "PGA Takes on Added Meaning," *Delaware County Daily Times*, July 25, 1961, 14.
4. "PGA Official Assails Mosk," *Los Angeles Mirror*, May 15, 1961, 25.
5. "Sifford's Record Too Poor—PGA," *Los Angeles Mirror*, June 22, 1961, 40.
6. "PGA Eliminates Controversial Caucasian Membership Clause," *Medford Mail Tribune*, November 10, 1961, 13.
7. Frank Eck, "Maybe Sifford Will Play Better Now," *The Daily Herald*, November 30, 1961, 22.
8. Stan Wood, "Race Clause Ban Hailed by Sifford," *Los Angeles Mirror*, November 10, 1961, 17.

9   Marion E. Jackson, "Sports of the World," *Atlanta Daily World*, July 14, 1962, 5.
10 Marion E. Jackson, "Sports of the World."

Chapter 14

1   F. M. Williams, "Former Tennis Great Althea Now Finds Golf Her Game," *Tennessean (Nashville)*, April 26, 1967, 28.
2   "Gotta Have Heart, Rhodes Has More," *The Evening Sun* (Baltimore), August 13, 1965, 33.
3   Jimmie Bowman, "Tee to Green," *St. Paul Recorder*, July 18, 1963, 8.
4   John Gates, "Gibson Out to Conquer Golf," *The Charlotte Observer*, March 31, 1965, 12.
5   Milton Gross, "'I'll Be Among Very Best,' Says Golfer Althea Gibson," *Buffalo Evening News*, April 4, 1964, 29.
6   John Bibb, "Sports Scope," *Tennessean (Nashville)*, July 9, 1969, 28.
7   Jimmy Davy, "Elder's Golf Success Beyond Early Dreams," *Tennessean (Nashville)*, September 11, 1970, 48.
8   Pat Harmon, "Elder Plays for His Teacher," *The Cincinnati Post*, July 7, 1969, 16.
9   Deborah Rhodes, personal interview with author, July 9, 2024.
10 Dick Young, "Young Ideas," *The New York Daily News*, April 2, 1967, 134.
11 Young, "Young Ideas."
12 Young, "Young Ideas."
13 Deborah Rhodes, telephone interview with author, June 21, 2024.

Chapter 15

1   Pat Harmon, "Elder Plays for His Teacher," *The Cincinnati Post*, July 7, 1969, 16.
2   John Bibb, "Elder Recalls Ted Rhodes' Fatherly Help," *Tennessean (Nashville)*, July 6, 1969, 61.
3   "Loses Buick Open to Hill," *Call and Post*, July 12, 1969, 11B.

4 "Kemper Capers," *The Charlotte News*, June 21, 1969, 6.

5 John Bibb, "Sports Scope," *Tennessean (Nashville)*, August 13, 1968, 15.

6 Bibb, "Sports Scope."

7 Frank H. Saunders, "What Really Happened to Lee Elder's Game," *Michigan Chronicle*, July 12, 1969, A1.

8 Bud Burns, "Rock Had a Soft Heart," *Tennessean (Nashville)*, September 10, 1969, 30.

9 Deborah Rhodes, telephone interview with the author, July 28, 2024.

10 "Ted Rhodes Dies," *The Atlanta Journal*, July 6, 1969, 53.

11 "First Negro Golf Pro Ted Rhodes Succumbs," *Call and Post*, July 12, 1969, 11B.

12 John Bibb, "Sports Scope," *Tennessean (Nashville)*, July 9, 1969, 28.

13 "Golf Opens Many Doors for Elder," *Newsday*, July 30, 1969, 37.

14 Maggie Hathaway, "Maggie Hathaway's Tee Time," *Los Angeles Sentinel*, July 10, 1969, B3.

Epilogue

1 Bob Denney, "From the Ring to the Course: How Legendary Boxing Champion Joe Louis Fought for Diversity in Golf," February 16, 2018, www.pga.com

2 Deborah Rhodes, telephone interview with author, June 21, 2024.

3 Craig Dolch, "Remy Has Played Key Role in PGA of America's Success," *Press Journal (Vero Beach, FL)*, April 7, 2016, 27.

4 Wendy Smith, "Sports A.M.," *The Tennessean*, November 27, 1998, 198.

5 Paul Henderson, "Golf's Fashion Masters," September 4, 2017, GQ-magazine.co.uk.

6 Vartan Kupelian, and Mike O'Hara, "Behind the Scenes," *The Detroit News*, April 20, 1997, 30.

7 Lee Elder, "My Shot, Lee Elder," August 27, 2019, Golf Digest.com.

8 Jim Gullo, "A Salute to Sweet Swinger," May 31, 1993, SI.com.

9 "Gotta Have Heart, Rhodes Has More," *The Evening Sun* (Baltimore), August 13, 1965, 33.

BIBLIOGRAPHY

"'Almost Threw It Away.'" *Charlotte News*, March 1, 1954.
"'You Can't Win' Negro Golfers Learn in National Tourney." *New Journal and Guide*, August 4, 1928.
"157 Golfers Poised for Richmond Open." *Santa Ana Register*, January 14, 1948.
"1950s Golf Champions in UGA." *Pittsburgh Courier*, July 14, 1951.
"4,000 Turn Out to Watch 24th Annual Midwestern Golf." *Chicago Defender*, July 14, 1962.
"A Keller Leftover." *Minneapolis Star*, July 21, 1953.
"A Son for Joe Louis." *Kansas City Times*, June 7, 1947.
"A Time to Remember the All-time Greats." *Philadelphia Tribune*, July 11, 1997.
"Al Zimmerman's 136 Leads Los Angeles Open Qualifiers." *Philadelphia Inquirer*, January 3, 1946.
"All Eyes Will be on Chula Vista as $10,000 Tourney Opens Next Thursday." *Chula Vista Star*, January 10, 1952.
"Bannerettes." *Nashville Banner*, September 11, 1926.
"Barred from Golf Tourney." *St. Louis Argus*, August 20, 1948.
"Barron Hikes All-American Links Lead." *Arizona Republic*, July 28, 1946.
"Barron Shades Vines to Take Chicago Golf." *Los Angeles Times*, July 29, 1946.
"Belle Meade As It Was in Heyday of Its Glory." *Nashville Banner*, October 13, 1918.
"Belle Meade Club Contributes Largely to Social Activities." *Tennessean*, May 27, 1923.
"Belle Meade Club to be Scene of Debut Party This Evening." *Nashville Banner*, December 9, 1939.
"Benefit Fund Nets Over $1,200 for Nashville's Rhodes." *Nashville Banner*, February 22, 1962.
"Benefit Planned for Ted Rhodes." *Pittsburgh Courier*, February 10, 1962.
"Best Amateur Golfers." *Boston Evening Transcript*, July 11, 1896.
"Bias Barred Golfers Ask $315,000 Damages." *California Eagle*, January 22, 1948.
"Big Sports Events of '48; and Disappointments, Too." *Tampa Bay Times*, December 31, 1948.
"Big Thrills Marked Sixth City Tourney Won by Ted Rhodes in 1949." *Chicago Defender*, June 24, 1950.
"Bill Spiller with Subpar 68 Takes L.A. Open Golf Lead." *Hollywood Citizen-News*, January 2, 1948.
"Billy Eckstine at Sunset Tonight." *Atlanta Daily World*, June 15, 1944.
"Billy Eckstine to Golf in Europe." *Detroit Tribune*, July 15, 1950.
"Billy Eckstine Wows Chicago." *Pittsburgh Courier*, August 26, 1944.
"Billy Eckstine's Ork Hailed as New Sensation." *Pittsburgh Courier*, August 19, 1944.
"Bing Crosby Given P.G.A. Membership." *San Pedro News-Pilot*, February 16, 1940.

"Bing Crosby to Use Ben Carter in First Film." *Michigan Chronicle*, August 12, 1944.
"Bradley Captures Montebello Event." *Nevada State Journal*, December 21, 1948.
"By-Law That Should Go." *Ventura County Star*, January 24, 1952.
"Caddies Will Have Their Inning at Golf." *Town Talk*, July 11, 1925.
"Camera Highlights From the Joe Louis Golf Tourney." *Michigan Chronicle*, July 27, 1946.
"Cars For the Negroes." *Morning News* (Savannah, GA), August 5, 1887.
"Charles Sifford Captures Atlantic City Golf Title." *New Journal and Guide*, June 26, 1954.
"Chicago Women's Golf Club to Honor Rhodes." *Philadelphia Tribune*, July 7, 1962.
"CIO Vice Presidents Criticize Professional Golf Ass. For Bias." *St. Louis Argus*, January 25, 1952.
"Clark, Middlecoff Pace Tucson Open Golf Field." *El Paso Times*, February 1, 1952.
"Cole Trophy Chase on at Belle Meade." *Nashville Banner*, May 20, 1926.
"Color Ban in Golf." *Oakland Tribune*, January 21, 1948.
"Country Club to Stage Top Golf Tourney." *Chula Vista Star*, August 30, 1951.
"Courier-Yorkshire Tourney Results." *Pittsburgh Courier*, August 16, 1947.
"Court Asked to Reconsider Golf Course Desegregation." *Nashville Banner*, May 2, 1956.
"Court Reinstates Negro Golf Players." *Scranton Republican*, August 4, 1928.
"Crosby Golf Tourney Listed as $5,000 Event." *Los Angeles Times*, November 12, 1941.
"Crosby to Use Ben Carter in First Film." *Michigan Chronicle*, August 12, 1944.
"D.C. Professional Wins the Mapledale Country Club Golf Tournament." *St. Louis Argus*, September 17, 1926.
"Death Notices." *Tennessean* (Nashville), March 18, 1929.
"Demaret Takes Early 36-Hole Lead in U.S. Open With 141." *St. Louis Star and Times*, June 11, 1948.
"Depression to Aid Golfers." *Tennessean*, May 22, 1932.
"Detroit Gets Joe Louis Golf and National Bowling Tourneys." *Michigan Chronicle*, November 25, 1944.
"Dinner Aids Golfer Rhodes." *Afro-American*, April 21, 1962.
"Down the Fairway." *Chicago Defender*, July 2, 1955.
"Down the Fairway." *Chicago Defender*, October 2, 1954.
"Down the Fairway." *New York Age*, September 25, 1954.
"Eckstine Band Makes $100,000 in 10 Week Span." *New York Amsterdam News*, October 28, 1944.
"Eckstine Grosses $30,000." *Pittsburgh Courier*, September 2, 1944.
"Elder Gate City Open Winner; Black Second." *Greensboro Daily News*, September 14, 1964.
"Encyclopedia of Cleveland History: Slaughter, Fleet." www.case.edu.
"Ernie Pieper Holds Lead in State Open Golf." *Los Angeles Times*, May 2, 1948.
"Fazio Choice in Fox Hills." *Daily News* (Los Angeles), November 2, 1945.
"Fechner Says C.C.C. Attacks Pressing Dual Problem." *Evening Star* (Washington, DC), April 4, 1939.
"Fires Par 72 in Negro Golf." *Pittsburgh Post-Gazette*, August 29, 1946.
"Five Local Golfers already Entered in June 18–20 Open." *Los Angeles Tribune*, June 14, 1947.
"For the Cup and Medal." *Chicago Tribune*, July 13, 1896.

"Ford's 200 Tops Golf." *San Francisco Examiner*, August 23, 1953.
"Foulis Wins Open Golf Championship at Shinnecock Hills." *Chicago Tribune*, July 19, 1896.
"Four White Men Arrested for Abuse to Negro Motorist." *Madison Journal*, August 24, 1951.
"Friction Flares Between P.G.A. Los Angeles Open." *Long Beach Press-Telegram*, January 24, 1948.
"Gambler Shoots Caddy in Texas." *Nashville Banner*, April 17, 1932.
"George May Thinks PGA Is All Wrong in Barring Negroes." *Fresno Bee*, January 24, 1948.
"George Van Elm Shows His Heels to Younger Men." *Nevada State Journal*, May 29, 1948.
"Gibson, Elders [sic] Win Titles in North-South Golf Meet." *Atlanta Daily World*, March 1, 1963.
"Golf Booms, 2,500 Needed for Pro Jobs." *Whittier News*, November 14, 1945.
"Golf Course Desegregation Cases." February 23, 2022, Golfblogger.com.
"Golf Crown to Wheeler." *Chicago Defender*, September 14, 1946.
"Golf Grows in Favor as Colored Clubs are Formed." *Philadelphia Tribune*, August 11, 1927.
"Golf Head Denies Ban on Joe Louis." *Napa Valley Register*, January 14, 1952.
"Golf's Stop Stars Set for Courier-Yorkshire Tournament." *Pittsburgh Courier*, August 2, 1947.
"Golfers Point to State Open in Fresno." *Fresno Bee*, May 5, 1940.
"Golfers Put Scare Into LA Open Field." *New Journal and Guide*, January 10, 1948.
"Good Field for Tourney." *Chicago Tribune*, June 26, 1906.
"Grant Defeats Louis in Chicago Amateur; Ted Rhodes Wins Open." *Atlanta Daily World*, September 17, 1947.
"Great Golf by Foulis." *New York Sun*, July 19, 1896.
"Great Lakes Sepia Sailors Applaud 'Freedom the Banner' by Negro Sailor." *Cleveland Call and Post*, July 10, 1943.
"H. Wheeler and Mrs. Siler Win National Golf Championships." *St. Louis Argus*, September 15, 1933.
"Harrison Paces Richmond Open." *Decatur Daily Review*, January 16, 1948.
"Hello Civilian! It's Joe Louis Off for Series." *Detroit Free Press*, October 2, 1945.
"Here's Tee Times for Open Tourney." *Hollywood Citizen-News*, June 9, 1948.
"History on the Links." *Akron Beacon Journal*, May 25, 1997.
"Hook 'Em 'N Slice 'Em." *Nashville Banner*, June 19, 1921.
"Hotel Majestic Is Golf Headquarters." *Cleveland Call and Post*, July 12, 1947.
"Houston Bars Negroes; EP Takes No Action." *El Paso Herald-Post*, January 29, 1952.
"Houston Open to Draw Top Golfers." *Pittsburgh Courier*, June 7, 1947.
"How They Finished in U.S. Open Golf." *Los Angeles Times*, June 13, 1948.
"Jackie Joins Swing to Burke Golf Sets Because of Policy." *Afro-American*, April 7, 1956.
"Jackie Praised by Press." *New Journal and Guide*, April 19, 1947.
"Jim Crow Laws: 1866–1955." January 3, 2011, BlackPast.org.
"Jim Crow Laws: Tennessee, 1966–1955." www.Blackpast.org.
"Jim Crow." *Butler Courier* (Alabama), December 20, 1883.
"Joe in Main Attraction at Tourney." *Detroit Tribune*, July 21, 1945.

"Joe Johnson Holds Pace." *Michigan Chronicle*, January 3, 1948.
"Joe Louis and Friends Take Golf Tournament Spotlight." *Arizona Sun*, January 25, 1952.
"Joe Louis and Ted Rhodes Win in UGA Tourney." *Alabama Tribune*, September 7, 1951.
"Joe Louis and the PGA." *St. Paul Recorder*, January 18, 1952.
"Joe Louis Appears as Guest on Benny Show Sun." *California Eagle*, November 8, 1945.
"Joe Louis Arrives in Los Angeles." *Anaheim Bulletin*, October 23, 1945.
"Joe Louis Blasts PGA for Bar of Negro Golfers." *Jackson Advocate*, January 19, 1952.
"Joe Louis Blasts PGA for Nixing Negroes in Tee Tourney." *Monrovia Daily News-Post*, January 14, 1952.
"Joe Louis Café Closes in New York City." *The Black Dispatch*, March 15, 1947.
"Joe Louis Challenges PGA Ban; Smith Denies Discrimination." *Long Beach Independent*, January 15, 1952.
"Joe Louis Due to Don Uniform on Wednesday." *Detroit Free Press*, January 13, 1942.
"Joe Louis Enters Phoenix Tourney Qualifying Play." *Arizona Daily Sun*, January 22, 1952.
"Joe Louis Featured by Makers of Chesterfields." *Pittsburgh Courier*, May 31, 1947.
"Joe Louis Gets 160, Fails in 'View' Playoff." *Dayton Daily News*, August 6, 1945.
"Joe Louis Hooks and Jabs in Dayton Golf Tourney." *Dayton Herald*, August 6, 1945.
"Joe Louis Opens 49-Day Training Session for Conn." *Hollywood Citizen-News*, March 8, 1946.
"Joe Louis Paired with Horton Smith." *Greensboro Daily News*, January 17, 1952.
"Joe Louis Surprise Entrant in Miami View Open Sunday." *Dayton Daily News*, August 5, 1945.
"Joe Louis, Tired of Restin', Itching to Slap Somebody." *Akron Beacon Journal*, July 30, 1941.
"Joe Louis, Two Other Negroes Battle PGA Golf Ban." *Arizona Republic*, January 15, 1952.
"Joe Louis Wins Tiff with PGA Officials." *Oakland Tribune*, January 16, 1952.
"Joe Respects Charles." *Dayton Herald*, August 2, 1947.
"Joe's Pro Scared." *Detroit Evening Times*, August 15, 1941.
"Junior Chamber Prexy Issues Hot Blast at P.G.A.; Promises L.A. Open To Retain Status." *Valley Times*, January 24, 1948.
"L.A. Open Golf Lead Piled Up by Ted Rhodes." *Hollywood Citizen-News*, January 2, 1948.
"Large Field to Compete in Louis Open." *Detroit Tribune*, May 17, 1941.
"Layout of Riviera Golf Course for National Open." *Evening Vanguard* (Venice, CA), June 11, 1948.
"List of Canadian Open Money Winners." *Toronto Star*, July 13, 1953.
"Lloyd Mangrum Strolls Away with Top Golf Prize." *Los Angeles Times*, December 23, 1946.
"Local Golf Fans Lucky for Tourney." *Californian* (Salinas), December 21, 1946.
"Local Golfer Returns to L.A." *California Eagle*, August 9, 1945.
"Locke's 66 Ties Oliver, Keiser; Bud Ward Out." *Chicago Tribune*, July 4, 1947.
"Los Angeles Golfer Breaks Course Record as Cleveland Tourney Opens." *Cleveland Call and Post*, August 16, 1947.
"Louis Amateur King; Rhodes Tops Pros in Courier Meet." *Pittsburgh Courier*, August 16, 1947.
"Louis Appears in Phoenix Open." *Arizona Daily Star*, January 22, 1952.

"Louis Engages D.C. Pro." *Evening Star* (Washington, DC), September 18, 1940.
"Louis Fans Hold Harlem Mardi Gras." *Philadelphia Inquirer*, June 26, 1935.
"Louis Gets Local Payday." *Minneapolis Star*, July 9, 1948.
"Louis Here, Figures He'll Win Title Bout." *Los Angeles Times*, February 13, 1946.
"Louis Making Vacation Pay Its Own Way." *Pasadena Star News*, October 27, 1945.
"Louis Retires; Ring Earnings Were More Than Three Million." *Los Angeles Sentinel*, July 1, 1948.
"Louis to Go to Tucson for Gext Tourney." *Arizona Republic*, January 23, 1952.
"Louis Will Stage Golf Tournament." *Detroit Free Press*, January 30, 1941.
"Louis Wins in Sixth; Referee Saves Carnera." *Chicago Tribune*, June 26, 1935.
"Louis, Rhodes Head 'Special Group.'" *California Eagle*, January 24, 1952.
"Louis, Vines in Golf Tourney." *Pittsburgh Courier*, November 3, 1945.
"Louis' Punches Stop Kracken in First Round." *Chicago Tribune*, July 5, 1934.
"Louis' Stable Has a Field Day Here." *Minneapolis Star Tribune*, July 8, 1948.
"Make Torch Out of Memphis Caddy." *Nashville Banner*, August 5, 1926.
"Mangrum Trips Hogan, St. Petersburg-Bound." *Hollywood Citizen-News*, February 26, 1946.
"Mangrum, Vines in Tie at Montebello." *Long Beach Independent*, December 22, 1947.
"Mapledale C.C. Opens Its House at Show." *Boston Globe*, April 20, 1927.
"Martin Wins Louis Open." *Detroit Tribune*, August 23, 1941.
"Middlecoff, Clark Share Tucson Open Lead." *Arizona Daily Star*, February 2, 1952.
"Mike DeMassey, Partner Lead." *Fresno Bee*, December 30, 1949.
"N.Y. Gets 7 Places in National Open." *Daily News* (New York), May 24, 1948.
"Nashville Golf Course Named for Teddy Rhodes." *Afro-American*, August 30, 1969.
"Nashville Pro Grabs Honors in Louis Open." *Detroit Free Press*, July 19, 1946.
"Nashville Professional Sets Record for Meet." *Pittsburgh Courier*, July 27, 1946.
"Nat'l Championship to End UGA Season." *Michigan Chronicle*, August 11, 1951.
"Nation's Golf Aces in Joe Louis Open." *Pittsburgh Courier*, July 20, 1946.
"Nation's Top Golfers Arrive for National Tourney." *Pittsburgh Courier*, August 24, 1946.
"Navy Service School Opens." *New Journal and Guide*, July 3, 1943.
"Negro Golf Club." *Bulletin* (Pomona, CA), December 23, 1925.
"Negro Golfer from Muncie in Tourney." *Muncie Evening Press*, August 27, 1949.
"Negro Golfers Advance with Amazing Strides." *Michigan Chronicle*, July 10, 1948.
"Negro Golfers Ask $315,000." *Salt Lake Tribune*, January 18, 1948.
"Negro Golfers to Have Open Tourney." *Portland Evening Express* (Maine), August 5, 1926.
"Negro Golfers Win Fight, Crack Color Line." *Cleveland Call and Post*, August 14, 1954.
"Negro Open Golf Tourney." *Brooklyn Times Union*, August 5, 1926.
"Negro Stars Honored by Newspaper." *Pomona Progress Bulletin*, February 13, 1946.
"Negro Takes Lead in 'Tam' All-American." *Tulsa Tribune*, July 31, 1952.
"Negroes Have Added Burden When Playing in Tourneys." *Johnson City Press-Chronicle*, June 14, 1963.
"Officials Shelve Richmond Open." *Oakland Tribune*, May 12, 1948.
"Ohio Manufacturer Hires Tan Golfer." *Afro American*, March 24, 1956.
"Old Dan Rice." *St. Louis Post-Dispatch*, September 29, 1844.
"P.G.A. Delegates Will Mold Plans for Big Tourney." *Palm Beach Post*, November 22, 1934.

"Pairings, Starting Times for First Day of U.S. Open Golf." *Long Beach Press-Telegram*, June 6, 1948.
"Palmer Piles Up Big Lead in Mexican Open Golf Tourney." *Lubbock Avalanche-Journal*, February 28, 1954.
"Palmer Sets Open Golf Pace." *Montreal Star*, February 26, 1954.
"Par Blasted in Ft. Wayne Open." *Journal and Courier* (Lafayette, IN), August 22, 1952.
"Paramount Golf Tourney Progress." *St. Louis American*, May 18, 1950.
"Pay as Pro Not Enough, Says Murphy." *Arizona Republic*, January 24, 1952.
"People in the News." *Pittsburgh Courier*, July 7, 1962.
"PGA Adjusting Rules to Allow Negroes in Meet." *Riverside Daily Press*, January 19, 1952.
"PGA Bars Rhodes, Hughes from St. Paul Golf Meet." *Alabama Tribune*, August 27, 1948.
"PGA Bestows Membership on African-American Pioneers." November 14, 2009, www.PGA.com.
"PGA 'Closed Shop' Negro Golfers Charge, Ask 250-G's Damages." *Santa Rosa Republican*, January 17, 1948.
"PGA Crisis: Joe Louis' Bias Claim." *Daily News* (New York), January 15, 1952.
"PGA Ducks 'Attachment' of Prizes in Richmond Meet." *Los Angeles Sentinel*, January 22, 1948.
"PGA is Issued an Ultimatum." *Wausau Daily Herald*. May 10, 1961.
"PGA Official Assails Mosk." *Mirror* (Los Angeles), May 15, 1961.
"PGA Outmaneuvers Negro Golfers by 'Paying Off' Richmond Tourney Winners with Blank Checks." *Michigan Chronicle*, January 24, 1948.
"PGA Pioneer Ted Rhodes Dies of Heart Attack." *Afro-American*, July 19, 1969.
"PGA Prexy Halts Snead from Playing in Mexico City Open." *Arizona Daily Star*, February 27, 1952.
"PGA Promises End of Tourney Jim Crow." *New York Amsterdam News*, September 25, 1948.
"Pieper's 70 Paces Open." *San Francisco Examiner*, May 1, 1948.
"Plan for Negro on Pro Golfdom." *New York Amsterdam News*, August 30, 1958.
"Pro Golfers Play and Parley in DC." *Pittsburgh Courier*, March 18, 1967.
"Pro Tennis Queen Now on Golf Scene." *Virginian-Pilot*, December 13, 1963.
"Pro-Amateur for State Open Lures Big Field." *Fresno Bee*, April 29, 1947.
"Qualifiers for L.A. Open Golf." *Valley Times*, December 31, 1946.
"Rags Rhodes Visits." *Tennessean (Nashville)*, September 19, 1949.
"Rain or Shine San Diego Golf Started." *Wilmington Daily Press Journal*, January 17, 1952.
"Registration Card." Frank Rhodes. City of Nashville, State of Tennessee, September 12, 1918. www. Ancestry.com
"Remembering the Old UGA Tour." *Black Enterprise*, September 1997.
"Rhodes Cards 284 in World Championship Tournament." *Atlanta Daily World*, August 16, 1949.
"Rhodes Cops UGA Title." *New Journal and Guide*, September 6, 1952.
"Rhodes Finishes Sixth in Tourney." *Pittsburgh Courier*, May 14, 1949.
"Rhodes Fires 11-Under Par 199, Cops Midwestern Tourney." *Michigan Chronicle*, July 24, 1948.
"Rhodes Gets Top Money in Houston." *New Journal and Guide*, July 5, 1947.

"Rhodes Goes Down Swinging." *Pittsburgh Courier*, June 19, 1948.
"Rhodes Golf Clinic at Fairway Range." *Asbury Park Press*, August 10, 1962.
"Rhodes in Nashville." *Michigan Chronicle*, September 24, 1949.
"Rhodes in the Money in L.A. Open." *Los Angeles Sentinel*, January 11, 1951.
"Rhodes Is Hot." *Fresno Bee*, May 4, 1949.
"Rhodes Leads Opening Round." *Wilmington Daily Press Journal* (California), January 2, 1948.
"Rhodes Places in Tam O'Shanter." *Los Angeles Sentinel*, August 18, 1949.
"Rhodes Retains UGA Open Title." *Pittsburgh Post-Gazette*, August 30, 1952.
"Rhodes Takes Cosmopolitan." *Pittsburgh Courier*, April 19, 1947.
"Rhodes Ties for 12th in Los Angeles Open." *Pittsburgh Courier*, January 18, 1947.
"Rhodes to Enter PGA Golf Tourney." *Los Angeles Sentinel*, October 23, 1947.
"Rhodes Wins Cleveland Golf Meet with 288." *Pittsburgh Courier*, September 7, 1946.
"Rhodes Wins Ray Robinson Open with 291." *Los Angeles Tribune*, August 14, 1948.
"Rhodes Wins So. Calif. Prize Money." *Pittsburgh Courier*, December 14, 1946.
"Rhodes, Gajda Blister Course at Tam O'Shanter Tourney." *Daily Illini* (Urbana, IL), August 1, 1952.
"Rhodes, Grant Win at Golf." *Chicago Defender*, August 23, 1947.
"Rhodes, Pro for Louis, Wins Boss' Tournament." *Detroit Free Press*, August 22, 1947.
"Rhodes, Roach, Gregory Win Golf Crowns in Windy City." *Pittsburgh Courier*, August 23, 1952.
"Rhodes, Spiller Drop $300,000 as PGA Drops Racial Bans." *Los Angeles Tribune*, October 2, 1948.
"Rhodes, Spiller Hit by Golf Bias." *Afro-American*, January 28, 1950.
"Rhodes, Spiller Out of Money in Los Angeles Open." *Cleveland Call and Post*, January 17, 1948.
"Rhodes, Wheeler Tied for Golf Lead." *Pittsburgh Sun-Telegraph*, August 30, 1946.
"Rhodes' 66 Listed as Threat in L.A. Open." *Michigan Chronicle*, January 7, 1950.
"Riviera—Hole by Hole." *Los Angeles Times*, June 10, 1948.
"Roberto De Vicenzo and Johnny Palmer Tie For Lead in Mexico Open Golf Tourney with 139." *Gazette and Daily* (York, PA), February 27, 1954.
"Rubaiyat Golfers Help Ted Rhodes." *Los Angeles Sentinel*, March 22, 1962.
"Russell, Nell Dodson." The Way I See It." *Minneapolis Spokesman*, July 2, 1948.
"San Diego Golf Open Jan. 17–20 Will Help Build 50-Bed Children's Hospital." *Escondido Times-Advocate*, January 4, 1952.
"San Diego Open Fights PGA Ban of Joe Louis." *Citizen-News* (Hollywood, CA), January 14, 1952.
"San Diego Will Host $10,000 Golf Open." *Escondido Times Advocate*, August 11, 1951.
"Scene of Open." *Los Angeles Times*, June 10, 1948.
"Second-Round Scores of U.S. Open." *Los Angeles Times*, June 12, 1948.
"Sentinel Sports Staff Selects Honor Roll of Outstanding Athletes." *Los Angeles Sentinel*, February 13, 1947.
"Service Men Benefitted by Local Program." *Nashville Banner*, October 9, 1941.
"Services Set for Rhodes." *Tennessean (Nashville)*, July 8, 1969.
"Shady Rest First Negro Golf Course." *Fort Worth Record*, August 27, 1925.

"Shelby Hosts Rhodes Golf on Sept. 11." *Tennessean (Nashville),* August 31, 1970.
"Sifford and Rhodes Get Golf Cash." *Chicago Defender,* January 21, 1956.
"Signing of Robinson Hailed by Fans Everywhere." *Afro-American,* November 3, 1945.
"Smash Color Lines in Major Golf Tournaments." *Michigan Chronicle,* June 6, 1942.
"Smith Speaks at N.Y. Press Club Dinner." *Pittsburgh Courier,* July 3, 1948.
"Snead Chars Riviera's Par." *Morning World Herald* (Omaha), June 8, 1948.
"Soldiers from Camp Forrest Celebrate Holiday Here." *Tennessean,* July 6, 1941.
"Spiller Threatens Suit If PGA Amendment Fails." *New Journal and Guide,* January 26, 1952.
"Spiller Wins Miami View Golf Toga." *Pittsburgh Courier,* August 13, 1949.
"Spiller, Rhodes Barred From Richmond Open." *Chicago Defender,* January 4, 1948.
"Spiller's Performance Amazes Top Golfers." *Afro-American,* January 10, 1948.
"Sport: May Time at Tam." August 17, 1953, www.time.com/archive.
"Sports in a Nutshell." *Minneapolis Star,* July 23, 1952.
"Stage Set for 1926 National Open Golf." *Commercial Appeal* (Memphis), July 4, 1926.
"Step Brothers' Al Williams Dies at 74." May 4, 1985, www.latimes.com.
"Steps Taken by PGA to End Race Discrimination in Golf." *Buffalo Evening News,* January 18, 1952.
"Ted Kroll Leads Golfers with 64 at San Diego." *Anaheim Gazette,* January 18, 1952.
"Ted Rhodes 68 Cops Fitch Golf." *Afro-American,* August 15, 1959.
"Ted Rhodes 275 Card Tops for Ray Robinson Tourney." *Detroit Tribune,* August 6, 1949.
"Ted Rhodes 280 Tops U.G.A. Pros." *Cleveland Call and Post,* September 8, 1951.
"Ted Rhodes Among Leaders as L.A. Open Draws to Close." *Michigan Chronicle,* January 14, 1950.
"Ted Rhodes Benefit Slated Here Tonight." *Nashville Banner,* April 4, 1962.
"Ted Rhodes Eyes 'Double Crown' in Joe Louis, Nat'l Open Meets." *Michigan Chronicle,* August 6, 1949.
"Ted Rhodes Finishes 3rd in Comeback." *Call* (Kansas City, MO) July 20, 1962.
"Ted Rhodes Finishes Fifth in Motor City." *Detroit Tribune,* July 10, 1954.
"Ted Rhodes Fires 66 to Win Cleveland Tourney." *Pittsburgh Courier,* August 23, 1947.
"Ted Rhodes Fires 67 to Lead in All-American." *Springfield Daily News,* July 31, 1952.
"Ted Rhodes First to Win Joe Louis, UGA Tourneys." *Los Angeles Tribune,* September 17, 1949.
"Ted Rhodes in St. Ann's Open." *St. Louis Post-Dispatch,* June 8, 1952.
"Ted Rhodes Joins Advisory Staff at Burke Golf." *Michigan Chronicle,* July 17, 1954.
"Ted Rhodes Makes Good Showing in Chicago Golf Tourney." *Daily Bulletin* (Dayton), July 31, 1946.
"Ted Rhodes Retains Pro Championship in Joe Louis Open." *New Journal and Guide,* August 30, 1947.
"Ted Rhodes Takes Early Lead in Canadian Open." *Montreal Star,* July 9, 1953.
"Ted Rhodes Tops Professionals in Ray Robinson Open with 291." *Atlanta Daily World,* August 3, 1948.
"Ted Rhodes Triumphs in Chi Golf Tourney." *Philadelphia Tribune,* June 16, 1956.
"Ted Rhodes Underdog in National Title Defense." *Los Angeles Sentinel,* August 25, 1951.
"Ted Rhodes Visits Golf Tourney of Paramount G.C." *St. Louis Argus,* May 18, 1950.

"Ted Rhodes Wins Houston Tourney." *New York Amsterdam News*, July 5, 1947.
"Ted Rhodes Wins in Texas." *Los Angeles Sentinel*, June 30, 1949.
"Ted Rhodes Wins Lone Star Open." *Pittsburgh Courier*, June 27, 1953.
"Ted Rhodes Wins Title, $700 in Windy City Open." *New Journal and Guide*, August 28, 1948.
"The Fairview Golf Club Top Philly Pioneer." *Philadelphia Tribune*, January 1, 1963.
"The Whole City Is Buzzing About Gala Golfers Ball." *Cleveland Call and Post*, September 1, 1951.
"Theodore Rhodes Wins Open in Joe Louis Golf Tourney." *St. Louis Argus*, July 26, 1946.
"Three Golfers Escorted by Police Play a Game." *Chicago Defender*, July 5, 1941.
"To Municipal Auditorium." *Call* (Kansas City), April 19, 1940.
"Todd's 65 Trails Mangrum by 1 in Tam Tourney." *Fresno Bee*, August 7, 1949.
"Topped Lawson Little." *Pittsburgh Courier*. January 20, 1951.
"U.S. Open Rich with Tradition Since 1894." *St. Louis Star and Times*, June 9, 1948.
"UGA Youth Winners." *St. Louis Argus*, September 9, 1960.
"Uncle Sam Hits Louis' Trust Funds." *Detroit Free Press*, March 12, 1954.
"Veteran Golf Ted Rhodes Dies; Taught P.G.A. Pro Lee Elder." *Philadelphia Tribune*, July 8, 1969.
"What Next?" *Pittsburgh Courier*, January 11, 1947.
"Wheeler Takes Golf Crown for 4th Time." *Afro-American*, September 6, 1947.
"Wheeler Tops Negro Golfers by 1 Shot." *Indianapolis Star*, August 28, 1948.
"Williams Jr., Takes Lead at Tucson." *Atlantic City Press*, February 3, 1952.
"Winchell Heard on 291 Stations." *Muskogee Daily Phoenix*, December 16, 1951.
"Winchell to Resume ABC Program Tonight." *Park City Daily News*, March 9, 1952.
"Winners of UGA Pro Purse and Scores." *Pittsburgh Courier*, September 13, 1952.
"Worsham, Hogan Lead in Open Play." *Boston Globe*, June 11, 1948.
"Writers Award Bing Richardson Trophy." *Oakland Post Enquirer*, January 10, 1950.
"Ziggy Johnson's Beige Room Cast Hit Swing Peak." *Chicago Defender*, December 25, 1948.
1920 United States Federal Census, Della Rhodes.
1920 United States Federal Census, Frank Rhodes.
1920 United States Federal Census, Mary Ellen Jefferson.
1940 United States Federal Census, Theodore Rhodes.
Adams, Julius J. "Negro Stars Snubbed in Bing's Open Invitational Golf Tourney." *New York Amsterdam News*, January 21, 1950.
Alexander, Chip. "Elder Still Working on Behalf of Minorities." *Grand Island (Nebraska) Independent*, June 4, 2008.
Alexander, T. H. "By the Way." *Tennessean*, December 21, 1926.
Allen, Shawn. "Citizen Rhodes." February 15, 2012, TheFriedEgg.com.
Anderson, Tom. "Cary Middlecoff Captures State Golf Crown." *Knoxville Journal*, July 14, 1940.
Aubrey, Coult. "Tennis Queen Althea Gibson Soon May be Golf Princess." *Morning Call*, October 9, 1961.
Barkow, Al. "Bill Spiller." December 2017, golfoklahoma.org.
Barkow, Al. "One Man's Mission." *Golf World*, January 18, 2008.

Bartlett, Charles. "$50,875 Meet Opens at Tam o' Shanter Today." *Chicago Tribune*, July 25, 1946.

Bartlett, Charles. "Barron Wins All-American Title; Vines 2D." *Chicago Tribune*, July 29, 1946.

Bartlett, Charles. "Hawkins Leads Western Open on 68." *Chicago Tribune*, June 29, 1962.

Bartlett, Charles. "Snead Fires 65, Wins Tam Golf with 271." *Chicago Tribune*, August 4, 1952.

Bartlett, Charles. "Ted Rhodes' 140 Tops Qualifiers for Open." *Chicago Tribune*, June 6, 1956.

Bartlett, Charles. "The Locker." *Chicago Tribune*, February 11, 1962.

Bay, Mia. "From Jim Crow to Now: On the Realities of Traveling While Black." March 25, 2021, LiteraryHub.com.

Becker, Bill. "'Old Charlie' Keeps Swinging." *Tampa Bay Times*, May 20, 1969.

Bell, Norman. "Louis Fights PGA's Golf Color Line." *Stockton Record*, January 14, 1952.

Bell, Norman. "Louis Irked by PGA Ban Against Negroes in Open." *Redwood City Tribune*, January 14, 1952.

Berry, Jack. "Lee Elder Leads Buick by a Shot." *Detroit Free Press*, July 6, 1969.

Bibb, John. "Sports Scope." *Tennessean*, December 18, 1968.

Bibb, Joseph D. "Popular Man's Burden." *Pittsburgh Courier*, November 24, 1945.

Blair, Frank T. "Frankly Speaking." *Long Beach Press-Telegram*, January 20, 1950.

Blair, Frank T. "Frankly Speaking." *Long Beach Press-Telegram*, June 9, 1948.

Bloom, David. "Memphian Wins Title Third Straight Year." *Commercial Appeal*, June 22, 1942.

Bowles, Billy and Tyson, Remer. "'Joe Louis' How He Touched a Generation." *Detroit Free Press*, April 13, 1981.

Brent, Elmer E. "Fourth Annual Golf Championship at Shady Rest Country Club Aug. 31." *New York Age*, August 24, 1929.

Briere, Tom. "Louis' Instructor Wins Elks Title." *Minneapolis Star Tribune*, July 8, 1948.

Brown, Clifton. "On Golf: One Man's History Rings Proudly." *New York Times*, March 1, 1998.

Burbridge, Eddie. "Joe Louis Scores on Jack Benny Show." *California Eagle*, November 15, 1945.

Burbridge, Eddie. "Layin' It On the Line." *California Eagle*, November 8, 1945.

Burbridge, Eddie. "No Fooling." *California Eagle*, November 8, 1945.

Burk, W. Jay. "Boros Fires Torrid 66 for Phoenix Open Golf Lead." *Arizona Republic*, January 25, 1952.

Burk, W. Jay. "Mangrum Holds Dominating Lead." *Arizona Republic*, January 27, 1952.

Burk, W. Jay. "Mangrum Posts One of Open's Most Decisive Wins." *The Arizona Republic*, January 28, 1952.

Burley, Bruce. "Woods' First Major Title a Sports Masterpiece." *Hartford Courant*, April 14, 1997.

Burley, Dan. "35th Street Goes Crazy." *Chicago Defender*, September 24, 1959.

Burley, Dan. "Confidentially Yours." *New York Amsterdam News*, November 10, 1945.

Burley, Dan. "Confidentially Yours." *New York Amsterdam News*, October 11, 1947.

Butchins, Carlos. "Martin Stages Late Rally to Win Joe Louis Open." *Washington Afro American*, August 23, 1941.

Byrne, Jim. "Burkemo Wears Pair of Purple Hearts." *Minneapolis Star*, July 18, 1953.

Carlson, Bill. "Five Locals Among 18 Under-70 in Keller Opener." *Minneapolis Star*, July 17, 1953.

Carlson, Bill. "Old Story for Rhodes…'and Then They Put Me with Snead.'" *Minneapolis Star*, August 25, 1956.

Carlson, Bill. "Snead, Ulrich Haunt Haas as 36 Crack Keller Par." *Minneapolis Star*, July 18, 1953.

Carlson, Bill. "Superior Eyes More Tourneys." *Minneapolis Star Tribune*, July 8, 1948.

Carter, Art. "PGA Lifts Ban." *Afro-American*, November 18, 1961.

Casey, Lawrence. "Old Master, Howard Wheeler, Takes Joe Louis Golf Title." *Michigan Chronicle*, August 4, 1951.

Casserly, Hank. "Hank Casserly Says." *Capital Times* (Madison, Wisconsin), June 24, 1948.

Chanin, Abe. "Joe Louis 'Goes Into Training' for Annual Tucson Open Meet." *Arizona Daily Star*, January 29, 1952.

Chilton, Ralph. "Boston National Golf Meet Looms as Challenging Item." *Phoenix Index*, August 16, 1941.

Clark, W. L. "Good Caddies Highly Important in Golf; Stars or Dubs May Slip Often, But 'Boys' Never." *Windsor Star* (Ontario), June 4, 1925.

Climer, David. "Ted Rhodes Blazed Trail for Golfers." *Tennessean (Nashville)*, February 19, 2010.

Cook, Debert. "Jim Crow Laws, Social Norms and Golf." March 25, 2016, www.africanamericangolfersdigest.com.

Cook, Debert. "Remembering the United Golfers Association." *African American Golfers Digest*, April 3, 2020.

Cook, Debert. "United States Golfers Association." April 10, 2019, AfricanAmericanGolfersDigest.com.

Covington, Aileen. "Off Tee to Green." *Valley Times*, January 19, 1948.

Cowans, Russ J. "Course Record Knocked Over by Ted Rhodes." *Chicago Defender*, September 11, 1948.

Cowans, Russ J. "Joe Louis Open to Dixie Pro." *Chicago Defender*, July 27, 1946.

Cowans, Russ J. "Joe Louis to Make Strong Bid for Amateur Golf Championship." *Atlanta Daily World*, July 10, 1947.

Cowans, Russ J. "Rhodes Will Not Defend Title in Joe Louis Tourney." *Chicago Defender*, August 13, 1949.

Cowans, Russ J. "Suit May be Reopened." *Chicago Defender*, July 7, 1951.

Cowans, Russ J. "Tam Tournament Gave Negro Golfers Chance to Compete On Big Time." *Chicago Defender*, April 12, 1958.

Cowans, Russ J. "Ted Rhodes Faces Tough Opposition to Retain Top Money Winning Post." *Michigan Chronicle*, June 10, 1950.

Cowans, Russ J. "Ted Rhodes Grabs Share of May Tourney." *Michigan Chronicle*, August 2, 1949.

Cowans, Russ J. "Two Birdies Paved Way for Victor." *Washington Afro American*, August 23, 1941.

Cowans, Russ. "Hughes Cards 297 to Win Joe Louis Golf Tournament." *Afro American*, July 28, 1945.
Cowans, Russ. "I Cover the Town." *Michigan Chronicle*, September 7, 1946.
Cowans, Russ. "Louis Puts Gloves Down for Clubs." *Chicago Defender*, July 3, 1948.
Cowans, Russ. "Sports Chatter." *Michigan Chronicle*, August 9, 1947.
Cowans, Russ. "Sports Chatter." *Michigan Chronicle*, August 23, 1947.
Cowans, Russ. "Sports Chatter." *Michigan Chronicle*, February 21, 1948.
Cowans, Russ. "Sports Chatter." *Michigan Chronicle*, July 27, 1946.
Cowans, Russ. "Sports Chatter." *Michigan Chronicle*, October 12, 1946.
Cowans, Russ. "Ted Rhodes Grabs Top Money in Dayton Open." *Michigan Chronicle*, August 9, 1947.
Crane, Omer. "Art Bell Is Crowned State Open Golf King." *Fresno Bee*, May 5, 1947.
Crane, Omer. "Fresno's Ralph Lomeli Cards 66 to Lead Open." *Fresno Bee*, May 6, 1950.
Crane, Omer. "Golfers' Invasion Will Start for State Open." *Fresno Bee*, April 27, 1947.
Crane, Omer. "Harris, Gage, Vines Will Play Off 282 Tie." *Fresno Bee*, May 8, 1950.
Crane, Omer. "La Jolla Pro, Fresnans, Lead Pro Amateur Play." *Fresno Bee*, May 4, 1949.
Crane, Omer. "Pieper Bolsters Lead in State Open with 207; Vines Trails w.ith 210." *Fresno Bee*, May 4, 1947.
Crane, Omer. "Quick Heads to Fresno to Defend Golf Crown." *Fresno Bee*, May 2, 1950.
Crane, Omer. "Quick Wins Open with Record Smashing 273." *Fresno Bee*, May 9, 1949.
Crane, Omer. "Vines and Pieper are Sub Par in State Open." *Fresno Bee*, May 3, 1947.
Crane, Omer. "Young Bill Nary Leads with 69 in State Open." *Fresno Bee*, May 1, 1947.
Crawford, Ray. "Golf." *Miami Herald*, June 3, 1973.
Cronin, Ned. "Ned Cronin." *Daily News* (Los Angeles), January 14, 1948.
Crouse, Karen. "Treasure of Golf's Sad Past, Black Caddies Vanish in Era of Riches." *New York Times*, April 2, 2012.
Curnow, Jack. "Eaton Nets 140 to Hold Lead in Southland Open." *Los Angeles Times*, November 4, 1945.
Curnow, Jack. "Eaton Paces Golfers in Southland Open." *Los Angeles Times*, November 3, 1945.
Curnow, Jack. "L.A. Open Golf Qualifying Set for Six Links." *Los Angeles Times*, December 24, 1945.
Curnow, Jack. "Snead's 68 Paces L.A. Open Golf; Nelson Fires 71." *Los Angeles Times*, January 5, 1946.
Curnow, Jack. "Star Golfers Clash Today in Los Angeles Open Meet." *Los Angeles Times*, January 4, 1946.
Curnow, Jack. "Vines Captures Southland Open Golf Title." *Los Angeles Times*, November 5, 1945.
Curtis, Charles. "Ben Hogan Reaping Rich Financial Haul." *Los Angeles Times*, March 6, 1952.
Curtis, Charles. "Golfagraphs." *Los Angeles Times*, December 2, 1951.
Curtis, Charles. "Hogan Fires 70 to Widen L.A. Open Golf Lead." *Los Angeles Times*, January 5, 1948.
Curtis, Charles. "Kroll Boosts Lead With Round of 69." *Los Angeles Times*, January 19, 1952.

Curtis, Charles. "Mangrum in Lead At Montebello – 136." *Los Angeles Times*, December 16, 1951.
Curtis, Charles. "Snead Leading Open With Record 138." *Los Angeles Times*, June 12, 1948.
Curtis, Charles. "Snead, Rhodes Shoot 67s on Riviera Course." *Los Angeles Times*, June 8, 1948.
Danner, Charlie. "Charlie Danner Says." *Nashville Banner*, June 10, 1948.
Darsie, Darsie L. "Riviera's Lengthy 10th Proving Hole for Sluggers." *Santa Ana Register*, June 10, 1948.
De Wan, George. "Pioneer Battles an Uneven Lie." *Newsday* (New York), February 28, 2002.
Delano, Frank. "In the Sportlight." *Long Beach Press-Telegram*, January 11, 1949.
Devine, Tommy. "Tommy Devine." *Detroit Free Press*, July 3, 1955.
Dixon, Ardelia B. "Hot Weather Pulls Us Out-of-Doors." *Cleveland Call and Post*, July 9, 1949.
Doyle, Joe. "Chicago Pro Wins Mermaid." *South Bend Tribune*, June 30, 1955.
Duncan, Arnott. "Dunkin' With Dunc." *Arizona Republic*, January 18, 1952.
Dunkley, Charles. "Negro Golfers Enter Richest Prize Test." *Journal Herald*, July 19, 1942.
Dunnell, Milt. "The Gibson Girl Has Many Talents." *Toronto Daily Star*, July 25, 1968.
Durden, Chauncey. "The Sport View." *Richmond Times-Dispatch* (Virginia), July 25, 1946.
Dyer, Braven and Finch, Frank. "Off the Links, Hogan's Just One of the Boys." *Los Angeles Times*, June 8, 1948.
Dyer, Braven. "Joe Louis Here for Vacation." *Los Angeles Times*, October 28, 1941.
Eck, Frank. "Joe Louis – Businessman." *St. Cloud Times*, April 22, 1947.
Evans, Orrin C. "'Good Sports' Golfer's Bow Their Heads." *Philadelphia Tribune*, August 9, 1928.
Feather, Leonard. "Billy Eckstine's Career a Glorious Roller-Coaster." March 10, 1993.
Fentress, J. Cullen. "Down in Front." *California Eagle*, November 6, 1941.
Fentress, J. Cullen. "Top Stars to Attend Courier Sports Fete in Los Angeles." *Pittsburgh Courier*, January 26, 1946.
Fullerton, Hugh Jr. "Roundup." *Times Herald*, July 19, 1945.
Fullerton, Hugh Jr. "Sports Roundup." *Waco Times-Herald* (Texas), December 18, 1948.
Fullerton, Hugh. "Sports Parade." *Pomona Progress Bulletin*, October 27, 1945.
Fuster, John E. "400 Golfers Registered at UGA National Championships." *Atlanta Daily World*, September 5, 1951.
Fuster, John. "Gallery Pulled Against Joe Louis in UGA Finals." *Alabama Tribune*, September 14, 1951.
Gaff, Glenn. "Haas' 64 Takes Keller Lead." *Minneapolis Tribune*, July 18, 1953.
Gallup, George. "Public Demands Continuation of CCC Camps." *Cincinnati Enquirer*, July 6, 1936.
Gammon, Wirt. "Just Between Us Fans." *Chattanooga Daily Times*, July 11, 1948.
Gifford, Ed. "Al Besselink Wins Joe Louis Open Meet." *Michigan Chronicle*, August 26, 1950.
Gifford, Ed. "From Tee to Green." *Michigan Chronicle*, September 17, 1949.
Graff, Todd. "The Clause That Closed." April 21, 2001, Greensboro.com.

Graham, Gene. "Negroes to Sue If State Refuses to Open Parks." *Tennessean (Nashville)*, January 26, 1956.
Graham, Renee. "k.d. Lang Dresses Up, Dumbs Down in Vogue Spread." *Commercial Appeal*, July 20, 1997.
Graham, Sheila. "Two Taylors Wed in 'Bride' Film; More Love Scenes for 'Valentino'; Niven to Star in Broadway Play." *Citizen-News*, December 24, 1949.
Graves, Lem Jr. "From the Press Box." *New Journal and Guide*, November 3, 1945.
Grayson, Harry. "Louis So Rich He Needs Money to Stay Solvent." *Ironwood Daily Globe*, August 19, 1950.
Grayson, Harry. "The Score Board." *Lancaster New Era*, February 2, 1952.
Green, Dudley. "Completing 35 Years as Belle Meade Pro May 28, Livingstone Retires Effective January 1948." *Nashville Banner*, May 9, 1947.
Green, Dudley. "State Final Cause Stir Among Belle Meade Caddies." *Nashville Banner*, July 12, 1941.
Green, Dudley. "Top on Driving Helps Campbell to Western Lead." *Nashville Banner*, July 10, 1959.
Green, Wendell. "Top Negro Golfers Organize Jim Crow Auxilliary [sic] to PGA." *California Eagle*, January 24, 1952.
Greenstein, Teddy. "Segregation on green." *Chicago Tribune*, February 9, 2009.
Greer, Thom. "America Loses Its Greatest Hero." *Daily News*, April 13, 1981.
Griffin, Jimmy. "Jimmy Griffin Sports." *St. Paul Recorder*, July 15, 1955.
Hall, Bob. "Hogan Assumes Command of L.A. Open." *Long Beach Press-Telegram*, January 4, 1948.
Hall, Bob. "Hogan, Worsham Set Open Pace." *Long Beach Press-Telegram*, June 11, 1948.
Hall, Bob. "L.B. Not Off Golf Tour." *Long Beach Press-Telegram*, May 12, 1951.
Hall, Bob. "P.G.A. Dissatisfied with Treatment in L.A. Open Golf." *Long Beach Press-Telegram*, January 13, 1948.
Hall, Bob. "Short Putts." *Long Beach Press-Telegram*, February 8, 1948.
Hall, Bob. "Short Putts." *Long Beach Press-Telegram*, January 19, 1950.
Hall, Bob. "Snead Confident of Open Win." *Long Beach Press-Telegram*, June 12, 1948.
Hall, Bobby. "Middlecoff Left Golfing Legacy." *Commercial Appeal* (Memphis, TN.), September 2, 1998.
Hancock, Dean Gordon B. "Between the Lines." *Atlanta Daily World*, October 5, 1947.
Harding, Halley. "Halley Harding." *Los Angeles Sentinel*, April 13, 1950.
Harding, Halley. "Halley Harding." *Los Angeles Sentinel*, August 11, 1949.
Harding, Halley. "Halley Harding." *Los Angeles Sentinel,* January 25, 1951.
Hathaway, Maggie. "First Black Pro Golfer Dead at 56." *Los Angeles Sentinel*, July 10, 1969.
Hathaway, Maggie. "Goodbye, Teddy Rhodes." *Los Angeles Sentinel*, July 10, 1969.
Hathaway, Maggie. "Maggie Hathaway's Tee Time." *Los Angeles Sentinel*, September 18, 1969.
Henderson, Edwin B. "Top Professionals Hit Discrimination in Golf." *New Journal and Guide*, January 19, 1952.
Henry, Bill. "Crosby Busy Figure in Sports Field." *Los Angeles Times*, January 31, 1937.
Hightower, Beth. "Porter Has Talent to Become Big Winner." *Sacramento Union*, June 13, 1948.

Hill, Herman. "Joe Leaves Coast: Oma Unimpressive." *Pittsburgh Courier*, December 7, 1946.
Hill, Herman. "Joe Louis, Lionel Take Honors in Big Radio Show." *Pittsburgh Courier*, December 1, 1945.
Hill, Herman. "PGA Damage Suit Set For Sept." *Pittsburgh Courier*, July 24, 1948.
Hill, Herman. "Top Sepia Golfers Lose in L.A. Meet." *Pittsburgh Courier*, January 22, 1949.
Hoenig, Bob. "The Inside Look." *Hollywood Citizen-News*, June 11, 1948.
Holloway, Lin. "From the Press Box." *New Journal and Guide*, August 30, 1947.
Holmes, Tommy. "Lip's Technique Pulls Victory Out of Fire." *Brooklyn Daily Eagle*, April 28, 1947.
Hough, Denny. "On the Sports Trail." *Evening Vanguard* (Venice, CA), January 2, 1948.
Hughes, Solomon. "Dozen Pellets Sent by Pro Aids Victory." *Michigan Chronicle*, July 28, 1945.
Hurt, Murray. "Gal Tennis Stars Take Opposite Paths – Reach Same Goals." *Rock Island Argus*, December 1, 1959.
Jackson, Cleveland. "Detroit Medic Defeats 1945 Titlist, Wins Forest City Golf Crown; Joe Louis Eliminated in Quarterfinals." *Cleveland Call and Post*, July 13, 1946.
Jackson, Marion E. "Negro Athletes Play Dominating Role in Turning Tide Against Racism, Bigotry." *Atlanta Daily World*, December 28, 1947.
Jackson, Marion E. "Sports of the World." *Atlanta Daily World*, July 8, 1951.
Jackson, Marion E. "Sports of the World." *Atlanta Daily World*, June 2, 1951.
Jackson, Marion E. "Sports of the World." *Atlanta Daily World*, June 14, 1949.
Jackson, Marion E. "Sports of the World." *Atlanta Daily World*, May 2, 1959.
Jackson, Marion. "Sports of the World." *Atlanta Daily World*, January 2, 1962.
Jacoubowsky, Ed. "Between the Lines." *Redwood City Tribune*, November 10, 1961.
Jacox, Cal. "From the Pressbox." *New Journal and Guide*, January 26, 1952.
Jenkins, Michelle, David Grannis, and Lynn. "Sunset Park." May 20, 2021, www.NolensvillehistoricalSociety.org.
Johnson, Charles. "Charles Johnson's Lowdown on Sports." *Minneapolis Star*, July 17, 1953.
Johnson, Raymond. "Little Rock and Chattanooga Pros Lead Local Qualifying." *Tennessean*, May 12, 1936.
Johnson, Ziggy. "Zagging with Ziggy." *Michigan Chronicle*, October 22, 1955.
Johnson, Ziggy. "Zig and Zag." *Chicago Defender*, March 3, 1956.
Jones, Billy. "Chicagoan Golfer Rallies for Title." *Tampa Times*, February 18, 1963.
Jones, Lucius. "Slants on Sports." *Atlanta Daily World*, August 16, 1941.
Juliano, Joe. "PGA to Honor Barred Black Players." *Philadelphia Inquirer*, August 20, 2009.
Kinney, Bill. "Along the Sport Trail." *Rock Island Argus*, May 15, 1947.
Knapp, Daniel K. "Charlie Keeps His Cool." *Los Angeles Times*, June 22, 1969.
Koch, Bruce. "Tom Bartolec's 69 Leads in Mangurian." *Democrat and Chronicle* (Rochester, N.Y.), August 27, 1961.
La Mar, Lawrence F. "'Born Happy' is Revived in L.A." *Jackson Advocate*, June 26, 1943.
Lacy, Sam. "A Round of Golf with Joe Proves He's a Good Boxer." *Afro American*, September 15, 1945.
Lacy, Sam. "From A to Z with Sam Lacy." *Afro-American*, August 27, 1949.
Lacy, Sam. "From A to Z." *Afro-American*, January 22, 1949.

Lacy, Sam. "Looking 'Em Over." *Afro American*, October 20, 1945.
Lane, Bill. "Swinging Down the Lane." *Michigan Chronicle*, January 13, 1951.
Latshaw, Bob. 'He Turns Misfortune Into Break." *Detroit Free Press*, July 5, 1954.
Lee, Bob. "95 Qualify for Rich L.A. Open." *Daily News* (Los Angeles), January 3, 1946.
Lee, Bob. "Hogan Dead Tired Champ." *Daily News* (Los Angeles), June 14, 1948.
Lee, Bob. "Snead's 68 Paces L.A. Open." *Daily News* (Los Angeles), January 5, 1946.
Lee, Bob. "Vets Take to Gold Trail in L.A. Open Tournament." *Daily News* (Los Angeles), January 1, 1946.
Lee-Smith, Hughie. "African American Sailors in the U.S. Navy." June 11, 2024, www.history.navy.mil.
Leigh, Fred. "Golf Sidelights." *Afro American*, September 2, 1950.
Lett, Frank Sr. "The 19th Hole." *Michigan Chronicle*, October 20, 1962.
Lewis, Dave. "Hogan in Record Win!" *Long Beach Independent*, June 13, 1948.
Lewis, Dave. "Once Over Lightly." *Long Beach Independent*, August 2, 1948.
Lewis, Dave. "Once Over Lightly." *Long Beach Independent*, January 10, 1948.
Lewis, Dave. "Once Over Lightly." *Long Beach Independent*, June 4, 1948.
Lewis, Dave. "PGA Clears City, Lions Club of Drawing Open Color Line." *Long Beach Independent*, January 19, 1950.
Lewis, Dwight. "Theodore 'Ted' Rhodes." October 8, 2017, tennesseeencyclopedia.net.
Little, Tom and Tom Sims. "Sunflower Street." *Tennessean*, August 1, 1941.
Little, Tom and Tom Sims. "Sunflower Street." *Tennessean*, August 5, 1941.
Louis, Joe. "'My Biggest Fight,' Says Louis…." *Daily Sentinel-Tribune*, January 16, 1952.
Louis, Joe. "Louis, Smith Air Views on Golf Tourney Feud." *Tampa Bay Times*, January 17, 1952.
Louis, Joe. "Write Hand." *New York Age*, January 28, 1950.
Lyle, George Jr. "Wheeler Tops Nation's Pro Golfers." *Chicago Defender*, September 6, 1947.
Lyom, Bob. "Blastin' Out." *Evening Vanguard* (Venice, CA), June 16, 1948.
Malloy, Jerry. "Bluejackets: The Great Lakes Negro Varsity of 1944." *National Pastime*, 2, No. 2, Winter, 1985.
Manimus, Hugh. "Teddy Rhodes Plays in L.A. Golf Tournament." *California Eagle*, January 9, 1947.
Matney, Bill. "Bill Matney's Spotlight." *Michigan Chronicle*, September 10, 1949.
Matney, Bill. "Howard Wheeler Expected to be Real Threat in Joe Louis Open." *Alabama Tribune*, August 6, 1948.
Matney, Bill. "Jumpin' the Gun." *Michigan Chronicle*, August 13, 1949.
Matney, Bill. "Jumpin' the Gun." *Michigan Chronicle*, July 2, 1949.
Matney, Bill. "Jumpin' the Gun." *Michigan Chronicle*, July 10, 1954.
Matney, Bill. "Negro Golf May Face Crisis If Louis Quits." *Michigan Chronicle*, January 31, 1948.
Matney, Bill. "Who are the 10 Greatest Athletes?" *Michigan Chronicle*, October 29, 1949.
Matthews, Les. "Mr. 1-2-5 Street." *New York Amsterdam News*, November 25, 1961.
Matthews, Les. "Sports Whirl." *New York Amsterdam News*, August 12, 1961.
Mayhew, Malcolm. "Tapped for Glory." *Fort Worth Star-Telegram*, May 24, 2003.
McAuley, Ed. "Barber Shoots Six-Under-par 64 to Lead Labatt Open Golf." *Gazette* (Montreal), August 21, 1953.

McAuley, Ed. "Barber with 132, Holds Stroke Lead in Summerlea Open." *Gazette* (Montreal), August 22, 1953.
McCallum, Walter. "Straight Off the Tee." *Evening Star* (Washington, DC), July 4, 1939.
McDermott, Barry. "Barry McDermott." *Cincinnati Enquirer*, August 13, 1968.
McGrane, Bert. "Open Cedar Rapids Golf Today; Nary Top Driver." *Des Moines Register*, August 27, 1949.
McGuire, Bobby. "Sifford Defeats Rhodes in 6th City Golf Open." *Detroit Tribune*, July 10, 1948.
McKay, Skibo. "Open Sidelights." *Tucson Daily Citizen*, January 30, 1952.
McMullen, Walter. "The Sport Trail." *Hamilton Spectator*, September 30, 1941.
McNally, Ray. "Ferrier Tops Early Finishers with 209 Score." *Tucson Daily Citizen*, February 2, 1952.
McTyre, Thelma. "Along the Fairways." *Chicago Defender*, February 26, 1949.
Mitchell, Ray. "Ted Rhodes Wins Gotham Tourney." *New York Amsterdam News*, August 16, 1958.
Monarrez, Carlos. "USGA to Salute Louis in 'Barrier Breakers' Exhibit." *Detroit Free Press*, February 19, 2012.
Monroe, Al. "So They Say." *Chicago Defender*, February 28, 1962.
Moore, Clayton. "Golforama." *Los Angeles Sentinel*, March 8, 1962.
Murray, Jim. "PGA Does Turnabout." *Los Angeles Times*, May 18, 1961.
Newland, Russ. "Three Play Off for First in State Open." *Modesto Bee*, May 8, 1950.
Newman, Claude. "Claude Newman Says." *Valley Times*, January 15, 1952.
Northington, Ted. "Carey Middlecoff Wins Prep Championship." *Commercial Appeal*, April 17, 1938.
Northington, Ted. "Middlecoff Wins Prep Golf Championship." *Commercial Appeal* (Memphis), April 17, 1938.
Nunn, William G. "Let's Take It in Stride." *Pittsburgh Courier*, April 19, 1947.
O'Dell, Bernard. "Golf Notes." *Michigan Chronicle*, August 4, 1951.
O'Shields, William. Pro Golf Bars Tougher Than Baseball's: O'Shields." *Atlanta Daily World*, February 12, 1948.
Oglesby, Joe. "In the Game from the Beginning." *Miami Herald*, February 4, 2001.
Ostler, Scott. "The Forgotten Story of the Man Who Pushed Professional Golfs Integration." *San Francisco Chronicle*, December 26, 2018.
Ottley, Roi. "Negroes Moving Ahead in American Business." *Pantagraph*, June 24, 1949.
Pack, Warren. "'New' Joe Louis Ponders Career as Comedian." *Daily News* (Los Angeles), October 23, 1945.
Panella, Bob. "Sports Row." *Citizen-News* (Hollywood, CA). January 15, 1952.
Payne, Barrie. "Bannerettes." *Nashville Banner*, June 7, 1938.
Pelham, Robert. "A Trip to Joe Louis' Camp – How He Came to Locate in Lakewood, N.J." *New York Age*, June 6, 1936.
Powell, Bill. "Cobb Offers Everybody Something." *Paducah Sun*, July 16, 1967.
Powers, Grant. "Primo Easy, Louis Wants Braddock!" *Daily News*, June 26, 1935.
Pye, Brad Jr. "Prying Pye in Prep Sportdom." *California Eagle*, December 20, 1951.
Pye, Brad Jr. "Prying Pye in Prep Sportdom." *California Eagle*, January 3, 1952.
Registration Card D.S.S. Form, 1, Theodore Nathaniel Rhodes, Ancestry.com

Reich, Howard. "Singer, Band Leader, Billy Eckstine, 78." *Chicago Tribune*, March 9, 1993.
Rein, Joe. "Joe Louis Isn't Broke but Lacks Ready Cash to Meet U.S. Tax Debt." *Buffalo Evening News*, August 30, 1950.
Rhodes, Ted. "US Open Scorecard." United States Golf Association Library, 1948 US Open.
Rice, Grantland. "Barranca-Bound Riviera Course Is Stiff Test for U.S. Open Golf." *Winnipeg Tribune*, June 9, 1948.
Richardson, Marty. "Let's Have Some Sports." *Cleveland Call and Post*, August 4, 1951.
Robinson, Edward. "Abie's Corner." *Los Angeles Sentinel*, October 14, 1947.
Robinson, Will. "Big Money Winners in '50 Were Rhodes, Wheeler." *Pittsburgh Courier*, April 7, 1951.
Robinson, Will. "From the Tee." *Pittsburgh Courier*, December 3, 1955.
Robinson, Will. "Golfs Great Names Set for Tough Grind." *Pittsburgh Courier*, July 1, 1950.
Robinson, Will. "Rhodes – The Master – Captures UGA Nat'l Tournament." *Pittsburgh Courier*, September 2, 1950.
Robinson, Will. "Rhodes Monopoly in Joe Louis Open Ends." *Pittsburgh Courier*, August 26, 1950.
Robinson, Will. "Rhodes Plays Top Golf Despite Many Handicaps." *Pittsburgh Courier*, July 17, 1954.
Robinson, Will. "Ted Rhodes Does it Again; Captures UGA Title." *Pittsburgh Courier*, September 3, 1949.
Robinson, Will. "UGA Golf Grind Begins With Penn State Open." *Pittsburgh Courier*, June 16, 1951.
Robinson, Will. "United Golf Association Arranges Summer Tournament Swing." *Pittsburgh Courier*, May 27, 1950.
Rowe, Billy. "Billy Rowe's Notebook." *Pittsburgh Courier*, April 19, 1947.
Rowe, Billy. "Billy Rowe's Notebook." *Pittsburgh Courier*, January 28, 1950.
Rowe, Billy. "Billy Rowe's Notebook." *Pittsburgh Courier*, January 20, 1951.
Rowe, Billy. "Billy Rowe's Notebook." *Pittsburgh Courier,* January 27, 1951.
Rowe, Billy. "Billy Rowe's Notebook." *Pittsburgh Courier*, March 19, 1949.
Rowe, Billy. "'Joe Louis Punch' Hits Stores in St. Louis." *Pittsburgh Courier*, May 10, 1947.
Rowe, Billy. "Notables from Everywhere Attend Big Fight." *Pittsburgh Courier*, June 29, 1935.
Rowe, Izzy. "Issy Rowe's Notebook." *Pittsburgh Courier*, April 9, 1960.
Rowe, Izzy. "Izzy Rowe's Notebook." *Pittsburgh Courier*, October 6, 1951.
Rule, Bob. "George Livingstone Starts His 34th Year Monday." *Nashville Banner*, May 27, 1944.
Rule, Bob. "Middlecoff Told Oehmig Friday He'd Win and Made Good That Threat." *Knoxville News Sentinel*, July 14, 1940.
Rule, Bob. "Tee Talk." *Nashville Banner*, April 17, 1940.
Russell, Fred. "Sideline Sidelights." *Nashville Banner*, February 8, 1939.
Russell, Fred. "Sidelines." *Nashville Banner*, June 25, 1948.
Russell, Nell Dodson. "The Way I See It." *Minneapolis Spokesman*, July 2, 1948.
Sadler, Grayce L. "Grayce's Gossip." *Michigan Chronicle* August 30, 1947.
Samuelson, Rube. "Draw Up A Chair." *Citizen-News*, January 17, 1952.

Saunders, Jack. "Champion Defeats Rhodes." *Pittsburgh Courier*, September 6, 1947.
Schoenfeld, Ed. "Great Field Set for $10,000 Richmond Open." *Oakland Tribune*, January 13, 1948.
Segal, Lewis. "Leonard Reed, 97; Tap Dance Pioneer and Producer." *Los Angeles Times*, April 9, 2004.
Sheppard, Bob. "United Golf Association." October 11, 2012, phillyburbs.com.
Shirley, Bill. "A Pebble Beach Event by Any Other Name Hard to Imagine." *Los Angeles Times*, April 24, 1985.
Simmons, Joe. "Rhodes Favorite in National Golf Meet." *Pittsburgh Courier*, August 17, 1946.
Sinclair, Murray. "Golf Pros Call El Rio Easiest." *Arizona Republic*, January 31, 1952.
Sirak, Ron. "The Master of His Craft." *Daily Herald-Tribune* (Grand Prairie, Alberta, Canada), April 14, 1997.
Sloan, Lloyd L. "Montgomery to Do Halsey Biog? 'Cold' Film for Frank." *Hollywood Citizen-News,* June 8, 1948.
Smith, Bob. "Louis Sees No Contender in Sight." *Dayton Herald*, August 4, 1947.
Smith, Horton. "…Smith Welcomes Joe to PGA Meet." *Daily Sentinel-Tribune*, January 16, 1952.
Smith, Joel W. "Rhodes, Louis Do It Again at Sixth City Golf Tourney." *Pittsburgh Courier*, July 15, 1950.
Smith, Wendell. "Jackie Robinson Wins 'Athlete of the Year' Honor." *Pittsburgh Courier*, January 4, 1947.
Smith, Wendell. "Knockdown Thrills Cubans." *Pittsburgh Courier*, March 15, 1947.
Smith, Wendell. "Martin Wins Detroit Golf Tourney." *Pittsburgh Courier*, August 23, 1941.
Smith, Wendell. "The Sports Beat." *Pittsburgh Courier*, August 16, 1946.
Smith, Wendell. "The Sports Beat." *Pittsburgh Courier*, August 16, 1947.
Smith, Wendell. "The Sports Beat." *Pittsburgh Courier*, March 22, 1947.
Smith, Wendell. "Wendell Smith's Sports Beat." *Pittsburgh Courier*, December 24, 1949.
Smith, Wendell. "Wendell Smith's Sports Beat." *Pittsburgh Courier*, January 24, 1948.
Smith, Wendell. "Wendell Smith's Sports Beat." *Pittsburgh Courier*, July 9, 1949.
Solinsky, Ted. "70 Negroes Play First Day at Shelby." *Tennessean (Nashville),* February 11, 1954.
Solinsky, Ted. "Negro Golf Course to be Equal of Any." *Tennessean (Nashville),* February 7, 1954.
Spriggins, E. Belfield. "Golf Gabbins." *Louisiana Weekly*, May 14, 1960.
Stabley, Fred Jr. "Flint Leader Making it on His Own." *Lansing State Journal*, July 6, 1969.
Steber, Bob. "Next Fight is Final – Joe Louis Says." *Tennessean*, November 3, 1948.
Stiles, Maxwell. "Rhodes Sets Early Open Pace." *Long Beach Press-Telegram*, January 2, 1948.
Stiles, Maxwell. "Stiles in Sports." *Long Beach Press-Telegram*, January 27, 1948.
Stiles, Maxwell. "Styles in Sports." *Mirror* (Los Angeles), December 11, 1951.
Stiles, Maxwell. "Styles in Sports." *Mirror* (Los Angeles), December 14, 1951.
Strafaci, Frank. "On the Trail of a Pioneer." *Miami News*, June 23, 1977.
Sullivan, Ed. "Manhattan." *Detroit Free Press*, June 3, 1936.
Sullivan, Prescott. "The Low Down." *San Francisco Examiner*, January 13, 1948.

BIBLIOGRAPHY

Super, Henry. "Joe Louis Is Worried About Golf and Harmonica." *Times Herald* (Olean, NY), June 16, 1936.

Swindell, J. Nathaniel. "Spiller Wins Sixth Miami View Tourney." *Cleveland Call and Post*, August 6, 1949.

Taft, Larry. "Hall Induction Humbles Former Maplewood Star." *Tennessean (Nashville)*, November 12, 2009.

Thompson, John H. "Theodore Rhodes Wins $1,000 Houston Open with Snappy 296." *Alabama Tribune*, June 27, 1947.

Tramel, Jimmie. "Bill Spiller." Los Angeles Times, *Tulsa World*, July 29, 2007.

Trentham, Pete. "Charlie Sifford Was Not the Best Black Golfer at Philadelphia's Cobb Creek Golf Club!" March 17, 2020, www.Trenthamgolfhistory.org.

Trost, Ralph. "Fore the Golfer." *Brooklyn Daily Eagle*, June 10, 1949.

Trutor, Clayton. "The Links Doctor." April 5, 2003, Memphismagazine.com.

Tucker, Randolph. "Soldiers Have First Week End of Fun Here After Maneuvers." *Tennessean*, October 12, 1941.

Turcott, Jack. "The Life Story of Joe Louis." *Daily News* (New York), October 20, 1935.

Turcott, Jack. "The Life Story of Joe Louis." *Daily News* (New York), October 27, 1935.

United States Supreme Court Plessy v. Ferguson N0 210, May 18, 1896, U.S. National Archives and Records Administration.

V. Rick. "Golf Ball Aerodynamics and the Effect of Altitude." March 2, 2017, www.titleist.com

Vinston, Warren C. "Chicago Prepares for National Golf Tourney." *Pittsburgh Courier*, June 24, 1933: 15.

Walker, Teresa M. "Who Was Ted Rhodes? Daughter Says Black Golf Pioneer Was Similar to Tiger." *Associated Press*, April 20, 1997.

Walker, Theresa. "Who Was Ted Rhodes?" *Daily News Journal* (Murfreesboro, TN), April 17, 1997.

Warden, Al. "Patrolling the Sport Highway." *Ogden Standard-Examiner*, February 16, 1948.

Warters, Jim. "Elder's Moment: Gains Masters, Sheds Tears." *Orlando Sentinel*, April 22, 1974.

Washington, Ches. "Ches Says." *Pittsburgh Courier*, January 26, 1952.

Washington, Ches. "'Comeback Trail Not for Me' – Joe." *Pittsburgh Courier*, January 14, 1950.

Washington, Ches. "Courier Sports Experts." *Pittsburgh Courier*, December 6, 1947.

Washington, Ches. "Joe Louis Set for Fight to the Finish Over Golf Bias." *Pittsburgh Courier*, January 19, 1952.

Washington, Ches. "Joe Louis Wins!" *Pittsburgh Courier*, June 29, 1935.

Washington, Ches. "Louis Punch at Bias Has PGA Jim-Crow Ruling Hanging on Ropes." *Pittsburgh Courier*, January 26, 1952.

Washington, Ches. "Race Discrimination in Big Time Golf Events Blasted." *Pittsburgh Courier*, January 28, 1950.

Washington, Ches. "Sifford Tells of Handicaps Facing Golfers." *Pittsburgh Courier*, May 9, 1959.

Washington, Ches. "Nation Hails Louis Greatest Ever." *Pittsburgh Courier*, January 17, 1942.

Wheeler, Elizabeth. "Golf Is Just Cricket For Powell." *Los Angeles Times*, September 25, 1976.
Whitaker, John. "Speculating in Sports." *The Times* (Munster, IN) June 26, 1955.
Whitaker, John. "Speculating in Sports." *Times* (Munster, IN), July 29, 1946.
Wilie, Louise. "U.S.O., Seeking Funds Here with Chest, Lauded by Idle Soldiers." *Tennessean*, October 13, 1941.
Wilkins, Roy W. "The Watchtower." *Los Angeles Sentinel*, April 17, 1947.
Wilkins, Roy. "The Watchtower." *Los Angeles Sentinel*, October 16, 1947.
Williams, Ted. "Joe Louis Golf Pro Takes Houston Open with Par 253. *Chicago Defender*, July 3, 1948.
Willis, George. "The Day Joe Louis KO'd Golf's Heavyweights." August 7, 2020, SI.com.
Wilson, Russ. "Red Norvo Swings on London Square." *Oakland Tribune*, June 3, 1962.
Wilson, W. Rollo. "Fifty Years of Progress." *Pittsburgh Courier*, February 25, 1950.
Wolf, Al. "Sportraits." *Los Angeles Times*, June 16, 1948.
Wood, Hal. "Harrison, Gage, Vines Tied for Title." *Honolulu Advertiser*, May 8, 1950.
Wood, Hal. "Negro Ted Rhodes Ties for Early Lead In Phoenix." *Fresno Bee*, January 24, 1952.
Wood, Hal. "Nelson Tops Fast Field." *Pasadena Star-News*, January 4, 1946.
Wood, Hal. "Nelson Tops Fast Field." *Pasadena Star-News*, January 4, 1946.
Wood, Hal. "Quick Wins State Open with 291." *Fresno Bee*, May 3, 1948.
Wood, Stan. "Cancel PGA Here Over Racial Issue." *Mirror* (Los Angeles), May 6, 1961.
Woods, Howard. "Across Town." *Chicago Defender*, March 9, 1946.
Woods, Tiger interviewed by Nantz, Jim. "1997 Masters Final Round Broadcast." April 13, 1997. www.YouTube.com.
Wright, James L. "Roosevelt's $2,000,000,000 Relief Bill Is Delayed." *Buffalo Evening News*, March 22, 1933.
Wynn, Linda T. "Leaders of Afro-American Nashville." ww2.tnstate.edu.
Young, A.S. "Doc." "Sport Show." *Los Angeles Sentinel*, January 28, 1951.
Young, Dick. "The Great Joe Louis Has Passed On." *Daily News*, April 13, 1981.
Young, Dick. "Young Ideas." *New York Daily News*, April 16, 1967.
Young, Fay. "End of Baseball's Jim Crow Seen with Signing of Jackie Robinson." *Chicago Defender*, November 3, 1945.
Ziff, Sid. "The Inside Track." *Valley Times*, December 19, 1946.
Ziff, Sid. "The Inside Track." *Valley Times*, December 19, 1946.
Zimmerman, Paul. "Sport Postscripts." *Los Angeles Times*, February 2, 1942.

ABOUT THE AUTHOR

Dan Taylor is a former award-winning television sportscaster. He is the author of several books that include *Baseball at the Abyss: The Scandals of 1926, Babe Ruth and the Unlikely Savior Who Rescued a Tarnished Game*; *Walking Alone: The Untold Journey of Football Pioneer Kenny Washington*; *Lights, Camera, Fastball: How the Hollywood Stars Changed Baseball*; *Fate's Take-Out Slide: A Baseball Scout Recalls Can't-Miss Prospects Who Did*; *A Scout's Report: My 70 Years in Baseball*; and *The Rise of the Bulldogs: The Untold Story of One of the Greatest Upsets of All Time*.

He lives in Fresno, California, with his wife and serves as Executive Director of the Fresno Athletic Hall of Fame.

INDEX

African American Golfers Hall of Fame   182
Airco Golf Course   164
Ambassador Theatre   135
Anderson, Howard   115, 119
Andreason, Dale   148
Apollo Theatre   27, 30, 32, 84
Astair, Fred   35
Augusta National Golf Club   2

Bacon's Arena   21
Baer, Max   22
Baldwin Hills Golf Course   46
Ball, Pat   25
Ballantine Beer   167
Balter, Sam   89
Barber, Jerry   151
Barber, Maxi   154
Barrow, Lillie   22
Barrow, Munroe   22
Basie, Count   156
Bates, John Lee "Pap"   12–16, 19
Bell, Art   46
Belle Meade Country Club   12, 13, 15, 18, 123, 160
Belli, Melvin   59
Berman, Irving   135
Besselink, Al   115, 118
Biltmore Hotel   139
Biltmore Yacht and Country Club   159
Black Golf Hall of Fame   181
Blackburn, Jack   79
Blair, Frank   89
Bolt, Tommy   183
Boros, Julius   105
Borthwick, Anderson   96
Bray, Conklin   63
Breckenridge, Paul   119

Brentwood Country Club   157
Brewster's Gym   22, 23
Brinke, Chris   39
Brion, Cesar   118
Brothers, Mac   17, 18
Broun, Heywood   22
Brown, Henry Justice   9
Bunn, Oscar   66
Burk, W. Jay   104
Burke, Jack, Jr.   139
Burke Golf Manufacturing Company   138
Burnham Woods Golf Course   161
Butler Cabin   2

Camp Shanks   32
Campanella, Roy   2
Campbell-Mithun, Inc.   155
Carter, Ben   92
Carter, Ed   157
Casper, Billy   143, 151
Castro, Fidel   159
Caywood, Frank   101
Cedar Rapids Country Club   121
Chickasaw Country Club   18
Chisolm, Scottie   91
Clark, Eural   97, 100, 104, 106, 134
Clark, Jimmy   124
Clark, Thomas   175
Clayton, Lew   67
Cleveland Arena   119
Club de Golf Mexico   121, 130
Cobbs Creek Golf Course   166
Cole, Nat King   144
Conn, Billy   37, 40
Coons, Hannibal   82
Cortines, Adolpho Ruiz   121
Corum, Bill   99

INDEX

Cowans, Russ   45, 82
Crosby, Bing   85–8, 91, 92, 94, 97, 100, 114
Crosby, Bob   33
Crosby, Larry   86, 87, 91
Cumberland Golf Course   141, 163, 169, 171, 173, 174
Cypress Point Golf Course   87

Davis, Sammy Jr.   144
Dawson, Johnny   72
Dedy, John   25
Delaney, Edward   62
Demaret, Jimmy   67, 72, 100, 131
De Vicenzo, Roberto   131
Dey, Joe   66
Dillard, Harrison   74
Diplomat Hotel   156
Donovan, Hugh   62
Dudley, Bill   61
Durante, Jimmy   67
Durein, Ted   87
Durocher, Leo   35, 87
Dyer, Braven   24
Dykes, Jimmy   87

East Potomac Golf Course   147
Eaton, Cal   69
Ebbett's Field   81
Eckstine, Billy   30, 139, 144, 166
Eisenhower, Dwight D.   81
Elder, Lee   119, 164, 167, 168, 173–7, 181–3
Eldorado Motel   169, 174, 176
Ellis, Duke   23
Evans, Stanley   23

Fairview Golf Club   40, 52
Faldo, Nick   2
Fazio, George   139
Federal Chemical Company   10
Ford, Joe   2
Ford Motor Company   22
Forest Park   168, 169

Fort Campbell   169
Fort Jay   29
Fort Lewis   168
Fort Washington Country Club   39
Fox Hills Golf Course   33, 65, 122, 155, 182
Frank's Famous Oyster and Chop House   27
Frederick Douglas Park   11

Gaff, Glenn   125
Gibson, Althea   91, 149, 163, 164, 169, 170, 180
Gibson, Leland   100
Gillespie, Dizzy   30
Gilliam, Jim   144
Gilliland, Ward   65
Goalby, Bob   3
Golden Lilly   83
Goldwater, Barry   103
Graffis, Herb   67
Grant, Judson   35, 46
Grayson, Harry   109
Green, Freddie   156
Greene, Correttea   119
Greenwood Lake   28
Griffin, Jimmy   128
Grimsley, Will   17, 19
Guinyard, Freddie   32
Gunter, Madison   56, 122, 158

Haas, Freddie   126–8
Hagen, Walter   24
Hampton, Lionel   111
Hancock, Dean   22
Harbert, Chick   138
Harding, Halley   92
Harding, Warren G. (president)   147
Harrison, Dutch   17, 138
Hartsfield, Zeke   43, 124, 147
Havana Military Academy   80
Hawkins, Robert H.   40
Hayworth, Rita   35
Henderson, Paul   182

Hightower, Beth   71
Hill, Herman   66, 74
Hillcrest Country Club   46, 139
Hogan, Ben   3, 36, 42, 43, 57, 58, 65, 67, 69, 71–4, 85, 92, 119, 136–9, 183
Hogan, Valerie   139
Holcombe, Oscar F.   47
Holmes, Tommy   78, 81
Hope, Bob   46, 65, 87, 122
Hotel Rice   105
Hotel Theresa   27, 28
Hughes, Bessie   125
Hughes, Solomon   31, 61, 125
Hunter, Willie   157
Hyland, Dick   86

Ickes, Harold L.   147

Jackson, Marion   102, 150, 154, 162
Jackson, William Hicks   12
Jacobs, Mike   24, 133
Jacox, Cal   76, 114
Jarvis, Al   89
Jessel, George   93
John, "Little Willie"   155
Johnson, Jack   79
Johnson, Joe "Ziggy"   83, 159
Jones, Roscoe   36

Keller Golf Course   124, 126
Key, Alyce   92
Kiner, Ralph   87
Klobuchar, Jim   125
Knox, Frank   29
Koscis, Chuck   31
Kraken, Jack   21
Kroydon Golf   167

Lacy, Sam   82, 138
Lafayette Hotel   150
Lake, George   93
Lake Venice Golf Club   171
Lakeside Golf Club   86
Lakewood Country Club   89, 93

Lanfield, Sidney   69
Langston Golf Course   24, 146, 180
Lefkowitz, Louis   157
Lincoln Golf and Country Club   139
Littler, Gene   131, 143, 148
Livingstone, George   19
Los Angeles Athletic Club   144
Los Angeles Country Club   33
Los Serranos Country Club   143, 151
Louis, Joe (Barrow)   8, 21–4, 26–32, 37, 39–42, 47–52, 67, 77, 78, 80–4, 88–91, 95, 97, 99, 102, 104–6, 108, 111, 112, 114–16, 118, 119, 121, 122, 134, 136, 139–41, 149, 165, 167, 174, 176, 181, 183
Louis, Marva   46
Luxford, Maurie   63, 88

Mains, Russ   70
Mangrum, Lloyd   37, 60, 65, 105, 106, 122
Mangrum, Ray   37, 39, 73
Manhattan Tap Room   140
Mapledale Country Club   40
Markovich, Dan   57–60
Marshall, Edison   25
Martin, Clyde   24, 26, 31
Marx, Zeppo   46
Mary Elizabeth Hotel   144
Matney, Bill   110, 114, 115
Matthews, Allen   103
May, George S.   41, 43, 60
Mayan Theatre   84
Mayfield, Shelley   129
McCormick, Bruce   35
McLaughlin, Ted   138
McMahon, Art   28, 61
McMurry, Jimmy   14
McPhail, Larry   37
Meadowbrook Country Club   141
Medina Country Club   160
Memorial Park   47
Menjou, Adolphe   35, 69
Metropolis Country Club   139

Miami Springs Golf Course   144
Middlecoff, Cary   18, 19, 86, 105, 130, 132
Miles, Marshall   32
Mills, Harry   139, 155
Mitchell, Judson   154
Mitchell, Ray   144
Monterey Peninsula Country Club   87
Morrison, Alan   124
Morse, Samuel F. B.   87
Mosk, Stanley   156–8
Murdock, Dana   62

Nantz, Jim   2
National Cemetery   177
Naval Station Great Lakes   29
Nelson, Byron   36, 42
Ness, William G.   21
Newcombe, Don   144, 181
Nicklaus, Jack   3, 174, 175, 177
Nova, Lou   27, 28
Nowen, Richard Pastor   10

O'Doul, Lefty   87
Oak Cliff Country Club   157
Oliver, Claudia (Rhodes)   83, 84, 93, 94, 135, 154, 156, 159, 169, 175–7
Olivet Baptist Church   12
Olson, Mike   124, 125

Paige, Satchel   49, 74
Palmer, Arnold   3, 4, 145
Palmer, Johnny   131
Paramount Studios   156
Parker, Charlie   30
Paycheck, Johnny   24
Pebble Beach Golf Links   85, 87, 91, 122
Pershing Hotel   82
Pete, Calvin   181, 183
Phoenix Country Club   103, 105, 106
Pile, Robert B.   155
Plum Hollow Golf Club   145
Polo Grounds   28
Porter, Eugene   154

Provident Hospital   28
Prysock, Arthur   144
Pye, Brad   102

Quail Hollow Country Club   174
Quick, Smiley   35, 57

Rackham Golf Course   24–6, 112
Raft, George   35
Rancho Santa Fe Golf Club   86
Ratliffe, Harold   4
Raynor, Harvey   149
Recreation Park   93
Red Run Golf Club   115
Reed, John Ed   17
Reed, Leonard   32, 46, 60, 134
Regal Theatre   30
Remy, Jim   181
Reneau, Lou Jr.   96, 97
Rhodes, Deborah   93, 144, 151, 169, 170, 176, 177, 181
Rhodes, Della   10, 11
Rhodes, Frank   10–12
Rice, Grantland   22, 24, 67
Richland Country Club   11, 18
Richmond Golf Club   55–61
Rickey, Branch   2, 77, 80
Riviera Country Club   36, 37, 65–70, 73, 74, 157
Roach, Joe   90, 160
Roberts, Clifford   2
Robertson, Dan   18, 19
Robey, Dan   47
Robinson, Jackie   2, 4, 49, 63, 77, 80, 81, 91, 138, 139, 144, 149, 159, 166, 168, 181, 183
Robinson, Sugar Ray   53, 90, 111, 112, 115, 116
Roosevelt, Franklin D. President   17, 29
Rose, Irwin   32
Rowe, Billy   84, 92
Rowell, Jonathan   59, 60, 63, 98
Roxborough, John   78, 79, 133
Rule, Bob   19

INDEX

Runyan, Paul   122
Rush, Dave   169
Ruth, Babe   21

Samuelson, Rube   81
San Diego Country Club   96
Sarazen, Gene   3, 60, 65, 67, 68, 119
Savoy Club   21, 27, 82
Sawyer, Pat   137
Schmeling, Max   23
Schneiter, George   55
Schoenfeld, Ed   61
Scott, Randolph   87
Searles, Calvin   26
Seaver, Charley   122
Seawright, Bill   115, 118
Seneca Golf Course   118
Seymour, Bob   68, 132
Shaefer Brewing Company   146
Shinnecock Hills Golf Club   66
Shippen, John   66, 180, 181
Short, Peter   156
Sifford, Charley   156–60, 163, 166–8, 174, 180, 181, 183
Sifford, Rose   176
Sinatra, Frank   81
Smith, Horton   89, 97, 98, 102, 108, 130, 131
Smith, Walter   23
Smith, Wendell   49, 82, 138
Smith, Wilfrid   21
Snead, Leon   82
Snead, Sam   3, 36, 43, 65, 67, 70–3, 119, 127, 138
Spears, Herschel   17
Speedway Gardens   27
Speeky, Walter   40, 161
Spiller, Bill   33, 36, 48, 50, 56–61, 63, 97, 101, 104, 106, 109, 112, 121, 134, 138, 142, 150, 156, 158, 159, 181.
Steel, Bill   58
Stern, Bill   42, 65, 68
Stroh's Brewery   22
Strong, Lou   158

Sullivan, Ed   23, 97
Sullivan, John L.   92
Summerlea Golf Course   129
Sunset Fields Golf Club   35–7
Sunset Park   16
Superior Country Club   111

T. T. Hockett & Sons   176
Tam O'Shanter Country Club   41
Tamarisk Country Club   138
Taylor, Jimmy   154
Ted Rhodes Golf Course   179, 181
Tennessee Golf Foundation Hall of Fame   181
Tennessee Sports Hall of Fame   182
Tennison Park Golf Course   167
Thompson, "Titanic"   168
Toski, Bob   105
Tucker, Forrest   87
Tucker, William   78
Tufts, Richard   71
Tuskegee Airmen   30

Ulrich, Wally   137
Union Station   7, 20, 59
US Rubber Company   167

Veterans Administration Hospital   117
Villareal Golf Club   160
Vines, Ellsworth "Elly"   33, 85, 123

Walcott, Jersey Joe   67, 74
Walker, C. J. Dr.   154, 159, 160
Ward, Alan   58
Warwick Hills Country Club   173, 175
Washington, Kenny   56, 91, 107, 141
Watkins, Bill   155
Watkins Hotel   35, 82, 155
Watkins Park   11, 16
Watrous, Al   31
Watson, Fran   61
Weissmuller, Johnny   69, 87
Western Avenue Golf Club   46, 60, 150, 158

Wethersfield Country Club 156
Weyman-Bruton Tobacco 11
Wheeler, Howard 25, 44, 49, 52, 100, 110, 112, 118, 119, 136, 137
White, Peggy (Rhodes) 177
Wiley, Red 60
Willard, Jess 79
Williams, Al 35
Williams, D. L. 176
Williams, Elmer 33
Williams, George 119
Williams, Joe 67

Wilshire Country Club 33
Winchell, Walter 95–7
Woods, Earl 182
Woods, Tiger 1, 3–5, 181–3
Worsham, Lew 71, 131, 132

Yankee Stadium 21, 22, 37
Yorkshire Golf Club 44, 49
Young, A.S. "Doc" 63, 76, 77, 82, 155
Young, Dick 170, 171
Young, Whitney M. 61, 62